Understanding TIAA-CREF®

Understanding TIAA-CREF®

How to Plan for a Secure and Comfortable Retirement

Irving S. Schloss
Deborah V. Abildsoe

This book has not been prepared, approved, or licensed
by TIAA-CREF or any affiliated organization.

OXFORD
UNIVERSITY PRESS

2000

\# 44541854

OXFORD
UNIVERSITY PRESS

Oxford   New York

Athens   Auckland   Bangkok   Bogotá   Buenos Aires
Calcutta   Cape Town   Chennai   Dar es Salaam   Delhi   Florence
Hong Kong   Istanbul   Karachi   Kuala Lumpur   Madrid   Melbourne
Mexico City   Mumbai   Nairobi   Paris   São Paulo   Singapore
Taipei   Tokyo   Toronto   Warsaw

and associated companies
Berlin   Ibadan

Published by Oxford University Press, Inc.
198 Madison Avenue, New York, New York 10016

Oxford is a registered trademark of Oxford University Press

Library of Congress Cataloging-in-Publication Data is available

ISBN 0-19-513197-5

1 3 5 7 9 8 6 4 2
Printed in the United States of America
on acid-free paper

Preface

We wrote this book for you, the TIAA-CREF participant. If we are successful, you will understand how TIAA-CREF (Teachers Insurance and Annuity Association–College Retirement Equities Fund) operates, how your account at TIAA-CREF accumulates, and what you need to know about your employer's plan or version of the TIAA-CREF menu of options. You will also know your investment choices and the impact that they may have upon your retirement. You will comprehend your distribution options, before and after retirement. Finally, if you are so inclined and if that is appropriate in your circumstances, you will know how to leave your account to your family.

In addition, we will try to give you some tools to track your account and plan your retirement. That process does not begin at some designated age. For decades, you may not regard retirement planning as even a remotely top priority item. Paying the bills, raising children, and career advancement will occupy center stage. But that does not mean that you should ignore the fact that, given a normal life expectancy, you may spend as much time being retired as you spent receiving a formal education. Generally, the earlier you start saving and planning, the more comfortable your last two to three decades on earth will be and the higher the probability your family will enjoy a substantial inheritance. Your labors will bear fruit for you and your loved ones.

We sincerely hope that this first edition will not be the last, and we welcome your feedback. With your help, later editions will prove clearer and more useful than their predecessors. We have tried to make this book as comprehensible, comprehensive, and even humorous as we could. We appreciate that you will need a working knowledge of the tax rules governing all retirement plans and some idea of the special rules that affect retirement plans for nonprofit organizations. We busted our britches to make those concepts as straightforward and even logical as we could. We hope that we have succeeded.

Any book represents a group effort in which many team members remain invisible. With a clear awareness of the contributions others have made, we want to acknowledge the help that we received from TIAA-CREF's staff. They reviewed the book for factual accuracy as to TIAA-CREF's product and procedures. They also kept us abreast of changes that were occurring at TIAA-CREF. That does not mean that this book bears TIAA-CREF's imprimatur. We are independent of TIAA-CREF, and the conclusions and the conceptual, legal, and factual errors that we reach in this book belong to us alone.

The tables contained in Chaper 36 were prepared using zCalc 2000, a product of Lexite Development LLC in Arlington Heights, Illinois. We also gratefully acknowledge the assistance of Brian and Cathy Skinner of Yale University, Robert H. Knapp of Northwestern Mutual Life, Sally Salancy and Lisa Davis of Tyler Cooper & Alcorn, LLP, and of our editors at Oxford University Press, notably Herb Addison. His good humor and patience proved inexhaustible.

Finally, we dedicate this book to our children—Tracy, David, Anne Cathrine, and Christian—in recognition of their individual and collective sacrifice in making this book happen and our unending love for them.

New Haven, Conn.   *I.S.S.*
February 15, 2000   *D.V.A.*

Contents

Understanding TIAA-CREF

Introduction

"The Key to Successful Retirement Planning Is Planning Ahead"
—TIAA-CREF brochure inviting participants
to seminars on estate planning

If you apprehensively perused the table of contents, you might think that we will explore what seems like an awful lot of peripheral issues. You can rest assured that this book's principal function remains to explain how TIAA-CREF works and how participants can derive the maximum benefit from their accounts. However, one cannot view TIAA-CREF in isolation, and we will cover related matters only to the extent that they bear upon the central focus of this book. Without some technical background, the TIAA-CREF literature and this book will remain incomprehensible. They need to be understood in the context of the legal and other rules that govern and shape TIAA-CREF.

This book does not provide an investment guide or a legal template for integrated retirement and estate planning. It does not contain a cookbook recipe for comfortable retirement. Aside from the fact that every situation is unique, the reason why it cannot serve those ends depends on the underlying issues to which we will make periodic explicit reference, but which should remain at the forefront of every reader's mind.

As the epigraph above illustrates, TIAA-CREF itself neatly summarizes the first issue that one needs to bear in mind. Retirement planning does not begin late in one's career. It starts as early as one can look up and begin to think about the long haul. Ideally, that process will germinate two to three *decades* before you plan to retire.

The second set of issues presents more complexity. They relate to time, risk, their impact on investment performance, the growth in one's TIAA-CREF account, and the resultant retirement income you will receive from the nest egg your hard work, investment diligence, and perhaps an element of luck generated. Everyone perceives risk differently, and the most that we can do is to alert you to these issues and to make you think or rethink some of your assumptions about how you should accumulate funds for retirement.

At the outset, the most important myth to dispel is that retirement represents the finish line. This misconception undercuts so much analysis and popular thinking that we must deal with this issue immediately. Even if one expects to annuitize one's entire account at, say, age 70, that does not entail accumulating as much as possible by that age and then freezing the size of the account and the income that it will generate. Everyone who reads this book will remember the recent decades of relatively high inflation and will recognize the problems created by that approach. Generally speaking, that strategy results in a fixed income whose purchasing power can only diminish over time. In addition to the toll taken by general economic inflation, your individual expenses may increase over time, either as a result of declining health, tax increases, your special needs, or other causes. You want your income to keep pace.

To take an example from our own backyard, in many Connecticut towns we vote annually on the budget by direct ballot referendum, and it is axiomatic that older voters will try to prevent any increase in their local taxes. Property taxes represent the one cost of living adjustment as to which they have a vote. They typically form a solid bloc of No votes. If the budget loses on the first referendum, we vote a second or even a third time. One town in Connecticut took eight referenda to adopt a town budget. Those on a fixed income will vote at every referendum, and their votes will probably not swiftly change as the size of the budget decreases with each defeat. As the amount of increase declines with each defeat of the budget, probably fewer of those living on a fixed income find the tax increase as pernicious as it appeared the first time around, and the number of those voting against eventually declines.

Nonetheless, whatever the merits of the tax increase, the retired person living on a fixed income finds them irrelevant. The retiree on a fixed income must make each dollar go farther in a world where, inevitably, the rest of society or economic conditions will raise costs that directly affect him or her. Parents with children in school will want to maintain or improve the quality of the town's educational system. Rightly or wrongly, that equates to more spending. Better police protection, road maintenance, and enhancements in other governmental services will propel taxes higher at the local level. Town employees need raises. Unless the town is experiencing continuous growth or rapid commercial development, these trends inevitably result in higher taxes. For the retiree, those represent the hard, cold facts. Some inflation occurs because of economic factors and some because of political factors, at one level of government or another.

Rather than view retirement as the end of the line, one has to recognize that, given one's likely life expectancy, one faces at 65 or 70 about a quarter century of continued dependence on the size of one's TIAA-CREF account or annuity and other retirement payments, as well as Social Security. That means that one cannot convert the account entirely into a fixed-income portfolio. Given the length of time that your retirement accumulation will serve as your major source of income, inflation will inexorably diminish the value of a fixed income. Buying lottery tickets or gambling to make up for that loss of purchasing power almost invariably produces a further erosion of one's economic base. Statistically, using those devices invites more losses.

For these reasons, a freshly minted retiree, absent serious health problems, remains a long-term investor with at least as much of an interest in the growth of his or her account as the newly hired Ph.D. The amount of exposure to the equity markets may differ in percentage or the equity investments may become more conservative as one ages. After all, the time horizon of the young teacher or researcher extends thirty or more years. In the worst case, the young can make up any losses with future contributions, and they benefit from the secular trend toward growth that gives them the luxury of withstanding even a prolonged storm in financial markets. For the retiree, the retirement account or annuity can only be replenished by recovery in financial markets. In other words, the retiree does not enjoy the luxury of as much time to compensate for declines in equity values. As a consequence, a retiree faces the dilemma of needing some equity component in the retirement accumulation, but not wanting more risk than is absolutely necessary. The trade-off usually favors conservative equity investments in larger, established businesses. They may lack the growth potential of the smaller company, but they also shed the accompanying market volatility.

In addition, for the working participant the TIAA-CREF accumulation represents just another asset, perhaps the largest one, but not the source of one's daily bread. For the retiree, the amount that was accumulated over one's career has to provide at a minimum three squares, a roof over one's head, and the other necessities of life.

On the other hand, the retiree need not become a victim of inflation or someone faced inevitably with a declining standard of living. The retiree needs some exposure to the equity markets in order to safeguard against an eroding income base. For those who do not annuitize, the postretirement account may actually grow, at least during the earlier years of retirement, rather than inevitably decline in value. For those who have CREF annuities, their income may grow, depending on investment performance. We will talk in more detail about retirement planning later, but the critical concept to grasp at this point is that the need for growth does not disappear when one retires or reaches age $70^{1}/_{2}$. It continues for as long as one draws breath.

This does not necessarily mean taking unacceptable risks. A recent study concluded that a portfolio comprised of 23% equities and 77% bonds did not involve more risk than an all-bond portfolio, but produced an annual yield of 2–3% more. Over the course of twenty years or more, that apparently small gap can spell the difference between a comfortable or a cramped retirement. Based on historical data, other studies have produced similar results.

This does not deny that the older one becomes, the more risk adverse one ought to be. But that does not mean that one avoids all risk. Often the safest investment in the short run will prove to be the most dangerous in the longer term. For example, we consulted with two clients who had begun contributing to TIAA-CREF in 1974, the height of the great 1973–75 bear market. One client concluded that the only prudent course was to invest entirely in TIAA. After twenty-three years, at age 57, he had accumulated $342,000. The other client, a canny English woman with about the same compensation, read the tea leaves differently. She allocated her contributions 75% CREF, or equities, and 25% TIAA, or fixed income securities. Her accumulation totals five times as much and is still growing. The first client may have enjoyed a good night's sleep for twenty-three years, but he now faces a major problem and a limited number of years to make up for a lot of lost ground. The second client must have endured some anxious moments, but she has reached a relatively calm harbor at the end of her working life.

TIAA-CREF quotes a study that $1 invested in government bonds in 1929 would have yielded $14 today. Stock investments would have yielded close to $1,400. Had one known when to move in and out of the stock market over the past seventy years, a form of clairvoyance not native to our species, one would have $2 billion today. Though startling, the last figure is irrelevant. The first two are germane. The stock investment yielded 100 times the safest investment one can make. Factor in inflation, and the safe investment lost ground. A retirement account does not equate to a savings account.

This line of argument puts two persistent rules of thumb into question. First, using the default allocation of 50% TIAA (fixed income securities) and 50% CREF (equity securities) simply does not make sense if one has three or four decades with which to work. For all but those on the cusp of retirement, this equates to tying one hand behind your back. It means that only half of one's contributions will enjoy the potential for growth that historically only equity investments have provided.

The second axiom is expressed in two differing but reciprocal formulae. The first version stipulates that one should have a percentage in TIAA equal to one's age; the variant postulates a rule of 100, namely that the percentage in CREF should equal 100 minus one's age. Both of these rules and the default selection cannot take individual variations into account. What may have been true in times of high interest rates and relatively high inflation cannot hold water in times of low interest rates and currently low inflation. What may hold true for the retiree with high fixed costs and a relatively small accumulation cannot apply with equal force to someone more fortunate who owns both a higher accumulation and other income-producing assets. For the latter individual, fixed costs may represent a small fraction of disposable income. If anything, all of these critically unaccepted precepts underline the need for more equity exposure than the default election in the early years and the fallacy of any investment formula that claims to cover every retiree. And both of them probably overstate the need for a fixed income for the retiree, again depending on the individual case.

So one does need to think about risk, one's real time horizon rather than some arbitrary signpost, and the requirements of growth throughout one's lifetime. One has to feel comfortable with the degree of risk that one is taking, but one should not ignore the risk that the passage of time will have upon an overly conservative choice of investment vehicles.

In short, one must always keep in mind the time value of money. During the accumulation phase, you will experience the power of compounding returns. Your estate planning should use the time value of money techniques contained in the Internal Revenue Code of 1986, as amended (the "Code"), to the extent appropriate to your situation. Unfair as it may seem, you will spend the last quarter or so of your life in a degree of comfort that will depend directly on how early you started saving for retirement. But then, where you end up in your fifties will largely result from choices that you made in your twenties. As we look back on our younger years, we often think, "If only I had known." This book tries to minimize the odds of your feeling the same way about your retirement planning.

In a modified way, retirees need to think in the same terms. Their time horizon may extend two or three decades, but they need some compounding from the time value of money in order to keep ahead of the cumulative effect of inflation and to be prepared for unforeseen future expenses. The time value of money does not stop operating when one leaves the workplace. Although its effects may be less dramatic, used wisely through savings and controlled risk, retirees can enjoy the balance of their retirement and do more of whatever activity intrigues them. One can never disengage risk and reward, but one cannot also uncouple time and its ability to make money either grow through prudent investing and early decision making or to dissipate its purchasing power through inflation if one pursues a fruitless search for utter safety. Although the great bulk of this book is spent discussing the intricacies and idiosyncrasies of TIAA-CREF, these themes remain beneath the surface and should lurk continually in your mind as you think about your investment decisions and the impact that they will have upon your life during retirement.

On a related point, the section on estate planning does not apply only to those readers at or near retirement. Your TIAA-CREF account will probably become your major asset, and the earlier you plan for its use during your lifetime and thereafter, the better your results will be. The savings in cost will loom large, and the benefits of early planning can prove to be substantial.

Nonetheless, this book cannot provide universal answers to every reader's situation. Your TIAA-CREF accumulations and your options with regard thereto depend upon the interplay among three sets of rules. The first appears in the Code, and we will discuss those generally. The second relates to the ways in which TIAA-CREF operates, and if we did not cover those topics, this book would lack content. The third resides in your employer's retirement plan rules, and they can vary widely. The menu that TIAA-CREF offers its participating institutions contains numerous choices, and almost every employer will react differently. You need to know what your employer's plan provides as to all material terms. Your employer's human resources or benefits office (or the equivalent) can give you a copy of the plan and, more readable, a copy of the summary plan description. In some cases, TIAA-CREF may know these rules, but their information may not be current or complete. You need to visit the appropriately named office to obtain those basic documents. Without that specific information, the discussion that will follow may appear at times abstract, general, and (no pun intended) academic. You want to know how these rules do and will apply to you, and only you can find out. Ask to be informed of any changes in your current employer's plan so that your knowledge does not become obsolete.

Implicit in the preceding paragraph is the distinction between (1) the plan under which your retirement accumulation grows and becomes available to you, and (2) TIAA-CREF, a plan provider. Your employer sponsors and directs the plan; TIAA-CREF only supplies the raw materials out of which the employer plan can be fashioned. Just obtaining TIAA-CREF literature will not, therefore, inform you about your retirement plan. That is a function of elections and options that your employer made.

Only if they are taken together can this book and knowledge of your employer's plan enable you to take more control over what will happen to you when you retire. You cannot make the right decisions if you do not have the facts. We will do our best with respect to the first two sets of rules. You must obtain the requisite information with regard to the third. Ideally, you should plow through the pertinent parts of this book (and you will only be able to judge relevance if you know your employer's plan) with the text of your employer's plan or the summary plan description at your side. You do not want or need an abstract discussion. You need a book that addresses your individual situation, and only you can supply the third set of rules that will have as much to say about your retirement as anything peculiar to TIAA-CREF.

Most of the preceding discussion has focused on the retiree looking backward. You also need to think about the time value of money during the accumulation phase while you are still working and looking forward. Generally speaking, the earlier you begin to contribute as much as you can to your TIAA-CREF account, the longer time will have to work on your assets and, in the biblical phrase, make them fruitful and multiply.

The effect of the time value of money can be illustrated by the following simple example. Suppose you have two individuals. The first elects to build his retirement account by putting aside $5,000 annually from age 25 to age 35 and then stops. The second defers contributing until he is 35, and he then adds $5,000 annually until he reaches age 65. Although the second individual contributed three times as much as the first, the first individual will have more accumulated by age 65, assuming that both of them earned the same return on their money. This seems and is counterintuitive, but that is the effect of compounding and allowing it to work as long as possible.

We emphasize this parable even though we are mindful of the expenses that one has to bear in what represent, on paper or in theory, the prime savings years. Although Aesop's fable about the ant and the grasshopper may date back thousands of year, the moral it points remains as true today as it did in his day. Taking a salary reduction—in effect, forced savings—ain't easy. It means doing without, and many of our readers will feel that, compared to their neighbors who are better paid in the private sector, they are doing more than their share of doing without. But for those who survive the summer and the fall, the winter of old age comes as inevitably to each of us as winter came to the ant and the grasshopper. Those who prepared and saved for colder weather earlier will fare better than those who did not. You must plan ahead, difficult as that can and often proves to be.

Yes, Social Security does exist. And yes, America may not longer represent a land entirely composed of rugged individualists (if it ever did). But too much reliance on governmental largesse poses such a obvious danger that we do not have to dwell further on that folly. Being an ant may not seem as much fun as being a grasshopper, but the fun stops for grasshoppers when autumn arrives. We may morally disapprove of the ant's response to the grasshopper's plea for help, but it reflects the harsh realities of life.

We hope that reading this book will enable you to thrive in all of the four seasons, recognizing that you may have less in the spring and the summer because you are putting by for the fall and for the winter. One day the warm sun of employment will wane, and we want you to be prepared for that day. Be an ant, hard as that existence may be at times when you feel you are entitled to make a little noise.

FINALLY, ALTHOUGH WE DISCUSS ISSUES OF INVESTMENT STRAT-
EGY AND PLANNING AND LEGAL MATTERS, THIS BOOK DOES
NOT REPRESENT OR CONTAIN EITHER INVESTMENT ADVICE OR
LEGAL ADVICE. NO READER SHOULD RELY UPON THE CONTENTS
OF THIS BOOK FOR ANY SUCH PURPOSE. FOR SUCH ADVICE, EACH
READER SHOULD CONSULT HIS OR HER OWN INVESTMENT ADVI-
SOR OR LAWYER. THIS BOOK DOES NOT DEAL WITH ISSUES OF
COMMUNITY PROPERTY. IT ONLY CONTAINS GENERAL OBSER-
VATIONS. YOU AND YOUR ADVISORS WILL NEED TO DETERMINE
THE EXTENT TO WHICH THESE OBSERVATIONS PERTAIN TO YOU.
NEITHER THE AUTHORS NOR THE PUBLISHER ASSUMES ANY
RESPONSIBILITY WITH REGARD TO THE INVESTMENT AND OTHER
DECISIONS YOU NEED TO MAKE WITH REGARD TO YOUR RETIRE-
MENT AND ESTATE PLANNING. NEITHER THE AUTHORS NOR THE
PUBLISHER SHALL HAVE EITHER LIABILITY OR RESPONSIBILITY
TO ANY PERSON OR ENTITY WITH RESPECT TO ANY LOSS OR
DAMAGE CAUSED, OR ALLEGED TO HAVE BEEN CAUSED,
DIRECTLY OR INDIRECTLY, BY THE INFORMATION CONTAINED
IN THIS BOOK.

TIAA-CREF

An Overview

Why Are Retirement Plans Different in the Nonprofit Sector?

Like so many facets of American life, retirement plans throughout the United States are now governed by the provisions of the Internal Revenue Code of 1986, as amended (the "Code"), as irrigated by the Employment Retirement Income Act of 1974 (ERISA). We did not write this book with the intention of making you an expert in these areas. If Anatole France thought that life was short and Proust was long, he would have gagged at the paper monolith that provides the rules by which Americans save for retirement, plans are operated, and retirement benefits are paid.

In any event, the nonprofit world falls under the rules laid out in Section 403(b) of the Code. TIAA-CREF offers Section 403(b) plans to its participating institutions. Many of the other popular types of retirement plans draw their names from the Code sections where they were created and are described. The Section 401(k) plan, the Section 457 plan for governmental employees, and others reflect their humble origins in the Serbonian bog of the Code.

Section 403(b) provides, in its most general terms, that if an organization described in Section 501(c)(3) of the Code (the subsection that describes the vast majority of nonprofit organizations) or a public school system (which may include a state university system) purchases an annuity contract for an employee, then the employer's contribution to the contract will not become income to the employee. Unlike other retirement provisions of the Code, Section 403(b) does not, except by cross-reference, speak in terms of a plan or a trust to hold contributions for retirement purposes.

Section 403(b) provides an alternative method of building a retirement accumulation. The employer may contribute to a custodial account that invests in mutual funds for the benefit of the employees. Section 403(b)(7) describes such an account as held by a financial institution that invests the account exclusively in mutual fund shares. This permits Vanguard and Fidelity, for example, to act as additional providers of retirement benefits to those in the nonprofit sector. They compete head to head with TIAA-CREF in the nonprofit sector, but are dwarfed by it in this particular market.

At many institutions, you may find that you can choose whether to invest in TIAA-CREF or in a custodial account with one of the major mutual fund families. Whichever choice you make, the most important determinant will be your assessment of likely future investment performance, and the provisions of your employer's retirement plan that will govern your account. Although a custodial account resembles an IRA or a Section 401(k) plan more closely than TIAA-CREF may, you are still enrolled in an annuity plan. When you reach retirement age, you will have to decide whether you want to annuitize your account or not, and that will depend on factors discussed later in this book. You may purchase an annuity through the provider of the custodial account or through TIAA-CREF. The difference stems from the basic orientation of the two types of providers. As explained in the next chapter, the orientation of TIAA-CREF leans heavily toward annuitization. The providers of custodial accounts may have insurance company subsidiaries, but they do not focus primarily on providing annuities.

We do not mean to slight custodial accounts, but they do not create the conceptual and practical issues that attend a TIAA-CREF account. In addition, the great majority of eligible participants elect to stay with TIAA-CREF, and in any event some employers do not offer custodial accounts.

Provisions dealing with employee contributions appear elsewhere in the Code and the reader constantly has to hop around tracking down cross-references, a maddening trait that makes the Code a perennial best-seller. You probably contribute to your account through a salary reduction agreement. Naturally, the Code limits the annual amount one can add in this way to one's TIAA-CREF or custodial account. For 1999, the limit equals $10,000, a figure that is annually adjusted for inflation. Your contribution reduces your taxable income, dollar for dollar, and lowers your income tax. As a tax-deductible item, your share in the buildup of your account consists of pretax dollars. And, as noted above, if your employer's plan meets the strictures of Section 403(b), its additions to your account will not turn up as part of your taxable income for the years in question.

In order to be eligible for this favorable treatment under Section 403(b), your employer's plan must meet many of the tests that are common to all qualified retirement plans and that will be dealt with in nontechnical fashion as this book unfolds. A qualified retirement plan means one that receives the same advantageous income tax treatment of the employer's and the employee's contributions described above—no taxable income from the employer's additions and tax-deductible contributions by the employee. Confusingly, the term "qualified plan" as used in the Code does not include an Individual Retirement Account ("IRA"), although they benefit from the same treatment.

A qualified retirement plan and an IRA share another income tax benefit. The income that they earn while the employee is still working is itself not subject to income tax. Without taxes on dividend or interest income or capital gains, these plans enjoy an enormous advantage over the taxable investor and will, other things being equal, tend to grow more quickly than one's savings and investments from post–income tax dollars, whose income and gains are taxed as they are earned.

Instead of current taxation, you will only pay income tax upon receiving distributions from the plan. In the grand scheme of things, taxation is deferred, but the accumulation compounds tax free until you retire or otherwise take lump sum or periodic distributions.

What makes a TIAA-CREF account confusing to many participants arises from its dual character. On the one hand, an annuity plan closely resembles a corporate pension plan that pays benefits to the retiree and spouse and then terminates upon the death of the survivor. On the other hand, it resembles an IRA, a Section 401(k) plan, and other types of plans because each participant has an individual account. Generally, as with an IRA, you make the investment decisions.

Unlike a corporate plan, where the benefit paid is a function of number of years worked and average salary for some number of years before retirement, the payments from the TIAA-CREF account will depend on the size of the account and other individual factors. The years of service and final compensation lurk in the background because they affect the time over which the account received the benefit of tax-free compounding returns and the size of the contributions that have been made over the years. Nonetheless, a shrewd or lucky investor who picks the right combination of TIAA-CREF investment options can wind up with a much larger account than a less fortunate or less skillful (from an investment point of view) but higher-paid fellow employee. In places where staff is enrolled in TIAA-CREF, it is not unusual to find that the janitor or a member of the building and grounds crew has a larger accumulation than a better-paid senior member of the faculty.

With the flow of quarterly statements, with daily information available by telephone or the Internet, the TIAA-CREF account most resembles, on a day-to-day basis, an IRA or a Section 401(k) account. During the accumulation phase, the resemblance often blinds participants to the fact that the end product of these apparently identical plans differs radically. Although it is possible to take an IRA and buy an annuity, this rarely happens.

An annuity is an insurance product. If one is observant, the insurance aspect of one's TIAA-CREF account becomes apparent from the nomenclature used by TIAA-CREF. On a quarterly statement, the contributions made by employer and employee are labeled premiums. The accumulation accounts are called annuity accounts. Every year, the participant receives an annual statement showing what the annuity at age 65 will be, based on certain assumptions.

As one would expect, the Code only makes the confusion worse. The $10,000 limitation on salary reductions that applies to Section 401(k) plans also applies to Section 403(b) plans. The same limitations on withdrawals from other retirement plans before age $59^1/_2$, the amounts that must be distributed upon retirement, and other general rules applicable to retirement plans also obtain in the nonprofit sector. The same rules regarding rollovers into IRAs also apply.

In one very important respect, the Section 403(b) plan differs from the IRA. An IRA is not a qualified plan, and therefore one cannot postpone receiving distributions after age $70^1/_2$. (Actually, the magic date, called the Required Beginning Date (the "RBD") in the Code, is the April 1 after you turn age $70^1/_2$, but we will follow the common convention and refer to the RBD as the date on which you reach age $70^1/_2$.) For reasons that will become clearer later on, you are better off thinking of the RBD as coming too early rather than too late. Like their counterparts in other qualified plans, TIAA-CREF participants can, if they are so inclined, defer taking distributions until the later of $70^1/_2$ or the actual date of retirement. If you want to work beyond age $70^1/_2$ and continue to draw a salary, you may do so without triggering the beginning of distributions from your TIAA-CREF account. You have postponed the RBD.

The trade-off for this additional deferral is that the life expectancy over which distributions must be taken is proportionately shortened. Although younger persons may find it hard to imagine working beyond age 70, many participants become so engrossed in their work or continue to enjoy it sufficiently that they willingly put off the day of retirement. As we will see, the ability to take advantage of this option, if the employer's plan does not mandate a retirement date, can in some circumstances materially enhance the size of the TIAA-CREF account and the size of one's retirement income. For other participants, deferring retirement does not reflect a choice based on job satisfaction, but on the need to accumulate more funds for retirement.

What the participant should do, therefore, is understand that, however much his retirement plan may resemble his corporate neighbor's, a Section 403(b) plan has a different orientation. Its intended end product is an annuity, a stream of income that will last for the lifetime of the participant and optionally someone else, typically a spouse, but that will terminate when the survivor has died. The corporate neighbor can, in many instances, take the vested balance in his pension account and roll it over into an IRA. He can do so whenever he changes jobs. Although he must take distributions at age $70^{1}/_{2}$, the distribution options available to him differ markedly from those availed of by most TIAA-CREF participants.

Like many other enduring philanthropic and public service concepts, the idea of TIAA-CREF germinated in the mind and fortune of Andrew Carnegie. In 1905, concerned about the poverty that seemed the common fate of retired teachers, he gave the then colossal sum of $10 million to fund the pensions of teachers at thirty universities. By 1918, it had become clear that the financial requirements for such a plan necessitated both teacher and employer participation and a larger financial organization. As a consequence, the Teachers Insurance and Annuity Association ("TIAA") was incorporated and licensed as a New York life insurance company.

From the outset, TIAA invested in interest-bearing securities and issued fixed annuities to retirees. For the first time, teachers had a pension plan that was oriented toward their needs. The annuity served the purpose of providing the retirees with lifetime income in what was then a benign inflationary environment.

In 1952, TIAA formed College Retirement Equities Fund ("CREF"), which was the first variable annuity company in the United States. CREF invests primarily in equities and has steadily increased the number of funds into which participants can direct their investments. As discussed in more detail below, the reason why CREF annuities are variable is that the amount paid out to participants will depend on the investment experience during the preceding year or month of the CREF fund or funds in which an individual participant may have invested.

Until 1988, TIAA-CREF exclusively served the educational and related spheres. In that year, the Securities and Exchange Commission opened that portion of the nonprofit universe to other providers, such as Fidelity and Vanguard. Despite those firms' marketing prowess, each of them only has approximately $25 billion under management in the nonprofit sector. By contrast, TIAA-CREF has over $260 billion under management and is the largest retirement plan in the world. At the present time, TIAA-CREF is estimated to own 1% of all of the shares traded on the New York Stock Exchange.

In the Taxpayers Relief Act of 1997, Congress ended TIAA-CREF's tax exemption. As a result, TIAA-CREF can now offer new products to its educational and nonprofit market base and to individuals generally. Participants and their spouses can now roll their pension plans from employment outside of the nonprofit sector into TIAA-CREF. TIAA-CREF now offers certain of its funds directly to individuals, either within or without its traditional customer base. For participants at TIAA-CREF institutions, this means that they can invest in TIAA-CREF products outside of their employer's retirement plans. If an employer limits the investment choices available to its participants, this new initiative by TIAA-CREF allows participants to gain access to some of those options.

The loss of the tax exemption has also had one other salutary effect. It has shown clearly that TIAA-CREF is a plan provider, rather than the plan itself. In common parlance, participants talk about having TIAA-CREF in a way that suggests that it is TIAA-CREF that operates the plan, provides the benefits, and structures the choices. Obviously, to the participant, who has a one-on-one relationship with TIAA-CREF, it appears to serve all of these functions. Putting to one side the general rules in the Code, the employer funds the plan with participant contributions added in. Rather than TIAA-CREF, the employing institution sets the basic framework of the plan: the vesting period, if any, the investment choices, the funding formulae, the ability to move some or all of one's account out of TIAA-CREF, the availability of alternative providers, and so forth. Finally, TIAA-CREF offers its services in a contract with the employing institution. The form of that contract offers an employer a wide range of options, and, as in a restaurant, the employer chooses the items it wants from the extensive menu. In our experience, many of the complaints that are leveled against TIAA-CREF really represent grievances with the employer's plan.

By dint of being the first kid on the block and ably filling a sizable niche, it has become the dominant player in the nonprofit sector's retirement team of providers. TIAA-CREF filled the need that Andrew Carnegie and others like him saw, and it pioneered the variable annuity concept. Generally speaking, it has tried to remain attuned to the needs of its participants, one of the characteristics of a market leader.

An annuity is a contract between two parties in which the first party, typically an insurance company, agrees, upon receipt of a specified dollar amount, to make periodic payments to a second party, typically one or two individuals, for an agreed upon period of time, starting either immediately or at some date in the future. The parties may define the stipulated period of time over which the payments will occur as (1) a definite number of years, (2) the lifetime of one or both of the individuals, or (3) a combination of (1) and (2). The recipient of the payments is defined as the annuitant. *Like any other legally binding agreement, an annuity represents an irrevocable choice.*

Annuities exist outside of qualified plans. Generally, they are labeled tax-deferred annuities, and the investor buys one with post-tax dollars. The annuitant has a number of payment options, including waiting until age 85 or taking a lump sum. Such a payment will produce income equal to the appreciation on the initial investment. The appreciation on the contract also enjoys a tax-free build-up, and only the growth is subject to tax.

In the qualified plan area, which is hedged about with more requirements under the Code, payments must begin as of the Required Beginning Date (RBD). A lump sum payment, if available under the employer's plan, will produce a similar bunching of income. However, in this case, the taxable income equals the full value of the account, none of it having been subject to income taxation before. One can avoid these dire income tax consequences by rolling over the lump sum from TIAA-CREF or any other qualified annuity into an Individual Retirement Account. Properly done, this can allow for further tax-deferred investing until the RBD. If you have passed age $70^{1}/_{2}$ when you effect such a rollover, even if you are still working, your funds reside in an IRA, not in a qualified plan, and you will have to begin taking distributions.

As financial products that depend upon life expectancies and that require that the issuer have a large pool of lives to minimize the risk of loss, annuities are insurance products that have been used in retirement plans for many years. In some Section 403(b) plans, the participants do not own their account, but contribute monthly to a commingled accumulation that will be applied to buy an annuity. At retirement, participants receive a lifetime stream of income. The annuity amount will depend not only on how much was contributed, but will also factor in other criteria such as seniority, age, and average salary. Many public school or state plans depend upon this basic structure.

By contrast, except for some group TIAA-CREF plans, you as a participant in a TIAA-CREF plan normally accumulate an account in your own name, which you may or may not annuitize upon retirement. Depending on your particular school plan, you have several distribution options from which to choose as well as several possibilities to withdraw funds before retirement. Most of the withdrawal options are revocable because you are merely withdrawing funds from your own account. All of the annuity options are irrevocable. When you choose to receive an annuity, whether through your retirement plan or through an insurance company outside of a retirement plan, you have bought a product for which you paid on the date the annuity contract is signed.

Annuities fall generally into two categories, a term annuity and a life (or lives) annuity. A term annuity will pay the stipulated amounts over a fixed period of time. When the term expires, so does the annuity. If you, as annuitant, die before the term is completed, then the payments will continue to be paid to your beneficiary until the term expires. If you die after the end of the term, clearly nothing remains to pass on to heirs or beneficiaries.

A life annuity pays the agreed upon amounts over the lifetime of the annuitant, no matter how long or short that life may be. If you, the annuitant, live well past your life expectancy, then you may indeed end up winning what is in essence a bet. You will receive more than the accumulation balance surrendered to the insurance company at the start of the annuity, plus earnings during the annuity's term. With life annuities, those who outlive their assets are subsidized by those whose assets, so to speak, outlive them. Those annuitants who end up living shorter lives than expected, thereby losing the bet, will of course not receive total payments equaling what they paid in, plus earnings during the unexpectedly short term of the annuity.

Let's look at an example. Say that you have accumulated $500,000 in your retirement plan, and you choose to purchase a lifetime annuity. The balance in the annuity account grows, by hypothesis, at 7% annually. Starting at age 70, you would probably receive approximately $48,000 a year for as long as you live. If you live to be 100 years old, then you will have received a total of $1,440,000 from the issuer of the annuity. Had you taken $48,000 a year from an account with a starting balance of $500,000, invested at 7% per year, then the account would have lasted only nineteen years and you would have received a total of $912,000. In this case, you have outlived your assets.

What happens when the annuitant lives a shorter than expected life? Let's look at the same numbers once again. In this example, however, you die prematurely after only five years. You would have received a total of $240,000, the insurance company would have come out at least $260,000 ahead on the contract. In this case, your assets would have outlived you.

To hedge your bet, you might elect a combination of the two types of annuity. In this instance, you would receive payments for a specified period of time, say, ten years certain or life, whichever comes last. The life feature protects you in case you outlive the term certain. Similarly, the term certain protects your heirs if you die before the term ends. The added guarantees of payments by the insurance company and therefore the greater likelihood of more payments in the aggregate will necessitate that the periodic monthly payments in a "life and term certain annuity" will generally be smaller than they would be under either a term or life contract.

In order for an insurance company to be able to guarantee that payments will be made for an undetermined number of years, it must both retain reserves as well as adjust the amounts it will pay based on the most probable statistical life expectancies of its annuitants. Your individual health situation does not have an effect on these calculations. Instead the insurer relies on the latest statistics showing how many more years a 70-year-old, for example, will live on average. It will then look at the amount of your premiums and an earnings factor in order to determine how much it can pay you for the rest of your life and remain solvent. In general, the more guarantees and stipulations in your favor, the lower the monthly payment amount the insurance company can make in order to honor its promises. You look at your own situation; the insurer looks at actuarial experience.

What Is a Fixed Annuity?

In the last chapter, we described the two types of annuities in terms of the periods over which they are paid. Annuities fall into two other major categories: fixed and variable. Within the TIAA-CREF universe, TIAA issues the former and CREF the latter, and we deal with them in that order.

The distinction between the two types of annuities boils down to this. A fixed annuity will pay you a fixed number of *dollars* on a periodic basis. A variable annuity (which will be discussed in chapter 5) will pay you a fixed number of *annuity units* on a periodic basis. The variability of the annuity payments derives from the changing values of the units, depending on investment performance for the previous year, quarter, or whatever length of time transpires between revaluations.

Honing in on the details, a fixed annuity is a legally binding contract that guarantees that you will receive at least a stipulated and presumably acceptable amount for either a predetermined number of years or the rest of your and potentially someone else's life. In order to understand how this type of a contract works, you need to know how the payments can be guaranteed and how your lifetime (using just one life for simplicity in this discussion) is measured for these purposes.

In order to be able to guarantee payments to a client, an insurance company must make sure that it has enough assets in reserve to be able to pay as promised many years into the future. Most fixed annuity contracts guarantee a rate of return or a minimum rate of return at the time the contract to begin annuity payments is signed. Although you may be paying premiums (making contributions) over many years, in many different interest rate environments, the guaranteed rate applied to your fixed rate annuity payments will be determined when you surrender your accumulation to the company in return for the agreed upon stream of payments.

What any insurance company or annuity provider counts on to meet its obligations is the time value of money. The company has investment income and a continuous flow of cash from premiums received from participants who are still in the accumulation phase. In order to guarantee that it will be able to make payments, the company must ascertain that a certain minimum of funds are invested conservatively to produce the necessary outflow of funds when participants elect to annuitize. To be able to make the necessary long-term payment commitments to you, the company must make long-term investment commitments that cannot be broken at short notice. It must match its income and the liabilities represented by its annuity obligations.

As more long-term investments are booked, the company loses liquidity. It needs to put its cash to work. As a long-term lender, it needs protection against the participants' becoming short-term depositors. Effectively this equates to preventing a run on the bank. If a sufficiently large number of participants decided to take their funds out of the fixed annuity pool and move them to another investment, say, CREF, then the company would have to liquidate its long-term investments. Such long-term debt is typically not traded on an active exchange or secondary market. If enough participants decide to move their funds, the company will have to conduct a fire sale of its investment portfolio, and it will not have enough assets to be able to honor contracts already signed. A provider of fixed annuities must either place limitations on the movement of funds or penalize its insureds heavily for any early withdrawals.

TIAA invests in publicly traded bonds and makes direct loans to corporate borrowers. It may also invest in real estate or commercial mortgages. These investments represent long-term commitments. They lack the liquidity of, for example, Treasury bonds. The theory behind TIAA's investment pattern lies in its ability to lock in better rates of return. In general, the less liquid an investment, the higher the return the investor can demand of the issuer. The lack of liquidity restricts the flexibility of the investor, in this case TIAA, to move in and out of the portfolio as the size of the premium pool grows or shrinks. *As a result, with two limited exceptions described where applicable, TIAA imposes a ten-year limitation upon the movement of funds, and, as described in more detail later, the funds exiting TIAA are paid ratably, that is in roughly equal installments, over the ten-year period.*

Receiving fixed annuity payments equates to a mortgage in reverse. Instead of making fixed payments of interest and principal over a period of years to pay back a fixed sum, you pay the fixed sum up front and receive payments of interest and principal equaling a fixed amount over whatever time period has been agreed upon. The amount you receive will depend directly on the size of the premiums you surrender to the company and the number of payments you have agreed to receive.

Looking at the moment only at your Retirement Annuity account, usually the bulk of your entire accumulation (the types of accounts to be described later), TIAA offers only two distribution alternatives from its Traditional Annuity account: life or ten-year term. TIAA calls the rate of return that you receive on your annuity the "payout rate." It reflects the rates of return TIAA achieved when you paid premiums or contributions into your account. It also varies depending on the proportion of your premiums that were paid in each year and therefore in different interest rate markets. That means that the payout rate on two fixed annuities issued the same day may vary, depending on when the annuitants paid premiums into TIAA and how large those premiums were proportionate to the size of the entire accumulation.

As of the time of writing, interest rates have fallen from where they had been over the last three decades, but TIAA's investments turn over slowly and you will benefit from the interest rates that TIAA negotiated over the life of your account. Once the payout rate is calculated and therefore your periodic payment determined, it will not change. It is guaranteed.

TIAA will reduce the interest you receive to cover internal expenses. Like any other insurance company, TIAA will also set aside reserves, typically termed "mortality costs," to ensure that the investment pool will suffice to cover payments that may be due to all annuitants who live longer than their life expectancy. These reserves also safeguard the insurer against the risk that its annuitants will live longer, on average, than projected in its mortality tables. If in any year TIAA decides that its current investments have yielded cash in excess of what it needs to cover expenses and its reserves, it will declare a dividend. Ordinarily, that will increase the amount that you receive from your TIAA annuity. Although a dividend is not guaranteed, TIAA has paid one in every year since 1948.

TIAA cannot know how long each annuitant will live. It cannot poll all of its annuitants to learn the state of their health, their hobbies and leisure activities, or the riskiness of the environment in which they live. Instead, an insurance company relies on massive statistics on life expectancy. When you, as an annuitant, choose a lifetime payment stream, TIAA will calculate the guaranteed periodic amount that you will receive based on your age when the annuity starts and your statistical life expectancy. For example, a 70-year-old today will probably live to be 86 years old, according to the Internal Revenue Service. In the technical jargon, a 70-year-old has a sixteen-year life expectancy.

Some companies may have statistics for their own client or plan participant universe that are more relevant for their annuity calculations. The numbers are probably not significantly different, however, from those compiled by the IRS. The insurance company is looking for an average life expectancy. If their statistics are accurate, they will judge the average age correctly most of the time, and the economic impact on the company from those who die older than expected will be offset by those who die younger than expected.

TIAA establishes its standard accounts to build up into conventional fixed annuities. For the reasons articulated above, you may only withdraw or reinvest the contributions you allocated to TIAA in the Retirement Annuity part of your TIAA-CREF accumulation through the purchase of a ten-year transfer annuity, called appropriately enough the Transfer Payout Annuity (the "TPA"). TIAA guarantees a minimum rate of return of 3% as of February 2000. In addition to the guaranteed rate, TIAA has the option to pay dividends from earnings in excess of the guaranteed return, and as noted above, it has paid a dividend since 1948.

TIAA offers two methods by which an an annuity is paid. The "Standard Method" pays the guaranteed return plus the dividend as earned. Assuming that the payments remain relatively level, the problem becomes one of coping with inflation. The "Graded Method" attempts to safeguard the annuitant from the effects of inflation. Instead of receiving a combination of the guaranteed rate on your annuity plus the full dividend in any given year, your payment will only reflect a 4% rate of return. TIAA will reinvest the excess dividend to buy more coverage for future years. As a result, the annuity starts with a lower monthly payment, but generates larger payments in later years to blunt the effect of inflation. TIAA "grades" the annual payments based on the increase in dividends as time goes on.

Interest rates generally exceed the inflation rate, investors not being interested in a negative return, and the graded payments should normally show a continued increase. However, if long-term interest rates remain at extremely low levels by postwar standards, the dividends on TIAA payments could drop below 4%. In that highly contingent scenario, the payments through the Graded Method could in fact drop. Based on the payments that TIAA has made from both types of distributions to date, it will take roughly ten years for the monthly payments from a Graded Account to exceed the monthly payments from a Standard Account. It would take probably somewhere in the area of eighteen years for the aggregate payments made by the Graded Method to exceed the total payments made through the Standard Method.

Although you may move from the TIAA Graded Method to the TIAA Standard Method, you may not move from the Graded Method to a variable choice within CREF nor from the Standard Method back to the Graded Method.

A fixed annuity has the advantage of providing a minimum guaranteed payment potentially for the rest of your life. In order to provide that guarantee, TIAA only promises a minimum return, enhanced by potential dividends that reflect the earnings on its entire portfolio. As a continuous investor, TIAA will own assets with returns that span a wide range of interest rates.

Here the long-term investments that TIAA has made protect you as an annuitant. Given the large amount of funds with locked-in rates from past investments, returns on fixed annuities will typically trail movements in interest rates and therefore exhibit less volatility. For example, if interest rates decline, fixed annuity rates will diminish but at a much slower rate. In this example, you would receive somewhat higher returns than then current interest rates. Conversely, if interest rates rise, the potential dividends will lag behind the rising rates, reflecting the longer-term investments at lower rates made by TIAA on its embedded capital. You are protected on the downside but cannot receive an immediate jolt on the upside. The guaranteed return remains TIAA's safety valve. It will be commensurate with existing interest rates when the contract is signed, not a rate that is substantially above or below existing market levels. Fluctuations in the dividend level will occur because of the differential between past and future investments and the interest rates that prevailed when you bought your annuity.

As mentioned before, a variable annuity will pay you, the annuitant, a stream of payments, each of which will contain an equal number of annuity units. The number of units per payment remains constant. The dollars received by you will depend on the market value of the units. With the value of each unit subject to fluctuation, your periodic annuity payments will, of necessity, vary. We will first define annuity units, look at how they are valued, and then look at your options within the world of TIAA-CREF variable annuities.

When you are making contributions to a CREF variable annuity account, you will earmark the CREF funds in which you want to invest. CREF divides your holdings into "accumulation units," whose value will depend upon the funds into which you have made your investments. Every time you make another contribution or pay a premium, to use TIAA-CREF parlance, you receive additional accumulation units in the applicable funds. The number of accumulation units each addition generates will depend on the size of the new cash infusion, divided by the price per accumulation unit of the applicable fund. In the same way, if you have an IRA or a custodial account that invests in mutual funds, each addition will translate into so many more shares of each individual fund. The number of additional units or shares (to use the IRA example) will depend on the value per unit or share. If you look at your quarterly statement, you will see the number of accumulation units you own in each of the funds you have selected.

When you decide to annuitize your CREF account, the accumulation units become annuity units on a 1:1 ratio. Depending on which annuity choice you make, CREF will then determine the number of annuity units you will receive each month. During each month and each year that the annuity continues to make payments, you will receive the same number of annuity units per payment period.

For example, suppose you have $500,000 invested in one or more CREF accounts and the value of each unit, for simplicity's sake, is $50. You then have 10,000 annuity units. If you chose a single life annuity and your life expectancy is twenty years, then you will receive 500 annuity units annually and slightly more than 1/12 of this amount units monthly. As with the fixed annuity, if you outlive your life expectancy, the flow of units will continue unabated, the value of each unit still dependent on investment performance. If you do not outlive your life expectancy, then the unused portion of your account becomes available to pay those who are longer lived. What those payments translate into in dollars and cents will depend directly on the investment performance of the applicable funds. If the investment performance has increased the value of each unit, then you will receive more dollars per payment. And the converse also applies.

Unlike the fixed annuity, a variable annuity does not carry a guaranteed rate of return. CREF promises only that the size in the distributions will directly reflect the returns of your investments minus fees and mortality reserves. With no guaranteed rate of return and payments that are directly related to investment performance, CREF does not need to restrict the liquidity of the investment choices either during the accumulation phase or during the distribution phase. The TIAA ten-year rule does not apply.

That explains, we hope, the annuity unit concept. How are the units revalued? You may choose to have your units revalued annually or monthly. If you elect annual revaluation, then each April 30, CREF will determine the average value of each unit during the preceding calendar year. This computation will determine the value of your payments for the next twelve months beginning as of the month of May. They will remain the same until the following April 30, when the process is repeated.

If you elect monthly revaluation, then each month's payment will depend on the average value of your units during the preceding month. In all likelihood, this will mean that every month's payment will differ, depending on market conditions. You may switch from one method of revaluation to another once annually, notifying CREF by March 31 so that the change can become effective as of the following May.

CREF offers the same types of annuity options that TIAA does— life or term. However, TIAA only offers a ten-year term for your Retirement Annuity account, probably the bulk of your accumulation. CREF gives you a range of up to thirty years, but the term cannot exceed your life expectancy as determined by the Internal Revenue Service mortality tables.

Within the TIAA-CREF system, you may change your investment choice while in the distribution phase once a quarter from one CREF fund to another if offered within your employer's plan or to the TIAA Traditional Annuity. However, you *cannot* change your annuity investment choice *from* the TIAA Traditional Annuity. The same limitations on the amount of liquidity that force a ten-year payment out of TIAA necessitate that once a TIAA annuity has started, TIAA cannot unwind its investments on a dime to reflect participants' change of heart.

CREF offers a wide variety of variable investment funds, all of which have performed well over time within their particular investment class. We will look at the various choices more closely below.

As you would expect by now, a variable annuity represents an irrevocable choice of your distribution method. Although you may change the investment base for your distributions, you may never cancel the annuity and take the remaining balance back.

The Accumulation Phase

This part of the book deals with the nuts and bolts of TIAA-CREF. This may sound as dull as dishwater. We will try to cover the facts as clearly and entertainingly as we can, but admit that the material contained in the several chapters that follow do not contain the stuff out of which best-sellers or beach books are woven. However, very few participants in our experience know very much about TIAA-CREF and the workings of their individual accounts.

It just happens that learning the information contained in this book does not fulfill any degree, job, or career requirement. In much the same way, law schools and medical schools do not teach their graduates how to run a legal or medical practice. That type of knowledge you learn in the real world, and this book provides more of that genre of information. It happens to be an important part of the real world for you, or it will be by the time you have finished reading this book.

Do not, therefore, skip over this section of the book. If you read the chapters of this book that apply to you and your plan, you should no longer remain bewildered by the apparent complexity of TIAA-CREF. Armed with that background, you will have the perspective to grasp the other, subtler, and perhaps more intellectually challenging aspects of the TIAA-CREF system.

You need to understand these details as they pertain to the plan in which you are a participant in order to become an informed decision maker, more particularly about some of the most important decisions that you will make in your life. The rewards may not arrive until the long run, when you retire. If you need more immediate gratification, then think in the following way. Master part II, and you will dazzle others at cocktail parties and other social occasions. You may even impress your spouse or significant other. Whatever your motives, remember that the old cliché about building on a firm foundation applies here as well.

On the other hand, each chapter may not apply to you. Your employer may not have group accounts, in which case you do not have to read about the Group Retirement Account or the Group Supplemental Retirement Account. On the other hand, you should read the chapters or sections describing the Retirement Annuity and the Supplemental Retirement Annuity, because that is what you've got, and you need to know the rules of the game.

Again, we have done our best to remain nontechnical, and we hope that our sense of humor has not begun to wear on you. *Read what you need, but be forewarned that if you skip too much, you may miss vital points in the discussion in the succeeding parts of the book.*

No one in his right mind will read this book at one sitting, not even the authors. But you need to plunge in and learn what applies to you and the plan that your employer maintains. This book deals in generalities. It cannot lay out the details of the eight thousand plans adopted by employers that use TIAA-CREF. We will describe the general aspects of the system in sufficient detail that you will be able to go from here.

Even if you commit this book to memory, the responsibility of dealing with your TIAA-CREF accumulation remains yours. You should ask for and receive, on a regular basis, your employer's plan or the Summary Plan Description (the "SPD"). At the very least, you should know the following about your employer's plan: the matching contributions, the investment options, the availability of the Supplemental Retirement Annuity, and the restrictions or lack of restrictions on moving your money out of TIAA-CREF upon retirement, should you desire.

You should read, keep, and file every quarterly statement that you receive from TIAA-CREF, and you should keep track of your progress in building an accumulation. God helps those who help themselves. This book is designed to make that task easier. *But the ball rests in your court, and it always will.* When you have read this book, you will, we expect, be a more knowledgeable participant, but you need to remain actively interested in what is happening and will happen to your account. We are talking about your last two to three decades on this planet, a sizable percentage of your life span. *Ask questions, demand answers that you understand, and remember that we are talking about your and your loved ones' lives.*

Two factors contribute to the growth in your TIAA-CREF account: contributions and investment performance. If you contribute as much as you can during your working years and at the same time make investment decisions that will give your account an opportunity to grow, you will create, *over time*, a substantial accumulation that will allow you to live comfortably in retirement. This presumes that we do not undergo some violent social or other cataclysm that no one can foresee.

The concept of contributions is fairly clear. You are increasing the size of your account by adding money on a regular basis. There are usually two sources of contributions to your account: your own additions through salary reduction, and additions made by your employer. An employer may "match" your contributions up to a certain percentage of either your salary or the amount that you are earmarking for the account. Some will make contributions to your account based on a percentage of your salary whether you contribute to the plan or not.

Your employer's retirement plan document will explain how much you may contribute from your own salary to your retirement account. It will also tell you how much your employer will be contributing to your account. A retirement plan with employer matches is arguably the most valuable benefit that an employer can offer. It represents, in effect, a tax-deferred salary increase or, as some might say, a salary for retirement. Just how large this "retirement salary" will become depends in many respects on you.

If you remember, one of the concepts we covered earlier (and will undoubtedly mention again) is the importance of putting money to work as *early* as possible. The time value of money idea works best for those who invest early on in the process and keep adding to the pot throughout their career. You have to keep in mind that your ultimate return will be a function of two variables: how much you put to work and when you put it to work. Indeed, this is where the employer match makes a difference. At times when you have less personal liquidity, an employer match may enable you to double the contributions to your account without further deductions that would otherwise be unaffordable.

In most plans, you may make contribution adjustments only once a year. Again, you should speak with your benefits office or look through a copy of your employer's plan document to determine at what point during the year this may be done. Usually, this limitation came into being in order not to create havoc for the benefits administrators and the payroll office. If you want to change your contribution amount, you owe it to yourself to find out the given month each year when this option becomes available, usually to be effective a couple of months later and at the beginning of the new year. Your employer may operate differently, however, and you don't want to miss out and delay your plans simply because you "forgot to check." Check!

The second part of the equation, making investment decisions that will give your account a chance to grow, offers a second challenge. You must look at the appropriate investment choices with your probable life expectancy in mind, as well as the age at which you will most likely begin drawing on your retirement assets. We will return to this theme later, but the issues described below should also be borne in mind as you make choices through the accumulation phase into retirement and beyond.

Right off the bat, you should know that even if you wait to retire until age $70^1/_2$, you probably have a healthy fifteen to twenty years of life yet to live. Although age may slow (most of us) down and increase the prevalence of sickness, for the great majority, age $70^1/_2$ does not represent the finish line, merely the beginning of the last part of the race. When one thinks through the implications of this statement, you will appreciate that growth in your income and in your underlying assets remains nearly as important a factor at retirement as it was in earlier years. Although preservation of capital carries more weight in later years, in most cases it should not be the only consideration when choosing an investment strategy.

Let's look at a few statistics. A Goldman Sachs study noted, "Three percent inflation would cut money's purchasing power in half in twenty-three years, and 4% inflation would take seventeen years." The IRS actuarial tables say that an individual aged $70^1/_2$ will most probably live another sixteen years. If you are married and your spouse is two years younger than you are, statistics indicate that one of you will probably live to be 90. A 3% inflation rate is historically low. During the years between 1960 and 1990, we saw inflation rates ranging from

3% to more than 12%. The current low-inflation, low-interest-rate climate does not represent a new era. The business cycle has not disappeared; we are simply experiencing an unprecedented postwar boom. Nor does the current favorable busines, climate represent some natural law like gravitation. We may well see a return to the rates of inflation that we experienced during the 1970s and 1980s. And, of course, the national average increase in the cost of living will rarely turn out to mirror your own experience.

In turn, the expectation of a longer life affects one's investment decisions. For years, the accepted wisdom was that retirement mandated the use of fixed-income investments, usually bonds, to preserve capital and assure income. If that wisdom ever accurately reflected reality, it could only have prevailed when life expectancy was considerably shorter than it is today. The challenge that you face as a retiree is not just how to preserve capital, but also how to keep your account growing so that you can weather a possible return to double digit or at least more rapid inflation without a collapse of your buying power.

The axiom about appropriate investments for the retiree requires reassessment. A top quality fixed-income investment, typically a bond with a coupon payable semiannually, will pay the same amount of interest each year until maturity. At maturity, you receive your initial investment amount in return. Although the payments you receive in the early years may seem acceptable, as time goes on, the effects of inflation will start eroding your purchasing power. Any fixed payment stream will *over time* lose the race against inflation. The payment stream remains fixed in size, but its value declines. How fast and how far will depend on general economic conditions. The likelihood that this phenomenon will impact your retirement obviously increases with your life expectancy. You are at risk for a longer time.

Everyone knows the risks inherent in the stock market where volatility can dramatically change the value of a particular investment. Historically, however, the stock market has appreciated at a pace that has exceeded inflation, in spite of short-term spikes up and down. The one thing fixed-income investments have *not* done over time is to maintain their value relative to inflation. Even those bonds paying relatively high coupons lose their purchasing power if they have a long maturity. Remember, it is not the number of dollars that changes; it is the value of a fixed number of dollars that is eroded by inflation. Each year, each dollar buys less than the year before. Stock market investments are also subject to dollar value erosion due to inflation. Inflation tends to decrease the value of intangibles, like stocks and bonds, and increase the value of tangibles.

The major difference between a fixed-income security and a stock investment boils down to whether one wants to be a lender or an equity participant. If you are lending to a company, the borrower wants to keep the cost of its loans as low as possible and the flexibility of its indebtedness as great as possible, especially if interest rates decline. Management of a company does not exist to enhance the value of its debt load. It is most interested in increasing the value of its, and therefore your, ownership.

This does not mean that one should put all of one's eggs in one basket. Diversification reduces risk, and perhaps only during the first half of one's career should you seriously contemplate owning an all-equity portfolio. Each of the TIAA-CREF funds is internally diversified, but you have to determine your own acceptable level of risk in choosing among the investment options available to you. You also need to assess general economic conditions. Proper asset allocation is a combination of lending (fixed-income) and investing (share purchase), and that will change as conditions change and as your situation in life alters over the years.

For all of these reasons, when you decide how to invest your retirement assets, think carefully about the nature of the investment you are making. Too many people think of investing in the stock market as putting money into a slot machine and pulling the lever. When you invest your retirement assets through a professional money manager, such as TIAA-CREF or other providers that your employer may offer in its plan, you are not gambling, but you are entrusting investment of your assets to fund managers whose business it is to look for growth within the risk parameters of the funds you choose. Which of those choices you make will depend on individual preferences and your personal assessment of the future of the economy and the markets in which investments will be made. TIAA-CREF and retirement accounts generally do not carry any immunity from the rule that the greatest rewards usually involve higher risk. The risk-reward ratio you prefer will depend on a number of factors that are locked up inside of you. This book can only inform; it cannot change hearts and minds.

Like the peculiar behavior of the dog in the night in the Sherlock Holmes story "Silver Blaze," one of the obvious but overlooked clues about the insurance orientation of TIAA-CREF appears in the names of the accounts that are given to the various accumulation alternatives available to you. Each account is labeled an "annuity," and each contribution is called a "premium." To avoid confusion you should note that what TIAA-CREF labels as an "account," you probably would call an investment choice or fund.

Stripped to the basics, your Retirement Annuity (or "RA") boils down to an accumulation agreement between you and TIAA-CREF. However, your employer's retirement plan limns the terms of this agreement. Although your employer determines most of the parameters of the agreement, TIAA-CREF does impose one or two requirements on the plan in the form of investment choices that we will touch upon below.

The RA generally forms the core of an employer's retirement plan. By making contributions to the RA, the employer can ensure that the benefits it provides serve their purpose. You will typically see a reflection of your employer's overall personnel philosophy in the structure of the RA. Some feel they have a responsibility to guarantee a lifetime cash flow for their employees and spouses and will require annuitization. Others maintain control through their contributions, the use of which is restricted to assure the employer that its funds will provide employee pensions. Some adhere to the philosophy that they are responsible for their retired employees only, and after the employee has died, the need for limitations vanishes and the employees' spouses or families can, as of that point, make the choices that are appropriate for their situation. In some instances, this being a free country, the family may not make the best choices, but the employer has discharged its obligations as it sees them.

Many institutions, however, seem to be moving in the direction of providing their employees with the opportunity of making their own investment and retirement choices, assuming that the individual employee can better decide on the appropriate path for his retirement than the employer, whose rules will cut across entire classes of employees. And indeed, some employers allow different degrees of freedom to withdraw funds from the RA at retirement, depending on the type of employee. Unionized staff may have an entirely different set of options than nonunionized employees, and these differences may appear in the collective bargaining agreement. Some employers allow their employees, or certain classifications of them, to withdraw their entire TIAA-CREF accumulation at retirement and to make their own decisions about appropriate investments among the myriad of alternatives now available. Freedom has its price, and we call it failure. Nonetheless, some employers permit their employees autonomy in shaping their retirement income and lifestyle, and they can choose where to park their funds in a manner that will, one hopes, provide for a comfortable and financially secure retirement.

We regularly find participants who believe that the strictures in their employer's retirement plan on their freedom to take their retirement funds and manage them originate with TIAA-CREF. It just ain't so. Generally, the only limitations imposed by TIAA-CREF appear in the rules regarding traditional TIAA and those inherent in annuities as a financial product. TIAA-CREF provides a very flexible model plan with numerous options from which an employer may choose. Some limitations may trace their lineage to the murky fens of the Internal Revenue Code. The great majority of limitations originates with your employer.

Having touched first on the area in which employers differ the most—the degree to which they will let employees take control of their retirement finances at retirement— we need to discuss three other major issues in order to understand the operation of the RA: employer contributions, investment choices, and the concept of portability.

First, as to contributions, Section 403(b) of the Code allows employers to match your contributions to your account within the plan. Annual addition by you and your employer may not exceed a given percentage (25%) of your income or $30,000, whichever is less. Employers enjoy a wide degree of latitude within that percentage limitation. They also can determine the extent to which they will match or exceed the employee's contributions. Each plan will differ on the method by which employer contributions are made, and there may be differentiation, for example, depending on your level of cash compensation. Again, you need to know your plan. You want to maximize the amount that your employer contributes to your retirement.

Plans fall into two categories: contributory and noncontributory.

This distinction turns on whether you have to contribute to the plan or not. Some employers will pay their contributions into the RA plan for your benefit whether you contribute or not, and they will deposit your contributions, should you choose to make them, into either the RA or the Supplemental Retirement Annuity ("SRA") described in the next chapter. From the employer's point of view, separating its contributions from yours simplifies its bookkeeping. From your point of view, if your contributions are allocated to the SRA, they escape whatever strictures the employer may place upon funds in the RA. Generally speaking, wherever the contributions end up, if you have a contributory plan and your employer's contribution will depend on yours, you want to max out your employer's contribution in order to leverage your contribution as much as possible.

In later years, many employers have also turned to outside investment product providers and offer their services either parallel to or instead of the insurance products provided by TIAA-CREF. If you choose one of these investment products, you will not be contributing to an RA. You will have a separate account with the investment firm, but it will exist within the overarching structure of your employer's retirement plan. Your employer may choose to allocate all matches to an accumulation in a TIAA-CREF Retirement Annuity, or it may choose to contribute the match to your account with the alternative investment provider. Again, this is depends on how your employer has constructed the plan.

The RA is unique in the world of retirement structures in that, generally, if you change employers, it is not necessary to make any changes in your RA investments. Provided that your new employer also has TIAA-CREF as a product provider and also offers an RA as part of the plan, your accumulation account at TIAA-CREF will most probably stay the same and you may receive contributions from your new employer into the same account. This feature is often referred to as "portability." (We will delve a little deeper into this concept later on.) When moving from one institution to another, it is usually not possible to continue contributing to an account with a provider other than TIAA-CREF. Not all schools provide the same alternative investment choices, and that clearly limits the portability of many custodial accounts.

Most employers' plans allow for immediate vesting. In other words, you may begin to make contributions from your salary and receive contributions from your employer into the RA from the first day you report to the salt mine, and you do not forfeit your accumulation if you leave your employer. In the for-profit sector, employers typically require that new employees wait a year or more before they can begin to take advantage of a retirement plan benefit; actual vesting of the employer's contributions may not occur until some years later. ERISA generally governs the vesting and participation features of most private pension plans.

Many employers who use TIAA-CREF for their retirement plan allow their participants to utilize most or all of the annuity accumulation funds offered by TIAA-CREF for qualified plan accumulations. Others, however, are more restrictive. They may reduce the number of investment options available. They may have lower or higher matching contribution percentages, and perhaps most importantly, they may place limitations on what you may do with your accumulation at retirement. Although TIAA-CREF offered ten annuity investment options in August 1999, employers are not required to offer all ten options to their participants through the RA. The only options that must be offered are the conventional, fixed TIAA account and, on the variable side, the CREF Money Market Account and the CREF Stock Account. It is important to contact your benefits office or read the most current version of your plan to know which of the investment options are available to you through your RA and what the employer's contribution, if any, may be.

In some of the other pieces we have written, we have referred to the RA as TIAA-CREF's "workhorse." The RA is the main accumulation account for any plan built up around TIAA-CREF annuities. Once the RA (or the Group Retirement Account, which is discussed later on) is in place, the employer can begin to look at other options to offer. We will try to cover most of these variations in the chapters that follow.

8

What Is Your Supplemental Retirement Annuity Account?

As the name indicates, a Supplemental Retirement Annuity (the "SRA") operates as an adjunct to your Retirement Annuity. If your employer offers an SRA, you have the opportunity to augment your retirement stash on a tax-deferred basis through a salary deferral agreement, provided you are within the contribution limitations stipulated by law. Again, your benefits office will be able to advise you as to how large a percentage of your salary you may contribute to your SRA. Not all institutions offer the SRA. If your employer is one who does, try your hardest to take advantage of this feature of your employer's plan. *It typically allows you to contribute the gap between the maximum contribution you can make under the Code and the permissible deferral of salary under the employer's plan.* If you have the funds, for obvious reasons you want to save as much as possible in the tax-favored setting of a qualified plan. Let's look at the other characteristics of an SRA.

The SRA is, like the RA, a contract between you and TIAA-CREF. The SRA does not fall under the employer's stipulations and limitations in the RA part of the plan. In the SRA, you may choose among the full range of TIAA-CREF investment vehicles. Furthermore, you may transfer any part or all of the accumulations in your SRA to an alternative investment. *This includes any accumulation you may have in TIAA.* This constitutes one of the few exceptions to the rule that traditional TIAA assets may only be transferred by using the TPA or a life annuity.

You contribute to an SRA through pretax salary deductions. You may decide how much you would like to contribute within the limitations established by the Internal Revenue Code regarding defined contribution plans. For the most part, the easiest way to determine the maximum contribution you may make is to confer with your benefits office. They should have the relevant numbers close at hand.

SRA funds are not subject to employer-imposed withdrawal or rollover restrictions, which may be the case with RA funds. They are, however (surprise!), subject to the rules of the Internal Revenue Code governing withdrawals from tax-deferred retirement assets. You may withdraw any SRA assets at retirement regardless of the employer's plan, and you may roll the assets out to another retirement account trustee (investment firm, bank, and so forth) and a different tax-deferred account. If you do so, you may have the funds managed or make your own investment decisions. You may also take taxable distributions without penalty as long as you are in compliance with applicable Code provisions, to be discussed later. To summarize the most important rules at this time, you should remember that, as a rule of thumb, any distributions taken before $59\frac{1}{2}$ will trigger a 10% penalty and distributions that fall below the level of mandatory distributions after $70\frac{1}{2}$ will trigger a 50% penalty on the shortfall.

As mentioned before, you should be taking advantage of a chance to set aside more funds on a tax-deferred basis if your employer does in fact offer an SRA option. As we delve further into retirement and estate planning, you will see how valuable tax-deferred assets can be. Given the compounding effect of time and a steady rate of return, even the smallest amount set aside on a regular basis can provide a tidy nest egg for retirement. Large retirement accounts do not come into being instantaneously, but grow like trees over time. The SRA invites you to save and to let the time value of money and compounding returns work in your favor.

9

What Are a Group Retirement Account and a Group Supplemental Retirement Account?

The Group Retirement Account (or "GRA") and the Group Supplemental Retirement Account (or "GSRA") resemble the Retirement Annuity account and the Supplemental Retirement Annuity account in many respects. There are, however, some fundamental differences between the group accounts and their nongroup counterparts.

Both the RA and the GRA are contracts with TIAA-CREF. Both function as the core of your employer's retirement benefit program. However, whereas the RA is formally a contract between TIAA-CREF and the participant, a GRA is a contract between TIAA-CREF and the employer. TIAA-CREF issues a certificate in your name indicating your participation in the group contract. Among the investment options available under the GRA and, of course, the GSRA, you still make the investment choices. As long as you remain with the same employer, the differences between a GRA and an RA will seem purely formal.

The critical concept is that your participation in the group contract occurs through your employer's relationship with TIAA-CREF. In an RA, you maintain the relationship with TIAA-CREF, the door to which is opened by your employer. As we mentioned above, you may normally continue adding to your RA account and continue to receive employer matches to your RA account, no matter which participating institution employs you.

In the case of a GRA, your participation is linked to your employment at a specific institution. You may or may not be able to incorporate your GRA accumulation into a plan offered by a new employer. In both the RA and the GRA style plans, your employer decides which of the TIAA-CREF investment choices you may choose from in addition to the TIAA standard account, the CREF Stock Account, and the CREF Money Market Account. Understanding the fundamental distinction between an RA and a GRA, we can now look at some of the specific differences between the two plan types.

There are options available to you through a GRA only. Unlike the RA, the GRA may offer the possibility of cashing out your accumulation or rolling it over income tax free to an IRA (nontaxable event) upon retiring or changing employers. This includes any assets that may have accumulated in a TIAA account within the GRA. This makes sense if you cannot carry over the GRA automatically to your new employer.

As you will recall, normally any assets accumulated in the TIAA standard account may only be withdrawn through the TPA or a life annuity. Your ability to move funds out of TIAA differs in GRAs in two respects. First, you may move all or part of the TIAA portion of your accumulation into another TIAA-CREF option over five years, rather than the standard ten-year term. You will receive a five-year TPA. Second, you have an option to withdraw your TIAA funds if you leave an employer who offers the GRA. At present, if you choose to roll over your assets accumulated in your GRA, you must do so, as to the TIAA portion, within 120 days of leaving your employer. If your employer offers this option, then you may be charged a 2.5% surrender fee by TIAA-CREF. This is similar to the surrender fees charged by other insurance companies outside of a retirement plan when you close out an annuity.

If you choose to maintain your assets in a GRA upon changing employers, you may as a rule do so. You can freeze your old GRA, adding no new funds to the account but letting the investment returns accumulate. If your new employer also offers a GRA option, you may be able to transfer your old account into the new GRA. In that case, you would receive a new certificate for a GRA. The certificate would identify you as a participant in the new employer's GRA plan and therefore eligible to receive matches and make contributions under the new plan.

The GSRA is also a contract between the employer and TIAA-CREF in which you as an individual may participate, and as a participant in the group plan, you are issued a certificate to that effect. As with the conventional SRA, you may choose among all of the investment options offered by TIAA-CREF. As with the SRA, contributions typically derive from pretax salary contributions and are not matched by the employer.

Under a GSRA contract, employers can offer a loan provision to participants. We will touch upon some of the technicalities of borrowing from your GSRA in the chapters dealing with preretirement withdrawals from your TIAA-CREF account. Although we deal with these issues later, we can say here that the merits of borrowing from a tax-deferred account are debatable.

In our opinion, unless your financial needs are dire, you should resist the temptation to borrow from these essential accounts. They represent funds that will support you when you no longer draw a salary. By borrowing against your retirement assets, you are mortgaging your future. In addition, you lose the opportunity to maximize tax-deferred growth at what probably is an early stage in the accumulation process. We have discussed the built-in advantages enjoyed by a tax-free investor; you want to take advantage of every opportunity of seeing these funds grow tax deferred. You also lose the compounding effect. From an investment standpoint, you risk losing some of the best periods of growth. Unfortunately, none of us is blessed with the ability to know when the market will surprise investors with one or more spectacular rises. Even in the most successful mutual funds, over 80% of their investors lose money. Rather than act as long-term investors, they try to time the market or take their funds out just in time to miss those spectacular days or weeks that provide most of the growth. If you borrow from your GSRA, you could end up emulating the hapless 80%. Obviously, emergencies may arise, but barring the catastrophic, the last source of loan funds you want to tap is your own.

The Teacher's Personal Annuity provides you an investment vehicle to accumulate retirement assets *out of after-tax funds.* Confusingly for our purposes, TIAA-CREF labels this type of annuity the "TPA." As you read the literature, do not mistake this option with the Transfer Payout Annuity (also called the "TPA"), the process by which funds move out of a traditional TIAA accumulation over a ten-year period. For clarity's sake, we will refer only to the Transfer Payout Annuity as the "TPA" and use the full name for the Teacher's Personal Annuity.

For all intents and purposes, a Teacher's Personal Annuity does not differ from a tax-deferred annuity that you might purchase from your local insurance agent or investment advisor. If you buy such an annuity from TIAA-CREF, you will invest in TIAA-CREF funds as opposed to funds offered by other annuity providers.

This chapter represents one of our few excursions outside of the qualified plan arena. Remember that the typical retirement accumulation builds through tax-deductible contributions on your part, contributions by your employer that do not increase your taxable income, and tax-free internal growth. You only pay income tax when you take distributions from your TIAA-CREF plan.

By contrast, you will fund the Teacher's Personal Annuity with money that has already been taxed as part of your taxable income. The account you create will also have tax-free internal growth. If you elect to annuitize this account, then the Code mandates a different method of taxation of each payment than prevails in the qualified plan. The principal of the account having been taxed once already, it escapes second taxation when it is distributed as part of each annuity payment. Only the still untaxed internal growth will incur a tax. For this reason, the industry description of such an annuity as tax deferred fits the facts like a glove.

Thus, the Code divides each payment into two components. The principal portion being returned to you will not incur a tax, and only the growth portion will be taxed as it is paid to you. The Code provides a formula for computing the two portions. *Even though the internal growth may have occurred in large part because of capital appreciation, as opposed to dividend or interest income, the Code treats the entire taxable portion as ordinary income.* You lose the benefit of the 20% capital gain rate, which may be lower that your marginal income tax rate. In evaluating the value of a tax-deferred annuity, do not lose sight of this Faustian bargain with the Internal Revenue Code.

The other downside to a tax-deferred annuity occurs if you die owning one. Ordinarily, the assets includible in your estate receive a step-up in basis from your original cost to the value, to simplify, as of the date of death. This lessens any capital gain or other income tax liability down the road when the asset is sold. No such step-up occurs with an annuity, and the untaxed internal growth remains liable to estate taxation and to income taxation upon distribution. The Code also limits the options available to your estate that might reduce estate tax.

Obviously, you should, as a rule, utilize every opportunity available to you to invest pretax dollars. In terms of economic efficiency, that will provide the most bang for the buck. The post-tax annuity only comes into play if you have the discretionary income to invest.

With that as an introduction, this chapter will provide an overview to nonqualified tax-deferred annuities within the TIAA-CREF universe.

In the Teacher's Personal Annuity, you have two investment choices: a fixed annuity that provides a set rate of return over an agreed-upon period of time, and a variable annuity. These alternatives have the familiar ring of TIAA fixed annuities or CREF variable annuities. However, within TIAA-CREF you do not have any investment choices to make if you choose the variable annuity. TIAA-CREF only offers the Stock Index Account for this product. By contrast, other providers offer a variety of investment vehicles.

In making these investments, you are not taking advantage of any tax benefits, and the Code does not restrict the size of your contributions. If you elect the Teacher's Personal Annuity, you also enjoy the opportunity of contributing through electronic transfers and/or salary deductions, which do not, of course, reduce your taxable income. You may also generally make lump sum contributions.

You may ask your insurance provider, in this case TIAA-CREF, to "surrender," that is, return to you, all or part of your accumulation at any time. Here be dragons. If you are under the age of $59\frac{1}{2}$, this payment will incur a 10% penalty tax on the untaxed earnings surrendered. Generally, partial surrenders are paid first from earnings and last from contributions or cost basis. Hence, if you are younger than $59\frac{1}{2}$ and wish to take a partial surrender, you will incur full income tax on the amount paid as well as a 10% penalty on the amount withdrawn. The only exceptions to the penalty occur in the case of death or disability, or if the payments are made in "substantially equal payments" over your life expectancy.

Once you have started to take annuity payments, you may not ask TIAA-CREF to surrender any of the funds. As with any of the annuity options in your retirement plan, the choice to annuitize is irrevocable.

Continuing the fast gallop through tax-deferred annuities, the first choice you face is whether you ought to invest in a tax-deferred annuity or seek to build a portfolio of other types of investments with your after-tax funds. The tax-deferred annuity holds out the advantage of postponing the incidence of taxation and increasing your retirement income. On the other hand, if you are already a participant in a retirement plan that emphasizes annuities, shouldn't you diversify the types of investments that you making? Your ability to grow that portfolio operates at a disadvantage because you incur taxes as you go on dividends or interest and capital gains. On the other hand, you have a wider range of investment choices, and the guaranteed rates of return on all tax-deferred annuities are usually well below market rates of interest. The account belongs to you, and you can make the investment choices. If you start to accumulate funds outside of your qualified plan when you are young, then the time value of money will probably result in considerable growth of capital to supplement your retirement needs or serve any other purpose that seems suitable to you.

In many instances, the tax-deferred annuity, which may seem attractive when you are young, does not appear so nifty when actual annuitization must occur. You then face a dilemma: either you take the annuity or you cash out. Unlike the TIAA-CREF annuity accounts within your employer's qualified plan, which the Code allows you to roll over into an IRA without income tax liability, *no such safe harbor exists in the tax-deferred annuity universe. If you take a full distribution in a lump sum, then the entire amount of growth that occurred since your investment began will be taxed as ordinary income (even if it represents capital appreciation) in the year of receipt.* Your marginal rate will probably soar through the range of brackets, and you will pay, typically, $33^{1}/_{3}$% to 40% of that growth to the Internal Revenue Service. You may minimize the tax burden by some stretching of the payments, but that still represents a high price to pay for regaining the flexibility that you could have enjoyed from the outset had you not invested in a tax-deferred annuity.

In a way, the choice mirrors the advertisements that an automotive parts manufacturer uses for its products: pay me a little now or pay a whole lot more later on. If you forego the tax-deferred annuity, then you will incur tax in relatively small bites. Capital gains will receive the benefit of their lower tax rates. If you decide to pay later, then you may pay more and end up with less after taxes. Capital gains will be taxed as ordinary income. Tax-deferred annuities create estate tax problems that are too technical to be described here, except as noted above, but they can result in both income and estate taxation.

The choice depends again on your value system and your tolerance for risk. It will also reflect your feelings about diversification and the need to build up assets outside of a purely retirement-based environment. Freedom has its price, and you may feel that you prefer to accrue as much postretirement income as you can through a stable of annuities, some variable, some fixed. At least you ought to know what your choices are and the implications of each of them.

"Portable," as defined in *Webster's Encyclopedic Unabridged Dictionary*, means "capable of being transported or conveyed." A portable retirement account would allow you to move it from one employer to another without any discernible detriment to you. As a rule, employers in either the not-for-profit or the for-profit sector rarely permit employees to bring retirement plans from previous employers to their new positions. On occasion, Congress has debated enacting legislation that would allow for the creation of individual pension accounts that could be moved from one employer to another.

Each employer determines what it considers to be reasonable to offer as a retirement benefit within the framework of the law (of course) and its own financial strength and personnel policies. Retirement plans from two different employers mix as well as the proverbial oil and water.

TIAA-CREF provides the exception that proves the rule. Given TIAA-CREF's dominant position as a retirement product provider and plan advisor in the not-for-profit sector, it has been able to bring a certain degree of uniformity to the thousands of plans it furnishes to participating institutions. Although few plans are identical, given the infinite variety of matching percentages and other idiosyncratic features characteristic of most retirement plans, every institution that utilizes TIAA-CREF incorporates a Retirement Annuity or a Group Retirement Account into its retirement plan. In addition, all plans using TIAA-CREF must offer at least the TIAA Standard Account, the CREF Money Market Account, and the CREF Stock Account.

Against that background, if you move from one employer who uses the RA to another employer who does the same, the transition will appear and, for accumulation purposes, will be seamless. Your RA account will reflect your prior accumulation, and it will increase as your new employer and you (if your participation is contemplated by your new employer's plan) make contributions in accordance with the new plan's terms. The same applies with respect to the Supplemental Retirement Annuity. If your new employer offers that as an option, your SRA accumulation will carry over, and you will be able to augment your retirement funds further with your own funds. Against the background of the for-profit sector, where typically a departing employee must leave his accumulation frozen or roll the fund into an Individual Retirement Account, in either case without making new contributions and relying on investment growth alone, the continuity provided by the universal acceptance of the RA or the GRA looms large in one's career and retirement planning.

TIAA-CREF acts, therefore, in some respects as a central book-keeping unit for all participating employers and, more specifically, for you as a participant. Note that these rules apply only to accumulations that you may have in TIAA-CREF products. If your present employer offers other institutions' investment funds and you have placed funds in these vehicles, you will most likely not be able to continue contributing to the same accounts with a new employer unless the same providers are part of the new employer's plan. Should that occur, that would, given the current market shares of nonprofit retirement plans, involve dumb luck.

If you cannot carry over those funds, they may continue to be invested and grow on a tax-deferred basis. For the sake of maintaining control and simplifying your life, you will most likely prefer to roll out those funds to an IRA. You will no longer be able to contribute to this account through your employee benefit plan, but you can monitor its progress more easily. On the other hand, if you like the investment performance you are getting from the previous provider, you can maintain your asset accumulation with the old employer's provider until it is time to take distributions. You are in the same boat as the typical corporate employee.

Even in these instances where you roll over your old accumulation into a new IRA, you may find some restrictions. Many firms have developed what they call "proprietary funds." All of the major mutual fund families and insurance companies operate funds in which you may not invest unless you do so directly through that company. TIAA-CREF and other annuities are proprietary funds. Hence, they lack portability and must be, in insurance parlance, "surrendered" before the value of the asset may be moved to a new account. Remember that, properly implemented, this transfer should not result in an income tax liability if you are moving retirement assets. It merely means that you must first turn your investment into cash before moving it and then reinvest it with the new firm.

In similar vein, TIAA-CREF funds are proprietary. If you want to move assets from TIAA-CREF to another firm, then you must first check to be sure that the plan under which these assets were accumulated will allow you to move your savings out of TIAA-CREF and roll them over to another company. If so, you must then have TIAA-CREF liquidate the funds and transfer the proceeds to your new account. If you are transferring TIAA-CREF retirement assets, then you will be moving the funds to a rollover IRA. If you are moving taxable investments from TIAA-CREF's taxable mutual funds, then you will be transferring to a taxable investment account with another firm. Any gains that have accumulated will be taxed at the point of transfer, as described in the section on tax-deferred annuities.

During your working career, your TIAA-CREF accounts will probably appear totally portable, subject to the incongruities between a GRA and an RA accumulation. You may find that your investment choices at your new employer are more limited than they were formerly. Of course, when you are working at institution A, its rules will control the amounts of contributions and the vehicles available to you within and without TIAA-CREF. TIAA-CREF will keep track of all of your Retirement Annuity accumulations in both TIAA and CREF as you move from one institution to the next. This means posting contributions to the ledger, but also allocating the earnings attributable to the time you served at school A and research institute B and the amount you accumulated while serving at hard labor at each of your employers.

As one typically learns at retirement, this means, that, in certain critical respects, your accumulation did not actually follow you from one institution to the next. *All assets accumulated at one institution and the growth thereon will always remain subject to the rules of that institution's plan.* Over time, those rules will probably change, and the current rules will apply to you as though you had retired from that employer, even though you may have accumulated your allocable portion of your accounts under another system of rules that may now be regarded as archaic.

The persistent quality of former employers' rules can lead to some confusion. You will not see any such differentiation of funds on your quarterly statements or annuity benefits projections. Potential differences in employer plan rules will only become apparent when you seek to take distributions, utilize some of the payment options, or even change your investments from one CREF fund to another.

In effect, your account consists of separate subaccounts, one for each employer for whom you worked. You can learn the true composition of your account by making an inquiry of TIAA-CREF, and you will not see that breakdown otherwise.

The abuse that this system is designed to prevent stems from the common misconception that if you worked for an institution with a very restrictive plan for most of your career and then move to an institution with a very flexible plan for your last years of employment, your entire accumulation will be subject to the rules of that last employer's plan. Not so. The assets contributed while working at institution A and the earnings thereon remain subject to the restrictive structure of institution A's plan. The somewhat smaller accumulation acquired while working those few years with institution B becomes the only part of the total accumulation subject to B's rules.

We have also seen many cases where the same scenario has worked in reverse. As of retirement, the participant is working for an institution with a series of restrictions, but the greater part of the participant's career was spent at a more permissive employer. Unexpectedly, this provides the participant with much more flexibility than originally expected. The different options available, especially regarding distributions, can reach significant complexity when an individual has worked at three, four, five, or more institutions during a career.

You may learn the provisions of your former employer's current plan by asking TIAA-CREF, but in many cases you may find that you will have to send letters requesting a copy of your former employers' plans in order to discover the current rules applicable to you. From experience, we know that this can become an awful pain in the neck, but there is no substitute for diligence.

Although the abuse being targeted is clear, this system can, at least in theory, lead to bizarre results. For example, suppose you worked for an employer from when you were 35 until you were 45 years of age. You retire at age 70. You invested in aggressive growth funds because you were young and retirement seemed as remote as the next ice age. The employer has a restrictive plan. For up to three and a half decades, your accumulation attributable to that employer has compounded and may now equal a disproportionately large part of your TIAA-CREF account. You would not think to ask that former employer for a pension, but its rules about pensions will govern what you can do when you retire with respect to the share contributed while you worked there as a young pup and the earnings thereon. In all likelihood, the increases in salary that have occurred in the intervening decades may diminish the effect of the compounding relative to the larger contributions that will probably be made as time goes by. Nonetheless, it seems odd that an institution with which one thought one had severed all ties retains this hold on your future.

Returning to more practical issues, before you change employers, you need to review how your retirement assets are apportioned. How much do you have in an RA account? How much have you managed to save in the SRA if your employer offers this possibility? Do you have any funds in a GRA or a GSRA, and if so would you like to roll them over to a new account with TIAA-CREF or would you prefer to pay the 2.5% surrender fee on the TIAA portion of your retirement assets and roll them over to a financial institution as a rollover IRA?

Although these considerations should not affect your career decisions, you should make a point of knowing the opportunities available to you under your present and past employer's retirement plans. What possibilities will your spouse have if something happens to you? Although TIAA-CREF does keep track of the different rules applying to your accumulation, you should keep a file with the governing rules of each of your employers' plans together with other important financial documents.

12

How Do TIAA-CREF Plans Differ from Employer to Employer?

As we indicated in the previous chapters, plans provided by TIAA-CREF can differ substantially from one employer to another. We have noted that some employers offer an Retirement Annuity account, others the Group Retirement Account. Contribution percentages will vary from one employer to another. Perhaps the most striking structural difference lies in the extent to which employers will give their employees options at retirement to withdraw funds from TIAA-CREF and take their futures into their own hands.

The range encompasses both extremes, from employers who require that a retiree annuitize to those who will allow a retiree to withdraw all of the TIAA-CREF accumulation and transfer it out to another financial institution. Some schools permit their employees to make such withdrawals at any time. Other schools will allow a retiree to withdraw a percentage of the RA accumulation that approximates the employee's contribution, the employer feeling that its contributions should remain within TIAA-CREF so that the original purpose of the employer contributions, providing a pension, will be fulfilled. An employer may place limitations on the ability of employees to take funds out of TIAA-CREF prior to retirement, whether through loans or other mechanisms available through TIAA-CREF.

These differences may stem from past experiences of bailing out retired faculty, the degree of the employer's paternalism, or the extent to which the employer believes that caution is merited when it comes to allowing faculty or other employees to make financial decisions. Fearing a recurrence or a rash of disasters, the employer may decide to protect the institution's endowment and the faculty's reputation by limiting the ability of retiring employees to gain control over their retirement funds and allowing only a partial withdrawal at retirement or perhaps none at all. Although this smacks of paternalism, saying in effect that the faculty, with its heads in the clouds and its bodies in the ivory tower, needs to be protected from itself, most employers also exhibit genuine concern for the well-being of the faculty and staff. That said, structuring a plan that will meet the needs of all employees represents a monumental undertaking. Similarly, fashioning a plan to meet the retirement needs of those with larger and those with more modest accumulations poses a substantial challenge.

Interestingly, in most cases restrictions appear only to apply to the participant. A surviving spouse or designated beneficiary may possess the ability to withdraw the full accumulation as soon as the participant ceases to draw breath. However, we have encountered exceptions to this rule, and you should know what your options are at various milestones. Other plan variations may allow participants full flexibility at retirement or even upon termination of employment at a particular institution. If you elect to opt out of TIAA-CREF, then you must effect an income tax–free transfer to another financial institution in the form of a rollover Individual Retirement Account.

13

When and How Much Should You Contribute to Your TIAA-CREF Account?

Given the time value of money, the answer boils down to early, often, and as much as you can. Remember that any contributions made to your retirement plan are deducted from your gross income for income tax purposes. The U.S. Treasury is subsidizing your accumulation of a pension account. Surprisingly, not all governmental largesse gets funneled into the pockets of large campaign contributors. Given enough affected voters, Congress will, from time to time, enact legislation with broad economic sweep. Separate from matters of politics and civics, of course, you want to leverage your contributions through your employer's match, another form of governmental subsidization.

We have dwelt on the time value of money. Inherent in that concept and what provides the driving engine is the power of compounding earnings and the exponential growth it can produce. You need to know the difference between compound and simple interest to become savvy about what is happening to your TIAA-CREF accounts. This may appear simplistic, but, in our experience, very few of our clients fully appreciate the difference in results that occur using the two different methods. So bear with us.

When calculating the return on a simple interest basis, you compute the amount earned in a given year, say 5% of $1,000, and put that amount, $50, in effect aside. You then reinvest the $1,000. If you continue this process for twenty-five years and then add all of the earnings to the $1,000, you will have the simple interest return. Your accumulation will total $2,250.

Compound interest assumes that instead of putting the annual earnings out to pasture, you add them to the $1,000 and immediately reinvest $1,050, using the previous example. At the end of the following year, you repeat the process. As you will see from the examples below, the differential in return is significant. As the rate of return increases, significant becomes staggering. Taking the prior example, a simple interest return yields $2,250 after twenty-five years. The return from compound interest would amount to $3,386. If the compounded rate of return were 10%, simple interest would return $3,500 and compound interest $10,835. The compounding effect now trebles the simple interest accumulation.

If, in addition, you add new money to the account every year, then the accumulation will obviously grow even greater. You have more principal on which the compounding effect can operate. The more time with which you have to work, the more powerful the effect compounding will have. As usual, a hypothetical example provides the best illustration and makes the abstract concrete. You should understand that investments do not typically grow at a uniform pace over a prolonged period of time.

We have two individuals. The first, a 25-year-old, call him Abel, contributes $1,000 a year to a retirement plan, earning a 10% annual return. After seven years, he stops contributing to the plan. The account continues, however, to earn a 10% compounded return. The 25-year-old expects to retire at age 65. A neighbor, also 25 and also expecting to retire at age 65, call him Cain, does not get started on a retirement plan until he is 32 years old. He starts when Abel stops. From that point on, Cain contributes $1,000 a year to the account until retirement at age 65. He also earns a 10% compounded return. Contrary to what one's common sense and intuition might dictate, the time value of money works so powerfully that both end up with the same amount in their retirement account, roughly $221,000. Abel contributed a total of $7,000; Cain contributed $33,000. Every dollar that Abel contributed did the work of $5 that Cain contributed.

Had either of them started at age 25 and continued contributing straight through until retirement at age 65 with the same 10% compounded return, he would have started retirement with an account balance of $442,599. The $40,000 investment grew eleven fold. Clearly, the money placed into the account *during the first seven years* earned half of the total return. For that reason, we voiced the concern about the rules of an employer left long ago having a profound effect on one's retirement options; compounding could, theoretically, make that part of your accumulation disportionately large. On the other hand, these simple cases underscore the critical importance of starting early, making time your ally and collaborator. Few factors work as powerfully as time, whether one thinks monetarily or geologically.

We all have a tendency to think that one can easily compensate for a small contribution foregone in the early years. In the world of compounding returns, as the example underscores, this proposition does not hold water.

Let's add another filter on to our simple and compounded interest examples. We need to factor in the effect of income taxes. By being able to defer taxes until distribution, you dramatically increase the rate of effective return on your account. To return to our shopworn 5% example, suppose that a 28% federal tax is imposed on your savings. Using simple interest, the net return diminishes from $1250 to $900. The $3,386 compound return declines to $2,421, a 50% decrease. In the 10% example, the simple interest amount falls from $3,500 to $1,800 and the compounded amount similarly falls 50% to $5,686. In the cases of the 25-year-old neighbors, similar investments in taxable accounts would yield account balances of only $86,356 in the first case and $123,862 in the second. You need to be a remarkable investor to outperform a plan that has the advantage of freedom from current taxes.

Now, let's add another dose of reality. Clearly, procrastination does not work. At the other extreme, you should not front load your account and then let compounding do the rest. However you look at the case of the 25-year-olds, optimal returns necessitate both using time and adding annual contributions of principal—in other words, more money. In the real world, investment returns do not occur uniformly over time. To paraphrase J. P. Morgan, the one thing certain about investment markets, stock or bond, is that they will fluctuate. If you make regular contributions to your plan, you will add funds at various points in the business and investment cycles. You are dollar averaging your costs and hedging against either a dramatic decline in the markets when you might wish you were elsewhere or a dramatic rise when you rejoice that you stayed the course. You have wisely concluded that market timing requires that one must be the seventh son of a seventh son or the female equivalent. No one possesses the divine foresight to be right four times over and over again. To win at market timing, you must know when to sell equities, what to buy instead, when to sell that, and when to buy equities again, selling at the peak and buying at the bottom. If you can consistently perform this feat of investment magic, we suggest that you might be in the wrong line of work, at least in terms of your compensation potential. If you choose to remain in a university setting, the administration will probably assign you the task of managing the endowment, a job that, given your innate abilities, should require less time than your current position and command better pay.

General principles aside, we do not mean to underestimate the difficulty of determining how many dollars you can or should be contributing to your plan at any point in time, given the competing interests for your money. We can only offer the bromide that you should contribute as much as you can comfortably afford. We all face short-term needs and long-term expenses throughout our lives. You will have college tuitions and down payments on houses to save for, plus the debt service on mortgages and the costs of weddings, vacations, medical expenses, cars, and any number of other items to pay.

At the risk of sounding like seventeenth-century Calvinists or Benjamin Franklin, you should decide early on to save a fixed percentage of your salary, which will be added to your retirement plan each month or pay period. As your salary increases or major changes occur in your life, the percentage may change, preferably upward until you are setting aside as much as the Internal Revenue Code will allow. You should coordinate your contributions with your employer's, especially if the plan is structured so that the percentage your employer contributes increases as your salary and contribution grow.

You will probably make out best if you define your contributions in terms of a percentage of salary. Your salary will change over time, and you do not want to lose the opportunity to contribute the same relative amount as your salary increases. (Nor pay too much in the rare case that your salary decreases. This would be primarily relevant to those who are working a shorter schedule but still qualify for plan contributions.)

The short answer, then, to our question at the start? Contribute as soon and often as you can, and contribute as much as you can comfortably defer. Contributing smaller amounts on a regular basis early beats waiting until you can put a large amount aside. You want time to work with you, not against you. You want time to be your friend and ally, not your adversary.

How Can You Learn How Your Employer's Plan Works?

As the text thus far has broadly and frequently stated, you need to know the details of your employer's plan. Generally, you have two routes to follow.

The first and most direct route is to contact your benefits office. In the institutions with which we have worked, admittedly a small cross sample, we found that the staff can outline and explain your employer's plan. Equally importantly, they can provide you with the latest version of the plan. Whenever changes occur in the plan, you should be notified as an employee. If you know how the plan operated during the *status quo ante*, you will understand the significance of any amendment to the plan's provisions. *At the very least, you should obtain a summary plan description, which is more nearly readable than the real thing, and read it. If necessary, be persistent.*

Remaining current about plans in which you have participated, but where you are no longer employed, poses more of a challenge. You should check with the relevant benefits offices from time to time just to stay up-to-date on any changes that may have been made. Although the impact that prior employers' plans may have will probably only occur at retirement, do not wait until then to learn the current status of the plan any more than you should wait until the day before you retire to begin thinking about your retirement planning as well as your choice of distribution method.

The second way to find out how your present or past employer's plans work is to contact TIAA-CREF. In most instances, TIAA-CREF will have the information that you need. Contacting TIAA-CREF with respect to a past employer's plans may garner the information you need with one phone call. If, however, you need a copy of the plan document for your records, you must contact the employer directly. Obviously, it makes more sense to contact your present employer directly if you need any information on the plan in which you are now participating.

If you are working with a professional estate-planning or retirement-planning advisor, provide him or her with any information you may have about your plans and where you have been employed throughout your career. As a TIAA-CREF participant, you have an asset that has a great deal of potential as a part of both your retirement and your estate, but also an asset that can change appearance depending on where you have accumulated your savings. Without that information, both you and your advisor are groping in the dark. You do not want answers in the abstract, but concrete solutions to your problems. Without knowledge of your plans, you are flying blind.

15 How Should You Allocate Your TIAA-CREF Contributions?

This question arises with the greatest frequency, and it ranks, as one would expect, as one of the most difficult to answer. We can only suggest general guidelines because your investment risk tolerance may differ from the next person's. Also, investment choices should reflect one's overall economic situation, and advertisements for online brokerage houses notwithstanding, not every form or method of investment suits every situation. In an age when most of us are at least aware of general movements in the market, if not actually participating in some way, most of us wish for a formula to provide the optimal investment mix for our particular situation. But investment management is an art, not a science, and there is no predetermined optimal solution or magic bullet.

We begin with what may seem self-evident. Your TIAA-CREF account represents a set of investment accounts. By that, we mean that it is not a risk-free savings account whose market value can never decline.

To illustrate, we had a client who was retiring after forty-eight years of teaching. He had directed all of his contributions into traditional TIAA. He had accumulated $1.1 million, which represents a tidy sum, but we remained puzzled that he did not express any regret about having missed out on all of the economic growth that had occurred in the United States since the beginning of the Korean War. Both he and his wife had lived through the Depression, and they had spent their formative years seeing the havoc wrought by the collapse of the stock market in 1929. Their TIAA accumulation came as close to being a savings account as they could have made it. We never mentioned what his accumulation might have been had he invested 50%, or even 25%, of his contributions in the CREF Stock Account. Crying over spilt milk four decades later seemed senseless, and the clients were happy. But they could never cotton, it appeared, to the fact that times had changed, and the trauma that had shaped their outlook would almost certainly never recur. In this day and age, you need to take more risk in order to glean more reward. You need to think like an investor, not like a passbook saver. Time had bailed out the client in this instance. His returns had proven modest, but they had compounded and gotten him and his wife to where they wanted. The other side of the Depression mentality came from the modest expectations that he had harbored about his retirement income.

We should interject a word or two on *investment* philosophy. We use italics here intentionally. "Investing" means a long-term placement of capital or funds. "Trading" is the term used for frequent—and in some cases, constant—buying and selling of funds, stocks, or other commodities; for those of us who do not buy and sell financial assets for a living, it means not being able to stick to our convictions. We refer to "day trading"; the concept of "day investing" borders on the ludicrous.

When you allocate funds to a TIAA-CREF account, you are not investing directly in the underlying securities held, for example, in the Stock Fund or the Equity Index Fund. You turn over your money to a professional, full-time money manager to make the buy and sell decisions for you. If you continually move your funds from one account to another, you are second-guessing the money manager's decisions. The fund manager is making decisions to buy or sell dependent on whether he or she sees certain assets increasing or decreasing in value, now or later. A fund manager has a three-to-five-year horizon, if not longer. Your assessment of their performance should be based on several years' results, in both up and down markets. When you invest in a fund, you are buying into the fund manager's ability to invest your contributions successfully in whatever market conditions may prevail. One swallow does not a summer make, and one quarter does not render a fund manager worthy or unworthy.

In the course of preparing this tome, we ran across an article on Dr. Daniel Kahneman of Princeton University and his work on the psychology of decision making. The author of the article interviewed Dr. Kahneman and asked him to relate his findings on the individual investor's buy/sell decision process. The article notes, "Psychologist Daniel Kahneman has devoted much of the last three decades to identifying and understanding the beliefs, biases, and preferences that influence individual decisions. Among the most common are optimism, overconfidence, hindsight, confusing chance with skill, and ignoring the big picture.... [A]s Kahneman has repeatedly shown in groundbreaking work on human nature, ... these 'tools' are not useful for thoughtful, rational decision-making. They are errors of judgement that often lead to poor choices and disappointing results."

That having been said, there are several sensible guidelines that may help. Generally, the younger you are, the higher the concentration of equity or stock investments you should have. You should also strive to achieve some variation in your investments. You probably need a core investment of fairly widely diversified blue chip or large capitalization stocks. You should consider also an allocation to more aggressive growth-stock investment as well as some international equity exposure. The key to safety in securities markets rests upon diversification. Each TIAA-CREF account will provide diversification within the defined universe of securities in which it invests; you also want diversity by placing your eggs into a number of different types of funds.

As you get older, you will probably give more prominence to the preservation of capital. However, keep in mind that even on the eve of retirement you will probably live another fifteen to twenty years, and that defines your true investment horizon. The downside of longevity, viewed economically, is your exposure to the same number of years of inflation. Although you will now be living on your retirement assets and need to limit your investment risks somewhat, you should still maintain an appreciable presence in the equities market. As we said before, a risk-free source of retirement income does not exist, and you need to hedge your bets so that you are not unduly exposed to market volatility or to the ravages of inflation.

Investment allocation is a dynamic process. Although you should not be making constant changes in your investment strategy, you should remain alert to the need for fine-tuning your asset allocation when you see major trend changes in the market or in your expected lifestyle. An increase in volatility does not entail that you should change your strategy from an aggressive to a more conservative allocation. As a long-term investor, you have to ride out the storms, bearing in mind that some volatility occurs on the upside. Investment changes based on short-term changes and moods in the markets tend to be emotional and founded on hastily compiled reasoning.

Many of the major fund families will tell you that most of the participants in their most successful funds have in fact at best broken even on their investments in these top performers. Instead of allowing their investments to grow with the fund, most investors will rush out after the market has dropped substantially and reenter only when the market has shown growth. Effectively, they are selling at the bottom and buying at or near the top. Generally, a few days or weeks create most of the market growth in any given period of time. Were it possible to know just when these periods were to occur, then we could all time the market successfully. No one can do this on a consistent basis. In investing, as in life, patience is a virtue.

TIAA offers two investment choices at present: the TIAA Traditional Annuity and the Real Estate Account. Both accounts are relatively stable investments.

The TIAA Traditional Annuity is the only investment option that offers a guaranteed return. The guaranteed level is generally low and can be changed, depending on prevailing market conditions. It provides an absolute bottom for those participants looking for a minimum return level, albeit well below existing market rates.

Although a guaranteed minimum can provide a feeling of security, you should understand that a minimum guarantee requires some form of compensation from the participant. As we discussed earlier, in order to provide participants with a guaranteed return, TIAA must make a series of long-term investments. The return on these investments must at least cover the guaranteed rate and, ideally, provide enough to pay a dividend. The TIAA board of trustees decides each year whether to pay a dividend and, if a dividend is to be paid, how large it will be. TIAA has paid dividends since 1948.

Once the dividends are announced for any given "dividend year," it will augment the guaranteed rate for that particular payment year. TIAA runs a March–February dividend year. Nationally recognized rating companies rate all insurance companies. The ratings are based on the ability of the insurance company to honor its claims and commitments to its clients. As of 1998, TIAA had top ratings from the four leading insurance-company rating companies based on its ability to pay its fixed annuity contracts. The ratings do not include commitments from any TIAA variable accounts or any of the CREF accounts.

TIAA creates the investment returns it needs to pay the guaranteed rate and a dividend by investing in publicly traded fixed-income investments with, for the most part, longer maturities but also by lending directly to commercial borrowers. In order to maintain a stable rate of return over time, these latter investments also involve long-term commitments, and they are therefore relatively illiquid. As a rule, such direct loans do not enjoy an active market and rarely change hands. Any buyer of such instruments will buy them at a discount to protect itself from the same risk of illiquidity after purchase.

Generally speaking, buying longer-term bonds enables TIAA to lock in higher rates. Such bonds carry a higher credit risk than short-term loans, and they risk a loss of value from inflation and rising interest rates. Once the purchase or loan is made, interest rates may rise or fall across the board thereafter. A rise in rates will not affect TIAA's ultimate return on the purchase, but it does mean that TIAA has locked in a rate that is no longer commensurate with the market. This will have an impact on the TIAA annuities that will be paid out in other interest rate environments than those prevailing at the time of investment.

If you have both a Retirement Annuity or a Group Retirement Account and a a Supplemental Retirement Annuity with investments in TIAA, you may have noticed that the SRA returns are on average about 0.5% lower than RA or GRA returns. This occurs because you can withdraw any funds invested in TIAA through an SRA at any time. The difference in yield reflects the cost of having that opportunity. By contrast, TIAA assets in either an RA or a GRA account can only move into a variable account or as a taxable distribution through either a ten-year annuity in a RA, a five-year or a ten-year annuity in a GRA, or a life annuity in either. Should you choose to annuitize the TIAA assets in an SRA, you may choose life or a fixed term from two to thirty years.

Although TIAA annuities are described as fixed, the guaranteed rate represents the only immovable aspect. It does not mean that you will receive the same amount annually for the term of the annuity. The amount paid will vary with the dividends declared, and that will depend on investment experience.

If you have TIAA assets in a GRA, then you may choose a ten-year annuity at any time. If you terminate employment and do not roll those assets over within 120 days of such termination or retirement, you may choose either a lifetime annuity or a term certain annuity of from five to thirty years. If your TIAA accumulation is in a GSRA and you elect to annuitize, then the same choices become available. Again, you need to know if these options are offered in your employer's plan. It may not incorporate all of the options offered by TIAA-CREF. Unless you affirmatively elect otherwise, TIAA will reduce your payments to reflect a 20% federal withholding tax.

TIAA also offers the TIAA Real Estate Account. This option has been available since the fall of 1995. Although offered by TIAA, the Real Estate Account is a variable annuity. As one would expect, the Real Estate Account invests about 70 to 80% of its assets in real estate, with about 20% to 30% invested in bonds and money market instruments to provide short-term liquidity. Unlike the TIAA Traditional Annuity, the Real Estate Account does not guarantee a return. Although it is separate from the TIAA general account, should redemptions by participants exceed the Real Estate Account's ability to provide cash, TIAA has stated that it will make the TIAA general account available to cover such requests for cash. As with any investment, you should review the most current prospectus and fund description to learn how the account is currently allocated.

Most of the assets are invested in commercial and industrial properties, multifamily properties, and in securities, such as mortgages, that are secured by or otherwise related to real estate. Returns will of course depend upon fluctuations in real estate markets, as well as changes in rent and lease levels, costs, potential environmental liabilities, and the ability of lessees and borrowers to pay their obligations.

A fund that invests wisely in real estate may provide an effective hedge against both inflation and adverse movements in the stock market. Although the Real Estate Account has a relatively short history, to date it has posted good returns. For these reasons, the Real Estate Account may serve as a good investment alternative. It offers more stability than an equity investment and more flexibility than the TIAA Traditional Account. New funds may be transferred into the TIAA Real Estate Account on a monthly basis. While you are still accumulating assets, you may move funds, in whole or in part, out of the Real Estate Account on a quarterly basis. Any withdrawals during retirement would take the form of either an annuity or the Minimaum Distribution Option. The annuity choices available to you from the TIAA Real Estate Account resemble those from the CREF accounts described in the following chapter. You can also roll over the funds into an Individual Retirement Account at retirement, but your flexibility will hinge on the provisions of your retirement plan.

17

What Are the CREF Investment Choices?

Currently, CREF offers eight different investment choices. They range from quite conservative to more aggressive investment alternatives. All of the CREF choices consist of variable annuity accounts; CREF has added new ones to its array of investment choices on a regular basis, as warranted by demand.

If you choose to annuitize your CREF accumulation, you may choose either a life annuity or a term annuity. If your CREF assets are in a GSRA account, then you may choose a term annuity of from five to thirty years. You may choose a term of two to thirty years if the assets are in a CREF Retirement Annuity, Supplemental Retirement Annuity, or Group Retirement Account. For reasons to be discussed in part IV, you cannot elect a term that exceeds the relevant life expectancies.

The CREF accounts fall into two groups: those linked to fixed-income investments and those linked primarily to equity or stock investments. Each of the accounts represents a pool of funds managed by one or several of the portfolio managers employed by TIAA-CREF in the same way that a mutual fund is managed by a portfolio manager employed by the relevant fund family. The fixed-income related accounts are the CREF Money Market Account, the CREF Inflation-Linked Bond Account, and the CREF Bond Market Account.

Each of the fixed-income related accounts invests in different variations of short-term investment-grade securitized debt, notes, and bonds. The account managers have parameters defining what maturities and what types of debt issuers they may pursue. Although fixed-income instruments tend to be generally less volatile than equities, you can lose money in a fixed-income fund. This can result from market developments and how the respective money managers have positioned their investment choices vis-à-vis the market. For that reason, these funds make up part of the variable annuity side represented by CREF.

The CREF Money Market fund is the least risky of the three funds. As in any money market fund, the investments are very short term, high quality, and liquid. It will tend, therefore, to follow interest rates up and down pretty closely. All of these desirable qualities have, of course, a downside: the return on the Money Market Account is probably the lowest over the long haul due to the relatively low investment returns for short-term paper. The CREF Money Market fund represents a good place to park your funds in times of economic or personal uncertainty. If you become concerned about your equity investments, would like to take profits, or anticipate a market correction, the Money Market Account may best serve those needs. It provides higher security of principal and flexibility for when you want to reenter the equities market. You can remove your funds from the Money Market fund at any time.

As of February 2000, the CREF Inflation-Linked Bond Account represents the newest addition to the CREF stable of funds. This account appeared soon after the U.S. Treasury began issuing Inflation-Indexed Securities. Not enough experience has accumulated with either the Treasury securities or the CREF account to permit an informed assessment as to how well they will fare as investment vehicles as inflation advances and recedes. It appears that this particular account may also invest in foreign governments' paper, as well as "other investments consistent with the account's overall objectives."

The CREF Bond Market Account offers a credit-risk profile similar to the Money Market Account. They both buy the debt of the highest-rated issuers. It does, however, encompass a greater exposure to market risk because most of its investments are longer term than you will find in the Money Market Account. Generally speaking, the longer the maturity of a fixed-income investment, the greater the volatility of the value of the investment in the market until maturity. A bond market account rarely holds its investments to maturity. They will for the most part be bought and sold over relatively short holding periods to take advantage of movements in the interest rate market.

Many feel that it is necessary to include exposure to the bond market in an investment portfolio. To the extent that you have access to individual bonds, they can play an important part in your portfolio mix. Within the TIAA-CREF universe, traditional TIAA comes closest to being a bond portfolio. You should understand that a bond *fund* does not equate to a *bond or even a bond portfolio*. A bond fund can and may carry as much market risk as an equity fund. The manager of a bond fund buys and sells bonds in the same way that the manager of an equities fund buys and sells stocks. Similarly, the returns on any given bond fund may not reflect the returns in the bond market in the same way that the returns on a stock fund may not necessarily reflect the returns of the stock market.

One can best conceptualize the Bond Market Fund as a commodities fund that buys fixed-income securities instead of pork bellies or orange juice or future contracts in those commodities. The returns depend on the fund manager's acumen in predicting the movement of the bond market and interest rates. Unlike an individual bond, a bond fund has no final maturity; nor does it have a determined interest rate payable at stated intervals. You have no guarantee of principal even if all of the investments are in government-issued or -guaranteed investments. A bond fund manager can lose money buying and selling bonds in the same way that an equities fund manager can incur losses even though the stock market in general has gone up. Although a bond fund includes many aspects of bond investment strategy, it does not replace bond investments.

CREF offers five equity accounts with varying risk profiles: the CREF Social Choice Account, the CREF Stock Account, the CREF Global Equities Account, the CREF Growth Account, and the CREF Equity Index Account. All of these accounts invest in equities that reflect the objectives as described in the literature and prospectuses from TIAA-CREF. Some engage in international investments, even though this may not be explicit from the name of the account. Most will use money market instruments to ensure that free cash is invested until the desired equity investments are purchased.

In terms of aggressiveness, the CREF Growth Account and the CREF Global Equities Account probably rank at the top of the available choices. Growth funds typically invest in newer companies with high growth potential or larger companies that have been severely undervalued by the market for some reason. Shares in these companies tend to be more volatile in price and often pay little or no dividends. Global accounts include not only international companies but also U.S. companies, hence the title "global"; true international funds will, as a rule, exclude U.S. companies and buy only foreign companies' stock. Currency movements and economic developments in countries outside of the United States will obviously affect global funds. Recent history provides numerous examples.

The CREF Social Choice Account may be more volatile than the more balanced CREF Stock Account and the CREF Equity Index Account. The Social Choice Account invests only in those companies that fit predetermined social, political, and ecological criteria. The account may avoid, for example, oil companies and others that may create ecological risks, tobacco companies, companies in the alcoholic beverage industry, the defense or weapons industries, and so forth. By restricting its investment choices by other than financial criteria, the account may be exposed to more market risk than a balanced equities account, which weights risk and volatility in its choice of investments.

The two CREF equity accounts with the least volatility are the CREF Stock Account, which was the original CREF account, first offered in 1952, and the CREF Equity Index Account. The Stock Account is an actively managed equity account. The Equity Index Account matches the Russell 3000 Index as closely as possible and, as such, is not independently managed. The Stock Account may invest in international names, while the Equity Index Account will not. The CREF Stock Account has been described as the largest single managed equity fund in the world, based on assets under management.

TIAA-CREF offers a good range of accounts to choose from for both the accumulation phase as well as the distribution phase. Its array of investment choices mirrors the basic range of investment choices covered by most of the major mutual fund families. You need to base your choice of accounts on your risk tolerance, your age and probable life expectancy, and your general financial situation.

If you have assets outside of TIAA-CREF or if you have other retirement accounts, ideally you should allocate your TIAA-CREF choices looking at all of your financial assets as one integrated portfolio. In that way, your choices should represent a reasonable complement to those other investments. You should strive to maintain flexibility in your investments so that you can make adjustments if necessary as your life changes or your perception and, on occasion, the objective reality of market risks alter. Although investing is a long-term process, it can never become static. In a changing world, you should be patient, looking for underlying value but recognizing that investing will remain a dynamic process.

Again, check with your employer's plan because not all of the above-mentioned funds may be available to you. When you do start looking at investment choices, always check the latest prospectus from TIAA-CREF because it will always carry the latest changes, adjustments, and other information pertinent to your selection of any particular account.

18

What Is the Transfer Payout Annuity?

We have alluded to the TPA from time to time, and now it gets the attention it clearly deserves. The TPA is literally an annuity, and it represents the mechanism by which funds are transferred from a TIAA accumulation to either one of the other investment choices in the TIAA-CREF family or as a taxable distribution after age $59\frac{1}{2}$ to the participant.

As we have discussed earlier, you can only withdraw funds from a TIAA accumulation in a Retirement Annuity through a lifetime annuity or a ten-year annuity while you are still employed. If you participate in a Group Retirement Annuity, your TPA may only have to run five years. If you wish to reallocate your investments while still employed, you would use the TPA to effect a multi-year transfer. TIAA will use then current annuity rates to establish the TPA and move it as you direct. As with any other type of annuity, you have made an irrevocable choice, with two exceptions described below.

In some instances, perhaps particularly around retirement, you issue simultaneous instructions for several different types of distributions. You must make sure that if you have chosen any annuity solutions, these will not restrict any revocable choices that you might wish to make. In short, you do not want to trip over your own feet. Let's look at an example.

You decide to take minimum distributions (for now, this is the smallest amount that the Code allows you to withdraw from your account in any year) from your TIAA-CREF accumulation at retirement. You may also decide that the large accumulation that you have in your TIAA account should all or partially be moved to one of the CREF investment choices. In order to make the change, you start a TPA from TIAA to CREF, ensuring that the desired amount plus earnings will be transferred to your new choice(s) over ten years. You need to insure that you have enough free funds not bound up in the TPA to cover the minimum distribution payments that you will be receiving during the next ten years. Otherwise, you risk a 50% penalty for underpayments. As each year passes, the amount transferred out of TIAA will become available for purposes of making the mandatory minimum, and some planning and the judicious use of arithmetic will emerge as essential.

If most or all of your accumulation is in TIAA, then the amount transferred to the CREF side may cover your minimum distribution requirement. In that case, you need to time the distributions during the year so that they occur after the funds have been transferred from TIAA. Conversely, you may have most of your accumulation on the CREF side already, and you use the TPA to transfer any residual funds that may be on the TIAA side. In this instance, the CREF funds will almost surely cover any minimum distribution requirements. You may also choose to use the TPA to even out any imbalances in your portfolio mix.

Funds may move from the CREF side to the TIAA side at any time. Going the other way requires ten years. You may think that we are pounding this point to death. Our experience to date indicates that many participants are unaware of these facts and unaware too that, once begun, the TPA becomes irrevocable. Clearly, you can reinvest your funds as payments are made; however, the investment choice is locked for those assets still in transit. The interest earned is set by TIAA each year. Roughly speaking, you will see a transfer of a little more than 10% of your transfer assets each year.

We mentioned above that the irrevocability of the TPA has two exceptions. First, you may convert your TPA contract to a life annuity. If you make this election, then the remaining balance in your TPA contract will fund the lifetime annuity. This choice is final. Second, you may combine a lifetime annuity benefit with the Retirement Transition Benefit, discussed in part IV. Those choices result in your receiving 10% of the balance in your account upon retirement or within the first year thereafter, and the remainder would convert to a lifetime annuity. Again, this choice is final.

To complete this discussion, we need to add some finishing touches detailing how the TPA is actually paid. You may elect to receive eleven payments, not just ten. The first payment occurs at the beginning of the first month after your contract is signed. This payment will equal 10% of your funds being transferred at that time. You will then receive one payment on each anniversary of the contract for the next ten years. Each payment will equal 10% of the remainder plus dividends, and the latter will vary to reflect interest market changes during the ten-year period.

You may elect not to take the initial 10% payment, but to receive payments on the ten anniversaries of the execution of the contract.

TIAA-CREF must receive these instructions in letter form when you send in your paperwork to start the TPA. You may change your choice of target for the transfers, either a new or different fund within CREF or to yourself if you are over $59^1/_2$ years old.

Finally, remember that your choice of investment vehicles for your TPA transfer funds will depend on your employer's plan. Before making any final decisions, make sure that your new investment choices are supported by your employer.

At first blush, you may think that we have descended from the mundane to the inane. However, we have had clients who did not read their statements at all and tossed them away unopened, and others who have told us that they found them partially or totally incomprehensible. Read properly, it becomes an extremely informative document. At this point, you may have enough insight to glean everything possible from your quarterly statements, but it may hide some subtle points of which you ought to be aware.

Starting at the top, your statements provide first an overview of your total assets listed by contract number, type of contract, and your total accumulation as of the end of the previous quarter compared to those figures for the end of the quarter before that. This shows you how your accounts fared during the preceding three months. This becomes your best mechanism for tracking how your investments are working out, subject to the caveat that you are only reviewing a three-month period in retrospect. An individual statement may not provide grounds for changing your asset allocation, but a collection of them may.

In each type of contract, for example, a Retirement Annuity or Minimum Distribution Annuity (MDA), you will see a TIAA and/or a CREF contract number listed. The letters in front of each contract number indicate in which type of contract the TIAA or CREF accumulations are growing. You will see a subtotal under each contract type, showing the total assets accumulated under that umbrella.

The next part of your statement to examine lists how your premium payments are allocated. The most recent form of statement appropriately names this section "Listing of Your Accumulating Contracts—Premiums." Again, you will see a list of your contracts grouped by type. On the far side of the page, you should see how much you have contributed to each contract during the quarter in question. You should also see how much your employer contributed to every type of annuity account other than a Supplemental Retirement Annuity.

Look carefully at the premium allocations and make sure that they reflect your current wishes and asset allocation. We have seen many cases where the participant has stated with complete conviction and in complete error that all contributions were going to, hypothetically, a CREF account. The participant then proudly points to the CREF account balance and claims that the tremendous growth in the CREF contract's size proves the point. Upon further inspection in the premium payment section, it often becomes apparent that the participant is still allocating 50% to TIAA and 50% to CREF, and the allocation never changed since the beginning of the participant's career. The enormous growth in stock funds during the last ten to fifteen years has had a similar effect on CREF accounts. Upon seeing the huge disparity in accumulation totals, many participants jump to the conclusion that part of the difference is attributable to their investment skill and they had made the adjustment they may have wished they had for so long.

In short, do not be fooled by the spectacular rise in equity prices and the low-interest-rate environment in which we have operated during the last few years. At the very least, you will recognize wishful thinking and distinguish it from reality. By checking your premium allocation, you can also determine if you want to make a change going forward in your asset allocation.

Finally, your summary page will give you separate totals of your TIAA and CREF accumulations as of the end of the preceding two quarters. You will also receive detailed pages for each of the contract types in which you are participating. These pages will include not only totals and premium payments, but also accumulation unit values and the number of units that you own in each contract. TIAA-CREF labels this part of your quarterly statement the "Quarterly Confirmation of Transactions." The detailed pages will also give you the percentage allocation of your premiums received during the quarter as well as a breakdown as to how much you contributed yourself and how much was contributed by your employer. You will also see any distributions made from annuities that you may have purchased or from your own assets through the Minimum Distribution Option.

You may also notice in your statement that when you either purchase an annuity or start taking minimum distributions, the lump sum applied in either case will be transferred to a new contract number (TIAA and/or CREF) and will be listed under a new contract type. In the example we have included, you will see that a sum converted to minimum distribution appears under the MDA contract type.

Do not get confused by the nomenclature used to define your contracts. You may note that your TIAA assets have a *contract* number, while your CREF assets have a *certificate* number. When discussing your accumulations over the phone with a TIAA-CREF representative, you may safely refer to them as contracts across the board. You may wish to refer to this chapter when you receive your quarterly statements.

Read your quarterly statements, at least the summary page. When you come right down to it, your quarterly statement only contains a few pages, and you ought to read the whole thing, now that you comprehend the contents. Compared to the professional literature you may be reading, the quarterly statement may appear virtually entertaining. In any event, you need to know how your accumulations in TIAA and/or CREF are doing and how your investments are keeping pace with the market. You also need to ascertain if they are growing at a rate that will suffice when you retire.

If you have ten or more years to retirement, you shouldn't let downdrafts in the market discourage you. You will be adding on a regular basis. Your quarterly statement confirms your actions. Read it, make mental notes, and file it for comparison.

Even those who are within ten years of retirement should not let one quarterly statement throw their investment plans out of kilter. As we have said from the outset, you are, statistically, still a long-term investor, and one statement should not give rise to abject depression or manic jubilation. You need to keep your equilibrium at least as much as your investments do.

Note any questions about allocations, accumulations, CREF unit values, and so forth, and give the 1–800 number a call. It only takes a few minutes, and the people on the other end of the phone are usually very helpful. If you have a trusted advisor locally, he or she may be able to help you appreciate the implications of your statements.

Once a year, you will receive a statement that projects the amount of the annuity you would receive if you retired at age 65, either by continuing to make premium payments at the same clip that you have to date or by making none at all. These statements presume a 6% growth rate as of 1999, some assumption being necessary to predict the size of anything years down the road.

The primary utility of this projection, while you are still in the accumulation phase, stems from its ability to give you some indication as to how close you are to fulfilling your income goals for retirement. Like any projection, this statement represents nothing more than a model, but you can use it as a yardstick as to whether your personal savings rate is on target or needs to be changed, usually in the form of an increase. Whatever you do, do not expect that the stock market gains we have experienced over the last decade represent a new norm. Although they have lasted far longer than generally predicted, they still reflect a historical anomaly and should not form the basis for your long-term planning. Wishful thinking may rank lower on the totem pole than such an extrapolation, but they are not different in kind, only in degree.

A final word on quarterly statements: how long should you retain them? If you have not made any significant changes in your allocations or distributions, then we suggest keeping the current year's quarterly statements until you receive your year-end statement. Keep this statement going forward and throw away the other statements for the year. If you retain each quarterly statement, however, you can gauge how volatile your investments are relative to that of the market as a whole. This can prove valuable information if you recognize that conditions change, including the composition of the funds in which you have invested, and that last year's performance may have only historical significance.

However, if you have made significant changes in your allocations or distributions, changed employers, want to track the premiums paid into your accounts, purchased a TPA, or done anything else out of the ordinary, then you should keep any statements reflecting those changes. If you have diversified your investment choices, saving the quarterly statements provides a retrospective look at which accounts performed up to expectations and which did not. You also need your statements to confirm that the developments in your account reflect not what you think you are doing, but what is in fact occurring.

Keep your statements in one place, filed chronologically. Remember, if something should happen to you, then you want your family or executors to be able to access your statements easily and not to have to sort them out.

Some people enjoy tracking the progress of their account. We have seen some impressive graphs that some participants have created for their accounts and kept at the front of the filing cabinet. It can be quite motivating to see how your account grows over time. When you look back over several years of participation, the short-term ups and downs will seem relatively small compared to the longer-term developments. What may seem like an excess of information can provide you with perspective on the entire accumulation process and prepare you for what lies ahead when you need to make choices affecting your retirement income.

What Happens to Your Statement
if You Have a Transfer Payout Annuity?

20

This also apparently routine topic produces its share of confusion, and we would like to dispel as much of it as we can.

We tend to think of the TPA as a transfer of funds in the same way that we think of movement of money from one bank account to another. If we choose to make the transfer over a period of ten years in relatively equal payments, then a balance will remain in the old account until the final transfer is made. A TPA is not a regular account. As with any annuity, you use a sum of money, in this case the amount you wish to transfer, to purchase a cash flow that will take place over a period of ten years.

When you *purchase* something, assets leave your account. Therefore, when you purchase a TPA, the assets deployed will disappear from your TIAA accumulation and be assigned a new contract number. You will, however, over time see an addition to your CREF accumulation (assuming that you are not receiving withdrawals directly) equal to the annual distribution from the TPA that you have purchased.

Some participants wonder why, after having chosen to buy a TPA, their TIAA assets suddenly drastically diminish or even disappear. In truth, this is exactly what has happened. These participants have taken those TIAA assets and used them to buy a new annuity. The assets do not leave your total TIAA-CREF accumulation. For purposes of calculating minimum distributions or if your employer is one of the schools that allows for only a partial or percentage rollover at retirement, the TPA assets still count. The TPA just reflects a redeployment of your assets.

The effect that the purchase of a TPA has on your statement probably furnishes the clearest example of the difference between an annuity choice and the Minimum Distribution Option described in parts IV and V. When choosing an annuity, you use your assets to purchase a product. When utilizing the Minimum Distribution Option, you are withdrawing your own assets from your own account that you are spending or investing as you deem appropriate.

21

How Can You Take Money Out of Your TIAA-CREF Account Prior to Retirement?

Assuming that your employer's plan allows, the Code provides you with a few methods to withdraw funds from your TIAA-CREF account prior to retirement. Generally speaking, a 10% penalty applies to withdrawals taken before one reaches age 59$^1/_2$. In this chapter, we discuss exceptions to this rule and the avenues that they open to you as a TIAA-CREF participant.

As one would expect, TIAA-CREF offers the means to accomplish what the Code permits. However, not every plan will. Generally speaking, the more protective—or if you prefer, the more paternalistic—the plan, the fewer the options it will offer to take early distributions or borrow against your accumulation. If the plan design posits that employees should not be allowed to mismanage—or more colloquially, blow—their retirement funds and should not, therefore, make any more investment decisions than absolutely necessary, the odds that the plan will contain flexible options decrease dramatically. If your employer's plan limits investment options and choices at retirement, the chances that the plan will provide escape hatches for early withdrawals plummet like a stone.

Returning to the Code and the general discussion, as with almost any rule, exceptions to the early withdrawal penalty exist, but they do not abound. With characteristic generosity, the Code allows for early withdrawal upon the occurrence of a personal calamity. Given most of the options, almost anyone would prefer ineligibility.

First, beginning the cataloging of disasters, if you die before age 59$^1/_2$, your estate or your beneficiary can take what would otherwise have been early withdrawals.

Second, you can achieve eligibility by becoming disabled. You are considered disabled if you are unable to engage in any "substantial gainful activity" because of a physical or mental impairment. You must demonstrate to the IRS that the impairment "can be expected to result in death or to be of long-continued and indefinite duration."

Third, you may withdraw funds from your Retirement Annuity, Group Retirement Account, or Supplemental Retirement Annuity penalty-free to cover medical expenses, providing that they are deductible for income tax purposes.

Fourth, you can take early withdrawals if you lose your job after age 55.

Fifth, if you are unemployed, you can take distributions to pay health insurance premiums.

Against this array of personal disasters and tragedies, the preferable route for taking early withdrawals remains a series of substantially equal payments for the life or life expectancy of the employee or the joint life or life expectancies of the employee and his designated beneficiary. To avoid the 10% early withdrawal penalty, the payments must continue for at least five years and terminate after the employee is over $59\frac{1}{2}$ years old.

Except for the final option, in normal circumstances, you will want to explore other possibilities for withdrawing funds from your TIAA-CREF account before retirement.

Some plans offer the opportunity of taking out loans from the Group Supplemental Retirement Account portion of your retirement account. Clearly, this limits the utility of this option to the minority of employers who use a GSRA rather than the more prevalent SRA. When you borrow from your GSRA account, TIAA-CREF imposes several limitations. You may only borrow up to 45% of your balance, and this cannot exceed the lower of (1) $50,000, or (2) 90% of the TIAA portion of your accumulation. You may transfer funds to the TIAA account to increase the calculation balance. You must maintain a balance in your TIAA account that is at least 110% of the loan amount. Loans only have a maximum five-year term, unless they are used to buy a principal residence; in that case, you can extend the term to ten years. Come hell or high water, you must repay the loan in full by your Required Beginning Date, that is, "RBD," April 1 of the year after which you turn $70\frac{1}{2}$ or if later, the date on which you retire. If not, the loan becomes taxable income and you face the 10% penalty imposed by the Code.

In almost every instance, you should regard your retirement account as the lender of last resort. This comment does not carry any moral disapproval but reflects the fact that, more likely than not, none of your investments is growing as quickly as your retirement plan. If you cannot repay the loan as scheduled, you may be taxed on the loan as if it were regular income and the outstanding loan balance will lose its tax-deferred status. Even worse, you may also get hit with a 10%

penalty for taking a pre–age $59^1/_2$ withdrawal. Before you borrow, check with your employer for current rates and parameters.

Just as some individuals do not have any credit source other than loan sharks, some TIAA-CREF participants may not have any other means of borrowing. Awful as the financial penalties of failing to repay the loan in timely fashion may prove under the Code, you will not have your knees broken or receive a custom fitting for cement overshoes. In a more serious vein, given an alternative, you will probably fare better if you leave your account alone and let it continue to grow rather than borrow from it and stunt its appreciation. Finally, depending on the purposes for which the loan is taken out and the proceeds applied, the interest may or may not be tax deductible.

TIAA-CREF offers more convenient and more widely available ways to withdraw funds from your TIAA-CREF account before retirement. In order, these options are Systematic Withdrawals, the Interest Payment Retirement Option (IPRO), the Retirement Transition Benefit (RTB), or a Cash Withdrawal. With the exception of the RTB, you can use these options to withdraw funds for consumption prior to retirement and to effect rollovers to Individual Retirement Accounts. We will discuss the RTB in greater detail later, but we will cover the Systematic Withdrawal, IPRO, and Lump Sum Payment, or Cash Withdrawal, in this chapter.

Again, the accessibility of all of these options depends on the applicable plan. The structure of your employer's plan will determine whether you can use any of these options, and the general rules of the Code on early withdrawal will also apply.

The Systematic Withdrawal allows you to withdraw a given amount on a regular basis from your account. You may only use the Systematic Withdrawal option in respect of your CREF assets, unless you are taking funds from your SRA or an Individual Retirement Annuity, in which case you may also access TIAA funds. You may continue to take Systematic Withdrawals for the rest of your life if you so choose. You should, however, think carefully about the effects this will have on your retirement balance. If you have already annuitized all or part of your account, then you may not use the Systematic Withdrawal on that portion of your account.

For those who choose the Minimum Distribution Option ("MDO"), the Systematic Withdrawal allows you to take out additional funds to cover special events, unforeseen medical costs, or any other use you deem appropriate. However, even if your elect the MDO, if your employer's plan limits your ability to withdraw your funds after retirement, it will probably contain restrictions on the preretirement access to your funds. If not, from the employer's point of view, the integrity of the plan risks being undermined by early withdrawals. With regard to Systematic Withdrawals, given the fact that they can be taken prior to or after retirement, the employer may, for the sake of consistency, simply prohibit them completely. Only then can the employee's or retiree's access to his or her TIAA-CREF account be limited to the share or percentage stipulated in the plan. The extent to which this logic will impede your flexibility will vary, depending on the degree to which your employer wants your ability to manage your own funds circumscribed.

The IPRO represents the only way to withdraw funds from your TIAA accumulation in an RA account without some form of annuity. The IPRO allows you to withdraw the earnings on your TIAA accumulation for your own use, providing that you have at least $10,000 of accumulation to use. You may not withdraw from the corpus of the account, only the earnings. The payments generally occur on a monthly basis. The amount that you will receive will equal the guaranteed rate on your TIAA accumulation plus the annual declared dividend.

When you decide to use the IPRO, you cannot use the underlying principal for any other transactions for at least one year thereafter. For example, if you have $500,000 in TIAA and you wish to utilize the IPRO on $200,000, then you may annuitize or set up the Transfer Payout Annuity on only the remaining $300,000 until one year after you terminate the IPRO arrangement.

Some additional restrictions apply to the IPRO. Only participants between the age of 55 and retirement can use it. Upon retirement, you must choose an income option that will preclude your use of the IPRO. When you start the IPRO, you must continue for at least one year. In short, it may serve as a means of supplementing income during the late preretirement years only. Furthermore, as with most of the options offered by TIAA-CREF, you must make sure that your employer does in fact offer this option in your retirement plan. Not all employers do, for the reasons set forth above.

With all of these options, bear in mind that you are raiding the cookie jar, and the funds will not support your retirement unless you can and do roll the earnings over to an IRA. On the other hand, if you use the funds to acquire a more valuable asset, then your choice makes sense from an economic point of view. Use of these options may fulfill pressing financial obligations or other needs; again, if possible, look at your short-term needs with a long-term perspective.

You may also avail yourself of the Cash Withdrawal, or the Lump Sum Withdrawal. Some plans will allow their participants to withdraw or roll over amounts of whatever denomination that suit your purpose. Most plans do not offer this option until you are either no longer employed by the institution or have actually retired. Once you have retired, you may also use this option, together with whatever other income option you have chosen, assuming that you have unannuitized CREF accumulations still in your account. The ten-year rule eliminates the use of TIAA funds for this purpose.

Aside from withdrawals from your SRA, the Cash Withdrawal option used in connection with a GRA provides the only mechanism to obtain a lump sum transfer of funds from your TIAA accumulation. This may only occur if you leave the institution's employ. If you wish to move the assets, then you must do so within 120 days of your termination of employment. You will be subject to a 2.5% (as of 2000) surrender charge or fee on any of the withdrawals coming out of your TIAA accumulation in the GRA.

In reviewing the preretirement options, you need to consider how electing any of these features will affect your postretirement lifestyle. Money withdrawn from the plan prior to retirement will obviously not remain in your accumulation to help you make ends meet after you retire. Growth in your accumulation because of continued contributions and/or market appreciation may mask this stark reality; a moment's reflection will convince you that your accumulation would have been even larger had you not opted to withdraw funds prior to retirement. Put another way, more dollars would exist within your accumulation to experience the same percentage of growth.

Again, assuming that the options exist under your employer's plan, you may find that you need to borrow money from your account in order to buy a house or to take early distributions in order to meet some financial exigency. You may not have a choice about what you do. Again, even if you face these circumstances, you should make your decision with all of the parameters of your decisions clearly in mind. In that way, you can gain some peace of mind that you made the right choice. If it were the only decision available at the time, you will know the consequences and will know what changes you will have to make to restore your accumulation to the point where you are comfortable with the thought that you have set enough aside to carry you through retirement. Put another way, if you had to dip into your savings to meet some special circumstance, then you will have to make adjustments to your contributions in the following years to compensate for the loss of principal, to use the term loosely, that you have incurred. The Code does contain provisions to deal with disaster and elective early withdrawals. It also offers opportunities to make late-in-the-day contributions that may exceed the normal limitations on your contributions and that you ought to consider seriously if the funds are available. Given the technical nature of these makeup provisions, they appear in appendix A, where they are described in some detail, being somewhat limited in application, so that you can plan accordingly.

Preparing for Retirement

How Should You Go About Your Retirement Planning?

For some, retirement comes as a wrenching experience, although this occurs less frequently due to the flexibility most participants enjoy as to when they begin their retirement. For most, retirement appears as a welcome relief, in part because they can design their retirement with more individual control than formerly. You can work part-time or on a reduced schedule. Administrative tasks can now be relegated to their proper place, and time can be used more efficiently and enjoyably. We have clients who intend to work and teach until their dying day and those, on the other hand, who count the days. Except for the first group, retirement does represent a major change in one's life, and economics may seem like the least of it. And in some cases, the issue of retirement income will pale beside other, more pressing concerns.

In writing this part of the book, we realize the obvious truth that TIAA-CREF participants will arrive at their retirement in different states of physical, emotional, and financial health. Those who possess large accumulations have more options and will receive, as a consequence, more consideration in these pages. Clearly, those who are not so fortunate also need advice and guidance. Against that background, those who are still working need to keep the future firmly and continually in mind. Today's sacrifice can avoid tomorrow's pinched future.

As is true of any activity, the outcome of your retirement planning will depend on your particular circumstances and your frame of mind. The first element in planning requires taking our old friend, time, into consideration. As you can tell by looking around you, the concept of retirement has changed over the last decade, if not longer. Not too long ago, retirement meant the definitive, unquestionable end of work—which was just as well, because one was often physically old and gray with relatively few years remaining. Now retirement may occur earlier, the population is longer lived, retirement may only involve the scaling back of working hours to free up leisure time, and the end of one career does not preclude the beginning of another. Retirees at age 70 have on average fifteen years of life expectancy. If they retire at age 65, retirement may amount to roughly 25% of their life span.

That is the good news. If you have harvested a sizable nest egg of assets, retirement can present new opportunities as well as further decisions about risk and time.

But all of us should remain mindful of the other side of the coin. Obviously, not everyone enters into retirement in the best of physical, emotional, or financial health. The averages may not have any bearing on your situation. More accurately, your situation may fall at one of the extremes that make up the averages.

For some, unfortunately, retirement planning may, for health reasons, amount to choosing among short-term solutions. In addition, the working years may have proven to be a period of unrelieved financial strain because of career constraints, unanticipated financial demands, the emotional needs of a family, illness, and so forth. Tragedy does strike, and you may have experienced a loss that statistically was unlikely, but did nonetheless occur. We are not Pollyannas, and we realize that, for some, the picture will not appear or be rosy. For some TIAA-CREF retirees, the last part of their lives will involve some financial struggle. Privation seems only remotely contingent. The accumulation of some TIAA-CREF funds, plus Social Security, should, we think, keep the wolf from all of our readers' doors. Retirement may lack the television image of sailing away into the sunset, but it rarely proves grim to those who have had productive working careers.

For those who only began working later in life, both the TIAA-CREF accumulation and the Social Security benefits may prove marginal or insufficient. Unsatisfactory as the answer may be, for those individuals, retirement may have to be deferred, further savings will have to be accumulated, and the workplace will remain their primary focus for more years than they might want, health permitting. If you are so situated, you need to remember that your savings cannot grow faster than in a tax-deferred environment, and that may require sticking with your job even if you want to be off doing something else. Only by continuing to work, if you can, *at a job where retirement benefits are offered*, will your retirement assets and therefore your retirement income hold out any realistic hope of growing significantly. If you can continue to work for your current employer, you probably can add to your TIAA-CREF accumulation. If your new employment does not offer such benefits, then you have no choice but to save and acquire assets on an after-income tax basis. Many of those who experience a difficult retirement usually chose to stop working as soon as the option became available, which was too soon, and then assumed that Social Security and a pension would take care of their needs. In too many instances, by not following the steps discussed in this part, they underestimated their needs or overestimated their real income; when that realization came, they had run out of time or options.

The lottery, casinos, and Internet stocks, although they offer the promise of instant return, represent unacceptable risks, if not certain loss. The house always wins, the states net money from lotteries, and betting on Internet stocks amounts to pure speculation or a more respectable form of gambling. The speed with which you can lose irreplaceable money can make your head spin. The news media occasionally report on the large number of casino customers who are retirees. Although we deplore their folly, we recognize that they hope to regain by gambling what they lost through poor planning, bad luck in some instances, or lack of choices in earlier years. This does not make them rational decision makers, but it does indicate the lengths to which necessity can drive those least able to afford to lose. To reiterate, if one begins to save and plan early, letting compounding returns work unimpeded, one should avoid this tenuous fate.

If health permits, a longer accumulation phase becomes the choice by default for those who have not yet managed to put enough by. For those with health problems, exploring a retirement arrangement and your postretirement health insurance options should occupy your attention. Eventually, you may have no alternative to sitting down with your employer face-to-face. Realistically, you may not possess sufficient leverage to structure a generous severance package, or your employer's retirement plan or the collective bargaining agreement may not allow individualized treatment. Mandatory retirement ages appear to be fading from the stage; however, if you face one, that will either require moving on to another job or making do with what you have managed to save.

Dollars and cents do not measure all costs. The opportunities for growth, travel, recreation, and so forth, that may be lost because you could not retire when you wanted do not lend themselves to economic modeling. They represent unquantifiable opportunity costs. On the other hand, continuation of your working life does not represent an unmitigated disaster. Aside from the monetary aspect, work provides structure and the chance to contribute to others' welfare. Dead-end jobs do exist, but the experience you have gained may enable you to surmount some of the obstacles that appeared insuperable when you were younger. We do not want to appear to be sugar coating what may remain a bitter pill to swallow, but you may have to make the best of necessity.

For those who are working without retirement looming, the recognition of the need to save appears to be on the upswing, whether as a result of lack of faith in Social Security's continued viability or concern about the number of years that one will have to make do on what one has individually managed to put away, helped in most cases by employer matching contributions. Oddly, even though we may feel that we go through much of our lives either stuck in a rut or fearful of falling into one, you can, with planning, continued good health, and discipline, make the last part of your life the one with the greatest range of choices since early adulthood.

For those who feel overwhelmed by loss of family or financial constraints so tight that you live hand to mouth without being able to set money aside for retirement, we urge you to examine some of the premises upon which you are living. You may find that the inability to save does not result entirely from circumstances over which you exert no control, but rather from the lack of defined long-term priorities and short-term cash flow planning. We do not say that to condemn, but rather to encourage those who sense that they cannot set money aside for retirement to step back and review their current spending against the longer perspective that thinking about retirement will provide. Few of us are born with silver spoons in our mouths, and few of us go through life with all of our needs and wants amply provided for. But few of us actually *need* to spend every penny we make, relying entirely on our employer and Social Security to look after us when we decide to hang up our sneakers. Such cases undoubtedly exist, but it is a mistake to assume that this description fits you and then tailor your spending habits to make sure that it does. You undoubtedly don't want to be told that you have to make do with less now in order to have more later, but in the great majority of cases, the old saws about saving remain valid. No one needs a sermon on the virtues of thrift or the perils of instant gratification because evidence of them exists all around us— for that matter, so do staggering amounts of consumer debt.

We all try to do our best. Nonetheless, if you are not making headway, then we suggest that you reexamine your situation. Consult a true financial planner, by which we mean someone who is not trying to sell a product, but who charges on a fee-for-service basis and can furnish you with a workable plan. From the beginning, Americans have believed that God helps those who help themselves, and despite the reforms of the New Deal onward, our system largely runs on that premise. We live in an individualistic society, and that carries with it the burden of caring for ourselves and those whom we love with little governmental assistance. In the end, the buck stops wherever you are reading this book.

With those sobering reflections in mind, you should be preparing for retirement well before the event. Viewed narrowly from the TIAA-CREF perspective, it means that you should try to increase your accumulation as much as possible. You want to leverage every dollar with employer matches. And you should invest your funds by balancing the risk-reward ratio as best you can, remembering some of the points made earlier about the applicable time horizon. If you can utilize some of the special catch-up contribution choices permitted by the Code and described in appendix A, then by all means do so. Congress must have recognized that those who work in the nonprofit sector don't get paid as well as those in private industry, and the years before retirement may represent the first time that an employee has some financial breathing room.

Fast forward: you are now on the verge of retirement, and these theoretical discussions have lost their timeliness and relevance. The next step in the TIAA-CREF process involves your finding out how much income your account will yield. First, you ought to look at what the annuity options are and how much they will yield, depending on which survivor option you choose, guaranteed terms, and so forth. Second, you should determine how much the minimum distribution option will yield (more will be said about this later.)

You then need to step back and look at the broader picture. You need to determine what, if any, other sources of income will remain available to you and, if applicable, to your spouse or your significant other after you retire. Whether this involves other income-producing assets or part-time work or a new career, your goal remains to ascertain how much you (singularly or plurally) will have to live on for the foreseeable future. You also need to know how much Social Security you will receive, depending on the age at which you start to withdraw from the system. Paralleling the private sector, Social Security will pay less the earlier you start and the longer that you can be expected to draw benefits.

This will give you a pretty good idea of what to expect on the income side of the ledger. You then need to look at your fixed costs: housing, utilities, insurance, and so forth. In the context of retirement, this term takes on two meanings. Eating is a fixed cost. No one can survive without it. But it is also variable because the cost of eating does not remain stable. Your choice of foods obviously also affects the cost of three squares.

Other costs are less volatile. If you own a home and the mortgage has been paid, then the costs of occupancy will only fluctuate with changes in local taxation and the needs for maintenance. Smaller housing may free up capital. For those who have lived in employer-provided housing, retirement may entail venturing out into the real estate market and buying a house. A better plan involves buying the house in advance of retirement, renting it to the extent it is not needed for living space, and thus having the process of amortizing the cost of the house well underway, if not completed, while supported by rental income and working income. Those same retirees may face the true cost of food for the first time too if the employer provides meals as part of the compensation package. This only emphasizes that one has to plan with a zero budget—that is, with no assumptions—and work up from there.

One has to go through the same discipline with all of the other necessities of life: utilities, medical costs, clothing, and so forth. Luckily, there are several good software products on the market that can aid in this process. These programs typically contain a module to plan for retirement, and they furnish excellent tools for planning purposes. These programs include Quicken, Quicken Financial Planner, and Microsoft Money, to name the most popular.

Everyone worries about the imponderable cost of medical care. We all fear senility and a long, dreary stretch in a nursing home that depletes our savings and ends our days. This concern obviously has roots in reality. We should not, however, overstate its importance. First, those cases represent a small percentage of the elderly population. Second, nursing home care usually lasts for a relatively short time. Third, if this remains a matter of concern, the insurance industry has developed long-term care policies that are inexpensive if purchased while one is in one's fifties and sixties. If you fear that you will face a prolonged stay in a nursing home, either because of family history or personal health reasons, again the time value of money mandates that you address this issue as early and therefore as inexpensively as possible. The insurance products undergo continuous evolution, and one has to look long and hard at them and the causes of mortality in one's family to make an educated guess about how likely it will be that the policy will be invoked and prove a viable investment of scarce dollars. The tendency in health care now points to more home care, and the policies now provide more generous coverage for such care.

Most of these policies only provide three to five years of coverage, daily and policy limits on coverage, and so forth. Although they defray the cost of nursing home care, they also serve as a mechanism for divesting one's assets and becoming eligible for Medicaid. In assessing eligibility, the state agency will, as mandated by federal law, look back three years for outright transfers and five years for gifts in trust to determine whether assets exist that can be used to pay the freight. Long-term care policies provide a window of opportunity to jettison your assets, protect your family financially, and have Medicaid foot the bill after the insurance coverage expires.

You can, therefore, make educated estimates about most of the costs of retirement and what your income is likely to be. How well you fared with your retirement account may determine the extent to which travel and other desired side effects of retirement will come your way.

However benign the inflation climate has been for the last several years, this state will not last forever, and one must budget for higher costs of living. And, again, this militates against the fixed retirement income that locks you in at the beginning of retirement and then has to carry you through, however long the journey.

In the end, planning for retirement boils down to the same disciplines as any other financial planning—quantifying what you have and what you need, then seeing how to structure your life to meet as many of your goals as you can. Early retirement may have to be shelved, employment or consulting after leaving one's long-term workplace may bridge the gap, but in any event, you have to be realistic and flexible. Part-time clerical work may represent an opportunity or a necessity, however much we may feel that it demeans our social status.

We realize in retrospect how uninformed we were in our early adulthood. In much the same way as the choices that we made in our twenties largely determine where we end up in our fifties, the choices that we make beginning in our thirties will shape where we end up at the beginning of retirement. If you are armed with this bit of foreknowledge, there remains time for adjustments, and two to three decades will probably prove available to accumulate savings. But if you have not taken advantage of the time value of money, then you face the more painful issues that surround the monetary cost of time.

First and foremost, this exercise does not occur two months before you plan to retire. Even when you are young and retirement seems decades away, you need to see how your account is doing and make sure that time remains your ally, permitting you to compound your accumulation.

You should begin focused examination of your retirement situation at least ten, and preferably fifteen, years before you anticipate that your career will end, and you should undertake a review periodically. Early in those years such a review might occur semiannually, and then more frequently as your personal countdown begins. If you wait until the eleventh hour, then you have lost the time needed to make any corrections to your mix of assets or to implement any plans to increase your income after retirement from other sources. Doing calculations every fifteen minutes nightly between three in the morning and dawn does not make for good decision making, and adding sleep problems to your agenda will not cure anything and will make you less productive.

So, at least ten years before retirement marks the point at which you need to take out your calculating tools to run the numbers. To reiterate, the earlier you begin to plan, the better the results are likely to prove. The prior chapter talked in general concepts, but we hope that you have done your best to contribute to your employer's plan. If you have been tracking the items that we are talking about, this task, though not the most pleasant, should not impose an unbearable burden. But above all, you need to be realistic.

You need to begin with your assets and see first what they are currently worth. Bear in mind that somewhere in your mix of assets, assuming a normal life expectancy, has to be a group of assets that will appreciate and that will throw off additional income. Your TIAA-CREF accumulation is one of those assets, but you need to look upon it as part of the asset mix and not in isolation. The purpose of viewing your financial and other assets in this way is to determine your overall asset allocation. How much is invested in fixed-income securities versus equities versus real estate? Which assets produce income and which represent nothing but expense?

Then comes the judgmental aspect—estimating what will occur to those assets over the next few years. This may seem like an exercise in futility (who, after all, can predict the future?), but you will be monitoring those assets, probably never more carefully than after you retire, and the amount of time that will go by before you revisit your projections will only amount to a few months, at most. As always with the equity portion of your asset mix (which one hopes is inside of your tax-deferred retirement accounts so that any capital gains will not detract from the size of your overall asset pie), you have to budget for market downturns and see how you would fare if the market declined 20% or 40%. That accomplished, step back and see if your asset allocation is consistent with your tolerance for risk and what impact a decline lasting from six months to two years in the value of your equity portfolio would have on your lifestyle. If you are investing those funds to provide a means of support years down the road and have a cushion, then the answer will probably be not much. Not that the experience will be pleasant; it was not from 1973 to 1975 when the market fell 50%, and there is no reason that the pain would lessen twenty-five years later. But if you have other assets allocated to other investment vehicles or low fixed expenses such as minimal or no debt service, the answer may come out the same. You can weather the storm and wait for better days.

Add in all of the income sources that either exist or are likely to exist over the course of the next few years. One would therefore add in consulting fees or any other source of what would have been outside income were you still working. Again, be realistic. These figures should not reflect a wing and a prayer. If you are married, you should, of course, make the calculations on a joint basis. Add Social Security and ask the Social Security Administration to give you a printout of your benefits when you retire. If you begin to draw benefits when you are younger than 70, then you will receive a schedule of benefits varying with the age you retire.

Then you need to do the same thing on the liability or cost side. If you have mortgage or credit card debt, that will have to be retired over some set schedule. You should figure in some amount of inflation—2 to 3% based on the current experience, 4 to 5% to provide a margin of safety because none of us buys the Consumer Price Index (at least not knowingly)—to compensate for the fact that the United States will not remain inflation free 'til the last syllable of recorded time. Look at the volatility of your personal costs of living, whether fixed or variable. If you factor in inflation from the get-go, you will be better prepared in terms of your investments and the path that your income will take when general inflation does ratchet up. You will also have adjusted for the fact that the CPI does not necessarily reflect the future increases in your personal cost of living. If inflation is less than you had projected, you will either enjoy more purchasing power or have free cash to save and invest. You need to add one final liability to the mix, and that is, of course, income taxes, including the taxes that will be generated by the distribution of your retirement account.

This description makes the process sound like a science, but it is also an art. The more realistic (or pessimistic, if you choose) you are, the better you can prepare for the unforeseen. No projection can ever take into account all of the events that will occur over time. After all, limits do exist on human foresight, and even in what may seem the calmer waters of retirement, surprises will occur. They may be pleasant, like an inheritance, or they may be just the opposite, like increased medical costs. Leave room in your budget for the proverbial rainy day even if you live in Palm Springs.

Most retirees take it as axiomatic that they do not want to be a burden on their children, who at this stage may be paying college tuition or have other problems of their own. On the other hand, you supported them, in part because of biological instinct, and have probably tried to make provision for them to inherit something. Providing grandparental assistance ought to earn some compensation. This should not enter into your calculations because you want to be and will need to be independent. But things do not always work out as we hope, and one needs to keep one's children in mind as, in effect, a last resort. For example, adding on to a child's house and living there may make financial and emotional sense from both generations' point of view. This does not amount to a recommendation, but rather a reminder that children are a resource if all else fails or if mutual dependence makes financial sense for everyone involved.

If you have planned well, you will enjoy, at least at the outset, an annual surplus. Some of that needs to be saved for emergencies and for extreme old age. Some can be used to enjoy the amenities that all of us would like to savor in our retirement years. Travel does broaden the mind, which also needs exercise, and you will need some diversion from the contents of, and the issues discussed in, this book. You will enjoy removing this book from your nightstand and diversifying your reading and uses of leisure time.

If the calculations show a deficit, then you may have to reduce your prospective standard of living during retirement, postpone retirement, or begin to take steps to work at some other job after you leave your the usual workplace. All of us will not play golf for the rest of our days, and it is not unusual to find retirees working due to their excellent work habits and the fact that they do not receive the full panoply of benefits that younger workers demand and need. That may make retirement seem less attractive than years of leisure, but one needs to remember that billions of years of evolution did not occur for the sole purpose of developing a creature that strives, at great individual and social expense, to put a small white ball into a slightly larger hole over an undulating field punctuated with small deserts, strategically placed trees, and other obstacles. In addition—and this is just a matter of personal opinion—work and personal involvement give our lives structure and meaning. You ought to have fun, but the issue boils down to how much or how expensive the fun will be.

Based on our experience with our clients, those who enjoy the greatest longevity appear to be those who remain active in their communities. That means physical and mental activity as well as social interaction. Those of us who live in the snow belt may yearn for milder winters, but we also need warm friendships and meaningful relationships and companionship. A tropical or desert climate and warm social interactions do not always coexist. Those who move to retirement communities wall themselves off from the rest of society. At first blush and even on further consideration, such a move may sound appealing, but, if one cannot afford it, that does not mean being cast into outer darkness. It may necessitate that you continue to work and remain involved in your communities, but you can also be ingenious about how you spend your time. Necessity is indeed the mother of invention, and you will not lose your ability to find rewarding things to do simply because you crossed an invisible line on the calendar.

Critical Intermezzo

24 When and How Should You Review Your Estate Plan?
A Primer on Estate Planning

We debated where to put this chapter. Logic seemed to dictate that it be placed at the beginning of part V. On the other hand, retirement planning and estate planning go hand in hand. When you think about it after you have read this chapter or in some meditative moment, you will realize that estate planning represents just another phase of financial planning and that type of long-term thinking forms one of the leitmotivs of this book. If we left this information to the end, we ran the risk that many readers would never make it that far or conclude, incorrectly, that they did not need to know what this chapter contains. Again, we cannot tell you what to do, but we can tell you the principal rules governing this area of the law and the options available to you as you work out an estate plan that suits your individual circumstances.

For most people, estate planning ought to begin with marriage and, at the latest, with the arrival of a child. At that point, you may view the process as involving little more than setting out your postmortem wishes, avoiding having a court decide on the guardian of your children, and sidestepping the arbitrary formulae that dictate what happens to your property should you die intestate, that is, without a will.

At every watershed event in your life, reviewing your estate plan borders upon the imperative. Circumstances change, and an estate plan cannot remain static. You may have put some of the basic building blocks in place when you last reviewed your estate plan, but your thoughts about your children or spouse, if any, about charity, and about the future will probably not remain fixed as you pass through life. In all likelihood, your assets will have increased, and every significant item requires planning to reduce taxes and to expedite its passing into the right hands.

When you are contemplating retirement or even after retirement, these issues assume more importance. Age obviously plays a role, and you have or ought to have a reasonable grasp of your financial affairs. In all likelihood, the assets that you now own will remain the same, although their value will fluctuate. Barring your winning a lottery, you can reasonably foresee any additional assets being added to your net worth or liabilities that will detract from it.

With that as a prologue, we need to make sure that everyone understands:

1. what estate planning is designed to achieve,
2. what will constitute your taxable estate,
3. what will pass to your heirs under your will and what will pass outside it, and
4. the basic gift and estate tax rules of the road.

This book can only provide a primer. Popular literature on estate planning abounds, most of it beside the point; some of it useful, even critical; and some of it dangerously wrong. Anyone who purports to have a method by which you can escape all forms of taxation is extending you an invitation to spend years in litigation and potentially the slammer. You will not emerge an estate planning expert at the end of this chapter, much to the relief of your friends and family who have come to love you as you currently are, but you will grasp almost intuitively everything that we introduce hereafter. You may need to return to this chapter to refresh your recollection, but at least you will know what you are looking for and why.

We begin with first principles.

Recognizing that no estate planner can create assets, certain precepts obtain across the board. The first seems obvious, but the obvious often bears repeating: the estate plan must provide you (and your spouse if you are married or your life partner) with financial security for the balance of your lifetimes. All too often, clients and estate planners of all stripes become so concerned about estate taxes that they lose sight of the fact that they are someone else's problem and that financial considerations always come first. Tax savings strategies only come into play when the basic needs have been met with a healthy margin of safety. Once that point has been passed, the Code offers numerous opportunities to save significant estate taxes; but those techniques, in order to remove assets from your estate, require that you surrender something of value. The gift tax value of that something may receive a healthy discount from fair market value, but nothing works if the economic foundation has not been laid.

On the other hand, you should understand what estate planning is not. Too often the term is taken literally to mean putting down in a will what will happen to property after one dies. The image of the family solicitor reading the will in an Agatha Christie novel gives a misleading and erroneous stereotype. Estate planning means the lifetime arranging of one's affairs to accomplish one's goals, ideally at the lowest tax cost. Structuring your estate planning so that everything occurs after you die provides a surefire recipe for not achieving tax or economic efficiency. In estate planning, as with investing, time should remain your friend and ally. Waiting until you have exhausted it will rarely produce enviable results. If one has the requisite margin of economic safety, then the time value of money techniques laid out in the Code can result in significant estate tax savings. But they assume the availability of time, and that does not exist in an estate plan contained entirely in a will. Whatever your religious beliefs, true to the First Amendment, the Code's estate tax provisions do not allow you to be born again, at least not for their limited purposes.

Second, in every instance, one must identify all of the assets that will make up the taxable estate. The Code defines this term broadly, but you can think of it as all of the property, real or personal, wherever located, that you own or over which you exercise powers that resemble dominion and control. With a few exceptions, those assets will pass from you to someone else, simply because you died. This concept will include items that you may not think of as assets, because they do not produce income and may not come into being until death. Life insurance provides the classic example.

Although you may wonder as you go through this process if you are worth more dead than alive, especially if you own considerable amounts of life insurance, you need to identify these subsurface assets that become part of your estate even if you would not regard them as assets in the ordinary course of life. They include death benefits of one kind or another, your interest in a trust, business interests that your colleagues must buy upon your death, a partial interest in the family summer cabin, and so forth.

You need to recognize that some assets, like one's TIAA-CREF account, other retirement assets, a life insurance policy, or jointly held property, will pass outside of your will. In the first three cases, this occurs because the designation of one's beneficiary operates as part of a contract between TIAA-CREF, the retirement plan provider or the insurer, and the decedent, you, and an existing contractual relationship will almost invariably trump your will. In the fourth case, the surviving joint tenant "takes" because that is the nature of that form of ownership. In effect, owning property in this form amounts to a contract between you and your joint tenants that the survivors will take the whole.

The will only operates on property that you own individually, free and clear of contractual obligations or arrangements that dictate what happens upon your death. You need to have the power to dispose of the asset. Good estate planning involves, then, looking at all of one's assets, seeing who owns what, and examining the form of the ownership. It also entails reviewing beneficiary designations for all kinds of contractual arrangements, including those mentioned above.

A word about probate and the avoiding of probate, with the caution that the procedures and rules differ from state to state. Your probate estate consists of those assets that pass under your will. For the reasons stated above, the concept of the probate estate does not encompass all of the assets that will make up your taxable estate. In addition, if your will directs that the residue of your estate pass into a trust, rather than having the trust in the will, the trust will ordinarily operate outside of the jurisdiction of the probate court. Most people have an image of the probate court drawn from Charles Dickens, with everything frozen in place while the probate process drags on interminably. That no longer represents the real world. Assets can be invested, income can be earned and distributed, and the family can function while the principal cause of delay, finishing up the tax process while waiting for the Internal Revenue Service and the state government to complete their audits, runs its course. In most instances, the estate stays open for about two to three years, and its role becomes pretty minor as the course of life continues. The executor may distribute all of the estate's assets, minus a reserve for taxes, well before the estate is wound up. Finally the moment arrives when all of the relevant taxing authorities have signed off on the tax returns. At that point, typically a final accounting is filed, the remaining assets are distributed, and the estate comes to an end.

Probate has its advantages. The court sets a date by which creditors must present claims against the estate or the claims will be cut off. It reviews the work and fees of the fiduciaries and lawyers working on the estate's administration. Most of the time very little actually occurs in the probate court as the estate is being settled, assuming that there are no disputes among the beneficiaries. If there are, the process can bog down, but that delay cannot be laid at the court's feet. If the will requires interpretation or some other cause produces conflict, the court will have to schedule and hold hearings. Again, the litigants would need to search for some forum in which to settle their disagreement, and the probate court usually requires less formality and expense than would be involved in full-scale litigation.

Returning, then, to issues of substance rather than procedure, in most cases the division of property and the use of beneficiary designations should serve to keep the surviving spouse in as good financial shape as possible. That usually means naming the survivor as the designated beneficiary of a TIAA-CREF account or as a joint annuitant. It means that the income from other assets should be paid to or be available to the surviving spouse, and the invasion of principal for at least health, maintenance, and support should appear in the estate planning documents. Only where you have substantial assets would you consider having other beneficiaries as eligible to receive income or principal during the life of the surviving spouse.

We now need to cover the basics of gift and estate taxation. This sounds worse than it really is. It all boils down to three rules of the road for most people. First, everyone has the equivalent of a gift and estate tax exemption of $675,000 in 2000 and 2001. Under current law, the exemption will increase, first by baby steps and then more rapidly to $1 million in 2006. The terminology to describe this feature of the law varies. Most accurately, it represents a credit against the estate tax that, when measured against the tables, produces the exemption or exclusion.

In practical terms, this means that each of us can leave this amount of property to whomever we want free of tax. If one can make gifts that utilize time in your favor, you can leverage the exemption and remove several dollars worth of assets from your taxable estate for every dollar of the exemption that you allocate to the transfer. Unfortunately, this subject falls outside the scope of this book, and we can only touch on the periphery of the issues.

Second, both the estate and gift taxes provide for an unlimited marital deduction. This allows for an infinite amount of funds to be passed from one spouse to the other without producing any tax. Unlike the exemption, which escapes taxation, this rule only defers taxation until the surviving spouse dies. Whatever passes to the surviving spouse will, if not spent or given away, be included in the survivor's taxable estate.

An estate plan most frequently fails to produce optimal results because it does not take full advantage of the estate and gift tax exclusion upon the death of the first spouse. If your estate plan does not take advantage of the exclusion, you or your heirs should not shoot the piano player, in this case the lawyer. Part of the cause may stem from the ownership of assets. You only get the benefit of the exclusion if you structure your assets so that you have individually owned assets to fund the exemption and you write your will or trust accordingly. In the same way that individually owned assets pass under the will, only individually owned assets can qualify for the exclusion. Most frequently, couples go for decades with simple wills that leave everything to the survivor or with all of their property owned in joint tenancy.

The defect in either of those arrangements stems from the fact that the unlimited marital deduction swallows the entire transfer; consequently, the exclusion for the first spouse to die never comes into play and is wasted. Upon the death of the first spouse, this estate plan produces no federal estate tax. However, it entails that the whole basket of assets will end up in the survivor's estate with only one instead of two exclusions to shelter the assets from taxation. The survivor's estate ends up in a higher tax bracket, and the unnecessary increase in tax that results will only grow with the exemption.

Let's take an easy example. If the total assets equal $1.3 million (the 2000 exclusion doubled), two estates that might have passed free of federal estate tax will, if all of the assets land in the survivor's estate, instead generate about $198,000 in Federal taxes and approximately $52,000 in state taxes, assuming that both spouses die within a short interval. Had the assets been owned and the estate plan drafted to take advantage of the two exclusions, the entire transfer would have generated no federal tax and probably no state tax.

On occasion, clients profess indifference, figuring that the exclusion, when fully implemented in 2006, will solve the problem. That strategy works only if one knows to a certainty the value of the combined assets upon the death of the surviving spouse. If they appreciate beyond one's expectations, the problem will reemerge, although the tax numbers will obviously differ.

While the leave-everything-to-the-surviving-spouse plan may have worked when the couple was young and childless (and often virtually asset free), it does not work anymore as you acquire assets. Instead, you want an estate plan that creates a trust that benefits your spouse or spouse and children and will not become part of the survivor's estate. The trust passes to whomever you choose, usually children, free of estate tax upon the death of the surviving spouse. Such a trust is called a "credit shelter trust" because it uses the estate tax credit or a "bypass trust" because it bypasses the estate of the surviving spouse.

If the trust has appreciated during the lifetime of the surviving spouse, the increased value will also pass free of gift or estate tax. Everything over and above the exclusion (or credit) should pass into a marital trust for the benefit of the survivor. This trust or outright bequest will eventually become part of the survivor's taxable estate and will be sheltered in whole or in part by the survivor's exclusion.

Now you have to make sure that the exemption trust and the marital trust will be funded. Naming the trust as the beneficiary of any life insurance policies, including the group term that employers typically provide, usually makes sense. Naming your spouse may exacerbate the problem of lumping all of the assets in the survivor's estate. Generally speaking, using insurance to fund the trust works best. First, for all intents and purposes, the trust will remain funded on paper only until the insured dies. Second, the existence of the trust will have no impact on your lifestyle. The trust then divides the assets into two separate subtrusts, the credit shelter trust and the marital trust. The marital share can pass to the spouse outright if that is your preference. Generally speaking, the trust wins hands down. It protects the assets from a later marriage, the surviving spouse's possible incompetence later in life, and from all of the hucksters in the world who will find little profit in approaching the surviving spouse directly.

The credit shelter trust escapes taxation in the second estate by just giving the survivor a life estate and none of the powers that would, under the Code, sweep the trust into the taxable estate of the surviving spouse. If other assets are there, including inside the marital trust, or children are young, the trust can spray income and principal among spouse and children. The benefit of the spray is best illustrated by college tuition. To minimize income taxes, the tuition can be paid to or for the benefit of the child, who is presumably in a lower bracket, rather than distributing everything to the survivor, who will then pay more tax in order to pay the collegiate freight.

You will have to select a trustee. Your first impulse might steer you in the direction of a family member. You should bear in mind that a trustee has two functions: a distributive function and an investment function. Most people focus on the former and ignore the latter, but the best-intended trustee needs to have something to distribute. In a trust that may last for decades, solid investment performance plays a critical role. We do not recommend an institutional or professional trustee for everyone or anyone, but the trustee, if not a qualified professional, needs to know that the trust will require a money manager. That individual or entity will ultimately affect the well-being of the people you care about most more than anyone else. The trustee has to monitor the performance of the money manager and make a replacement when appropriate. Too much is riding on the money manager to invite casualness in the initial choice and future retention.

You can name your spouse as the sole or as a co-trustee. The first alternative can spawn some problems. In order to avoid having the credit shelter trust included in the survivor's estate, defeating the trust's purpose, the spouse can only invade principal under what the Code calls an "ascertainable standard." This means criteria framed in terms of health, maintenance, and support. Truly discretionary distributions, for travel, by way of example, are out of bounds unless they can be funded out of income only. Having a second trustee, who can be a child, allows for truly discretionary distributions. You should recognize, however, that your child has a conflict of interest. The less that is distributed to the surviving spouse, the more the children will inherit. Most parents trust their children to that extent, but one should know that this can in isolated situations cause untold grief.

This describes a plain vanilla estate plan. The survivor gets the economic benefit of all of the family assets, and the estate tax is reduced through the use of two exclusions. We mention a variant on this structure because it introduces a useful, if not critical, tool to the kit. One can leave everything to the surviving spouse, especially where the combined assets hover near the exemption amount, and give the surviving spouse the power to disclaim part of the inheritance into a credit shelter trust. If one meets the generally simple rules for a "qualified disclaimer," then the transfer will not constitute a gift. The disclaimer has many other uses, but it provides a mechanism for taking a later look at the situation and doing what is most tax efficient at the time. It avoids the need to foresee precisely what the future holds and builds more flexibility into the estate plan.

Single individuals also need to review their estate plans. Again, you need to gather up in your mind all of the assets that will constitute your taxable estate and decide who will inherit what. Beyond that, most of the work consists of making sure that the beneficiary designations on life insurance policies, and so forth. are correct in terms of carrying out your intentions. You obviously want to check that any individual beneficiaries still want, need, or deserve an inheritance. If you are planning to make a charitable gift as part of your estate plan, then you should probably make a discreet inquiry of the intended charity as to how the gift should be structured and whether the charity will honor your wishes about the use of your gift. One needs finesse to remain anonymous if you ever want to spend a dinner hour in peace. Charitable giving—which one would think is relatively straightforward—has, through the complexities of the Internal Revenue Code, become a specialized subject whenever one makes anything other than an outright bequest. In the part of this book dealing with estate planning, we will discuss lifetime giving with a retained life use, but you should become familiar with the charitable remainder unitrust and annuity trust if you are seriously considering a charitable gift and want to retain or increase your income.

The last area of concern (usually conceived as the first) revolves around what the next generation will inherit. The issues encompassed within this topic will be dealt with in detail in part V of this book. Nonetheless, one should know that the principal issue that confronts TIAA-CREF participants with sufficiently large accumulations is whether they want to enjoy the security of an annuity or, feeling that they do not need a safety net, to leave their accounts to children or other family members. Achieving the latter result requires making a series of interrelated decisions and preparing an estate plan with customized language. At this point, the only issue you need to worry about is whether your account is large enough or you have other assets that will make your retirement comfortable and, secondarily, allow you to extend the life of the account beyond your lifetime and that of your annuity partner or spouse. In many instances, the size of retirement assets of one kind or another dwarfes the other parts of the estate. Consequently, in those cases, the issue of inheriting the account will have a direct impact on and play a major role in your retirement and estate planning, and you should at least dip into part V before you make any irrevocable decisions that may preclude passing your account on to your children.

As the prior paragraph intimated, retirement planning and estate planning do not represent two different disciplines or mental processes. If, as is becoming increasingly prevalent given the great bull market of the 1980s and 1990s, retirement assets amount to virtually all that you own, you should recognize that the two types of planning have to become internally consistent and have to be viewed as two aspects of the same issue. Retirement planning deals with the assets before the death of the surviving spouse, and estate planning moves the clock forward to determine what happens to the same assets upon the death of the surviving spouse or annuity partner. For the last reason in particular, if retirement does not outright compel review of your estate plan, it makes eminent good sense to revisit your planning.

Finally, we need to double back, so to speak, to the third basic rule. It arises under the gift tax. Every year, you can make a gift to whomever you choose in an amount of up to $10,000. In tax terminology, we refer to this feature as the "annual exclusion." If you are married and your spouse consents to the gift, the limitation rises to $20,000 per donee annually, even if all of the property belonged to one spouse. In one of those charming abuses of the language that represent some of the hallmarks of tax practice, the consent of the spouse produces "gift splitting," when in fact it is just the opposite.

Earlier, we said that the difference between the gift tax and the estate tax boiled down to one of timing. One does not just dismiss time. If you can afford to make gifts, then all of the appreciation that the donated asset accrues inures to the benefit of the donee. It passes to your recipient free of gift or estate tax. As we will discuss later, there are ways to leverage the annual exclusion and the gift and estate tax exemption so that they produce outstanding results. But realistically, one cannot think about making gifts until you know that your financial house is in order and that your financial security is assured. It comes down to the same unfairness that the well off have options that those less fortunate do not. But if you have the choice, you need to know it, and you need to know how to take advantage of what good fortune and the Code have provided you.

To anticipate a later chapter, the rules discussed above presume that both spouses are American citizens. If only one of you is not an American citizen, different rules apply, and you need to know them and incorporate them into your estate planning documents.

That ends the primer, but please do not try this at home. We have only touched on the fundamental tax issues. Few areas of the law yield as many unwanted tax or administrative problems from nuances of language and sloppy draftsmanship as estate planning and administration. No will leaves our office unless it has been reviewed by two lawyers, preferably experienced partners in the firm. Estate planning self-taught does not present any likelihood of reward. This is one area in which you need an experienced and knowledgeable lawyer if you want to avoid a potential catastrophe. We want you to follow the bouncing ball as we continue our discussion, and that is all. Every week, dozens of cases and rulings appear in which implementation of an estate plan ran afoul of the Internal Revenue Code. The Internal Revenue Service's position may not prove reasonable or right, but who wants to spend money on unnecessary legal and accounting fees when the ultimate objects of your bounty are left waiting or are left with less?

Against the mural of overall estate planning considerations, we turn now to the distribution options available from TIAA-CREF. That subject will take up part IV of this book. Like part II, it comes closest to required reading if you want to understand TIAA-CREF.

The TIAA-CREF Distribution Options

**PART
IV**

What Is the Retirement Transition Benefit?

In this part, we describe the various distribution options that are available for the withdrawal of your TIAA-CREF accumulation after you have retired. The rules governing almost all of these options originate in the Code. Again, we will try our best to describe them in nontechnical terms.

The transition from a working environment to retirement poses financial as well as emotional challenges. The financial adjustment probably seems the most daunting to teachers who have lived on campus for most of their careers. Even those who own their homes may face substantial change. You may decide to buy a smaller house. For any number of reasons, you may move after you retire. You may need to buy a car or major household appliances. Even in less extreme cases, you may require a one-time cash infusion to make the transition into your new lifestyle. In our society, every major life change seems to necessitate the spending of money somehow.

If you choose the Minimum Distribution Option and have assets in the CREF portion of your account, you can easily meet this financial challenge (again, assuming that your employer's plan permits). You can use the Systematic Withdrawal option to take out funds necessary to make the transition into retirement. If, however, you have decided to annuitize some or all of your TIAA-CREF assets, you may find that the initial payments do not suffice to overcome that initial financial hurdle. Recognizing that issue, TIAA-CREF offers the Retirement Transition Benefit to those who have annuitized their assets, but who will need more than their initial annuity payment to pave the transition into retirement. TIAA-CREF limits the RTB to 10% of the assets that you are annuitizing in retirement. You will receive this sum in one payment, and you can then apply it to meet your needs.

Although this payment can obviously prove highly beneficial, you should keep two issues in mind. First, although there will be no penalties imposed by the Code on the use of the RTB, all of the payment will constitute taxable income. You should calculate the impact that this one-time wallop of income will have upon your income tax liability, state and federal, and therefore how much of the RTB will end up in your pocket, net of taxes. Second, if you exercise your right to take the RTB, this will obviously affect the size of your future annuity payments. If, for example, you have $500,000 in your retirement account and you are annuitizing the whole amount, then you will have received an estimate from TIAA-CREF as to what your initial annuity payments will be. If you avail yourself of the RTB for the full 10%, then you will receive $50,000 at retirement. Other things being equal, this will immediately reduce your remaining balance to $450,000. TIAA-CREF will then base your future annuity payments upon this diminished balance.

If your financial needs are pressing, then you may not have a choice as to whether you ought to take advantage of the RTB. If the RTB will fund an opportunity to increase your net worth and income substantially, then it may prove a timely invasion of capital, assuming, of course, that the investment produces what it promises. Even if you find yourself in dire straits, you ought to work out completely the trade-off between the immediate payment and the reduction in income that you will receive in future years. To the extent that you can minimize the amount that you withdraw, the 10% representing a ceiling, clearly that will mitigate the impact upon the future payment stream upon which you will depend for a number of years.

You should ask for a recomputation of your annuity, depending on the amount that you intend to withdraw through the RTB. See how the difference affects your projected lifestyle in retirement. If you also bear in mind that you are losing the compounding effect on the funds that you take out of the system, you will know all of the facts you need to make an informed judgment about the appropriate course of action. The comparison between the two annuity estimates, with and without the RTB, will quantify the impact that the upfront withdrawal will have in the long run when those funds are no longer working for you.

26

The Heart of the Matter
What Sorts of Annuities Does TIAA-CREF Offer?

For those of you who are considering annuitizing all or part of your account, this chapter and the next may prove to be the most critical and, we hope, helpful. We will lay out the different options available, the implications for each choice, and the issues that you need to consider in picking an annuity.

At first blush, the choice may appear straightforward, but you are making decisions about life expectancy, the trade-off between a higher initial payment versus a lower monthly payment that may last longer, and the benefit that will inure to your heirs. The decision is not as easy as it seems, and we will try to give you the information you need to make a rational choice. Again, you are making a choice about the future, and the best you can do is to make the most informed guess about what lies before you.

However bewildering the choices may seem when they appear on your annual benefit statement or, more pertinently, when you are making a decision that will affect your retirement income, you need to start with the simple premise that TIAA-CREF offers basically two types of annuities: annuities measured in years and annuities measured by one or two lives. On the TIAA side, the first group of annuities are labeled annuities for a term certain. CREF labels its analog annuities for a guaranteed period. Most of the options represent hybrids of these two basic types.

We begin by discussing the annuities with a term certain. They present the fewest conceptual difficulties, although the wisdom of electing this option will depend on the greatest number of independent factors.

TIAA offers only two types of annuities: a ten-year certain annuity or a lifetime annuity. No alternative exists between these two extremes. As you will readily perceive, the ten-year certain annuity carries with it the risk that you and/or your annuity partner will live longer than ten years, and you will have lost your retirement income.

The choice of the term certain only appears to make economic sense in two situations. The first probably does not occur with any degree of frequency. It involves the unusual case where you are absolutely certain that neither you and/your annuity partner will survive the ten-year term. This could occur if both of you are in poor health. The only other scenario that comes to mind involves delaying retirement so long that you are both well beyond $70^{1}/_{2}$ and your life expectancies can confidentially be predicted to be short. In such an instance, a lifetime annuity would wind up paying less because payments would cease upon the death of your survivor if you have an annuity partner, or upon your death if you do not. Instead, if you elected the ten-year certain annuity, the remaining years' payments would pass to your heirs.

The second case probably does not arise with any frequency either. If it does, you can never know whether it makes sense without running the numbers in your individual circumstances. The term certain may make a shrewd choice if you have significant other assets that you want to invest for long-term growth. You need a source of income until your proverbial boat comes home, and the TIAA ten-year certain option fills that void. This strategy appears shot full of pitfalls and uncertainties, unless you also have other assets that will carry you through if the anticipated investment return does not pan out or requires longer than ten years to reach your goal.

Absent these two unusual circumstances, the choice of a term certain TIAA annuity contains the potentially unacceptable risk that the annuity payments will cease before you do and you will have outlived your assets. Theoretically, you could save some of the payments after paying income taxes and guard against that risk, but that would involve heroic sacrifice, iron discipline, an extraordinarily high annual annuity payment, or other sources of income. The acceleration of the payments into a decade will, of course, generate a significant income tax liability, and you will need presumably a substantial part of the remainder on which to live. That does not provide much margin for savings. That approach contains so many problems that it makes the lifetime annuity a slam dunk in all but the most unusual cases. If you elect a lifetime annuity, TIAA becomes your vehicle for forced savings, and the earnings on your savings do not incur any income tax until distributed. Even if you could save something from the ten-year payment stream, it would not, all things being equal, generate as great a return as would occur in a tax-free investment environment.

Under the guaranteed period CREF annuity, CREF will pay you a given number of annuity units for an agreed upon number of years. CREF offers ten-, fifteen-, and twenty-year guaranteed period annuities. If you choose the guaranteed period option without turning it into one of the hybrids described below, then you are electing that you and your annuity partner, if any, will receive payments over the agreed upon period. At the end of that period, all payments stop, and your annuity income comes to an abrupt halt. If expository prose contained a repeat symbol like musical notation, we would insert it here to cover the drawbacks to those choices.

The one restriction imposed by CREF on your choice of guaranteed period depends on your age and your joint annuitant's age. The Internal Revenue Service will not allow you to choose a guaranteed period that is longer than your life expectancy or the joint life expectancy of you and your annuity partner as set out in the IRS mortality tables.

As we have indicated before, the more guarantees, or in this case the longer the guarantee, the more TIAA-CREF, or any other insurance company, will reduce each periodic payment to hedge its risks. In this case you have elected an option that will continue even if you and your annuity partner both die before the expiration of the guaranteed period. What you have bought with this option is the certainty that the payment stream will continue despite early death or deaths. Should that occur, the remaining payments will pass to your heirs, and your assets will have fully paid their way. TIAA-CREF does not obtain the use of your funds to offset the long-lived annuitant's demands on the system, and therefore the monthly payments decrease to reflect the unavailability of your assets to the insurance pool.

Life annuities represent the second major choice among the TIAA-CREF annuities. The underlying concept seems simplicity itself. As long as you and your annuity partner, if any, live, your annuity will be paid. Clearly, this option provides lifetime income, and you and TIAA-CREF stand on opposite sides of a bet as to how long the measuring life or lives will prove to be.

The single life annuity represents the purest form of the lifetime annuity. This choice will pay you a monthly benefit for the rest of your life and then cease immediately at your death. No beneficiary can exist for this type of annuity, because, tautologically, you will be the only income recipient. From the insurance company's perspective, such an annuity represents a pure play based on the current mortality tables.

From your point of view, especially if you are married or have dependents, this option carries the most risk. Sign the contract today and get hit by a meteorite or the proverbial bus tomorrow, and nothing will ever be paid. Your entire accumulation returns to the insurance pool to support payments to longer-lived, possibly nimbler, and undeniably luckier annuitants.

TIAA-CREF's obligations to make payments on the basis of only one life results in this type of annuity providing the largest monthly payments of all of the annuity choices. Put another way, at the end of your measuring life, TIAA-CREF does not have a continuing contractual duty to keep making payments until either another person dies or a fixed period expires. Your choice has reduced its risk, and your reward shows in higher monthly installments. Statistically, TIAA-CREF knows that, on average, the number of payments that you will ultimately receive will be less than if you had chosen a guaranteed period or an annuity partner to whom payments would have to continue after you had died. You may beat the odds, but TIAA-CREF has a sufficient number of other annuitants similarly situated who will not, so that the extended payments to you will not affect the financial integrity of the insurance pool. Obviously, if projected investment returns fall or overall longevity increases, then TIAA-CREF will adjust by lowering the amount of the monthly payments, probably across the board, to those who are just starting their annuities. If the life expectancy of a 70-year-old doubled, we cannot see any alternative, assuming that investment returns remain constant.

Life annuities resemble insurance policies in reverse. A life insurance policy receives its funding from a stream of premiums that typically add up to less than the face amount of the policy. Upon your death, your beneficiary receives a large lump sum payment based on the premiums paid plus earnings thereon. The life annuity works as a direct opposite. Instead of your beneficiary receiving a lump sum at death, you fund the annuity with a large up-front premium out of which flows the periodic stream of payments that terminates with the end of the measuring life. They clearly fall within anyone's reasonable definition of a life insurance product, and they share the same underwriting assumptions about longevity and the need to balance the premium against the stream of anticipated payments to minimize the insurer's risk. The amount that you ultimately receive on a monthly basis will directly reflect TIAA-CREF's past and anticipated experience with its annuitants' lifetimes.

The most frequently chosen options consist of the hybrids, annuity choices that combine elements of both basic types. The most popular is a lifetime annuity coupled with a guaranteed period. The attraction of this option comes from the fact that it provides lifetime income even if one lives to be very old and a stream of payments to one's heirs if one does not. The most frequently chosen variant is the annuity measured by two lives with a guaranteed period. This choice protects both husband and wife, the typical profile, against the other's dying and their heirs against both of them dying early. Again, this increases the likelihood that the annuity stream will continue for a longer time than the single life annuity, and the monthly payment declines as a result.

At this point, simplicity ends. We are talking, after all, about real life, and one can only simplify so much. We know that, as a matter of law, the longest guaranteed period will reflect and cannot exceed applicable life expectancies. But now you have to choose whether the survivor will receive a continuation of the same monthly dollar benefit or some lower figure. Once again, you have to balance probabilities and the trade-off between high monthly payments at the outset versus the odds of receiving an attenuated stream of lower payments after the death of one of the joint annuitants. You can make any of the choices below without a guaranteed period if you find the risk acceptable that you and your annuity partner will not outlive your assets.

The three hybrid variations of annuities are all based on joint lives, i.e., you and your annuity partner. The first option provides "Full Benefit to Survivor," subject to variation depending on the amount of annual dividends declared. With this option, the agreed-upon dollar sum (TIAA) or number of annuity units (CREF) will continue to be paid to you or your joint annuitant until both of you have passed away. Unless the two of you die before the end of the guaranteed period, upon the death of the survivor the payments cease; the annuity ends with no remaining balance due to beneficiaries. This choice provides the greatest security and the lowest monthly payments as a result. From TIAA-CREF's point of view, this option vastly increases the odds of the initial payment stream continuing for a longer period of time than, taking the paradigm, a single life annuity.

The second variation provides a "Half Benefit to Survivor." In this arrangement, you and your annuity partner will receive an agreed-upon monthly amount or number of annuity units as long as you are both alive. Should you predecease your annuity partner, then he or she will receive half of the monthly benefit that you both had been receiving up to the time of your death. If your annuity partner predeceases you, however, then no change in the amount paid or the number of annuity units paid will occur. By selecting this option, you are betting that you will outlive your annuity partner. This may create some friction at the time you retire, but it enhances your odds of receiving extraordinarily considerate treatment from your annuity partner for the rest of your life. Obviously, if your health is not as good as your partner's, this represents a dumb or vicious choice. If your annuity partner's health has deteriorated substantially, you may choose to take the risk and pick this option.

The third variation is the "Two-Thirds Benefit to Survivor." Under this option, TIAA-CREF will reduce the monthly annuity payment by one-third upon the death of *either you or your annuity partner*. Here the calculation or bet that you are making varies dramatically from the other two hybrid choices. Your annuity partner is receiving a larger benefit upon either death than under the Half Benefit to Survivor option if you die first, but you are doubling the odds that the reduction will occur by accepting the fact that either death will trigger a lower payment. This choice makes sense if you and your partner are both in excellent health, recognizing that the unexpected does happen with some frequency.

Aside from extraneous factors, such as other sources of income, other assets to cushion the effect of a lower annuity payment, or overt differences in states of health, the election of the type of annuity most appropriate to your circumstances will probably depend on the age differential between you and your annuity partner. If your annuity partner is ten or more years younger than you, then you will probably want to pick an option that continues the income flow at as high a level as possible after you die. The Half Benefit to Survivor option does not make sense, given the odds that you will predecease your annuity partner. If you are both roughly the same age, then you may want to elect Full Benefit or the Two-Thirds option because you will have a hard time betting which of the two of you will die first.

The choice becomes more complicated if you try to estimate longevity based upon an educated hunch. Absent the situation where one spouse is clearly failing faster than the other, you are venturing into the unknown, given the possibility of the sudden onset of illness, the silent killing disease, the risk of accident, and other variants on the same theme.

As mentioned before, the annuity variant that pays the largest percentage of your accumulation, after fees and mortality costs have been subtracted, is the single life annuity with no guarantee period. In your TIAA-CREF materials, you will see that TIAA-CREF treats this monthly payment as the benchmark against which all other variations are compared. We do not differentiate between TIAA and CREF annuities because the relative percentages do not vary.

If you then imitate TIAA-CREF and refer to the single life annuity for a 60-year-old as 100%, then you can compare the monthly payments from the other types of annuities in terms of a percentage of a single life annuity. As table 26.1 shows, the older you are, the larger the reduction in payment you will experience from the single life calculation. For example, if you are 60 years old, have chosen a TIAA Standard Method Annuity, and choose to add a ten-year guarantee to your single life annuity, you would receive 99% of the full pay. Elect a twenty-year guarantee, and you will receive 95%.

If you choose to have a joint participant with full benefits to both, then the monthly payment dwindles to 90% and so on as the guarantees and the level of continuing payments increase. If you are 70 years old, then as you can see from tables 26.1 and 26.2 the payments amount to 96% and 86% for the single life variations and with an annuity partner of the same age, 85%, 92%, and 94%, depending on the survivor's benefit.

The relative percentages for TIAA Graded, Real Estate, or CREF variable annuities appear as slightly lower. This protects TIAA-CREF against the variable nature of these investments and their need to lock in the monthly payment in your annuity contract. To compare the variations, you need to check the tables and refer to your most recent TIAA-CREF brochures. These numbers will vary from time to time, depending on TIAA-CREF's actual investment experience.

Table 26.1

Relative incomes from various options and guaranteed periods

Note: The percentages in Tables 2 and 3 are based on the dividend rate applied to premiums received and annuitized between January 1 and June 1, 1999. rates for other vintages would produced different relationships among staring ages and income options.

TIAA Standard Method

Your Age	One-Life Annuity			Two-Life Annuity with 10-Year Guaranteed Period			
	No Guaranteed Period	10-Year Guaranteed Period	20-Year Guaranteed Period	Your Annuity Partner's Age	Full Benefit to Survivor	Half Benefit to Second Annuitant	Two-Thirds Benefit to Survivor
60	100%	99%	95%	60	90%	94%	96%
				65	92%	96%	100%
				70	94%	97%	104%
65	100%	98%	91%	60	84%	91%	92%
				65	87%	93%	95%
				70	90%	95%	100%
70	100%	96%	86%	60	77%	87%	85%
				65	81%	89%	89%
				70	85%	92%	94%

How to Use This Table

Suppose you are 65 years old and your spouse is 60. If, under a one-life annuity with no guaranteed period with TIAA's Standard Method, you'd get $1,000 monthly, then with a 20-year guaranteed period you'd receive $910 monthly ($1,000 x 91%), and under a full-benefit, two-life annuity with a 10-year guaranteed period, you'd get $840 monthly ($1,000 x 84%).

The older you are, the more income a given accumulation will generate, based on the same income option.

Table 26.2

Relative incomes from various options and guaranteed periods

TIAA Graded Method, TIAA Real Estate Account, and all CREF accounts

Your Age	One-Life Annuity			Two-Life Annuity with 10-Year Guaranteed Period			
	No Guaranteed Period	10-Year Guaranteed Period	20-Year Guaranteed Period	Your Annuity Partner's Age	Full Benefit to Survivor	Half Benefit to Second Annuitant	Two-Thirds Benefit to Survivor
60	100%	99%	95%	60	88%	94%	96%
				65	91%	95%	100%
				70	94%	97%	105%
65	100%	98%	91%	60	82%	90%	90%
				65	86%	92%	95%
				70	90%	94%	100%
70	100%	96%	86%	60	74%	85%	83%
				65	79%	88%	88%
				70	83%	91%	94%

How to Use This Table

Suppose you are 65 years old and your spouse is 60. If, under a one-life annuity with no guaranteed period with TIAA's Graded Method, or any of the variable accounts, for your initial payments you'd get $1,000 monthly, then with a 20-year guaranteed period you'd receive $910 monthly ($1,000 x 91%) monthly, and under a full-benefit, two-life annuity with a 10-year guaranteed period, you'd get $820 monthly ($1,000 x 82%).

The older you and your spouse are, the more income a given accumulation will generate.

What Are the Advantages and Disadvantages
of the Different Annuity Choices?

27

As you consider the various options described in the previous chapter, you need to remember that your situation is unique. From experience, we know that you will probably bounce ideas off people whom you know well, who know you, and certainly whom you trust. Beware, however, advice from a well-meaning friend who may have just made a decision and whose situation may be slightly or even significantly different from yours, but who feels confident that her choice is by far the best. All too often those who may have made a choice, right or wrong, will defend it vigorously and seek confirmation through the conversion of others. Although we have not undertaken a scientific survey, empirical evidence suggests that the louder the defense, the likelier it is that the decision was wrong.

In less dramatic situations, we have seen cases where peer pressure or "peer fear" has led to decisions that did not make good economic sense. If you are choosing an annuity, you are making an irrevocable choice with major implications for you and typically those whom you love. Be skeptical, become as informed as you can be, and work through the exercises described in part III. Recognize that limits do exist to human foresight, but the limits on human insight are less constricting. If you have an annuity partner, the choice ought to work for both of you, and you should both feel comfortable with your decision. Again, leave yourself enough time. Medical consultation may be required in order for you to make a final decision. If you have planned for retirement, then the election of an annuity option should not pose an insurmountable challenge. To the contrary, the choice should comport with that planning, subject to any last-minute second thoughts. Above all, do not sin in haste and repent at leisure.

As we mentioned before, if you can obtain advice from a professional outside of the TIAA-CREF organization who can look at your and your family's issues independently with an unemotional approach, you will increase the likelihood that you will make the appropriate choice. You need to recognize that no one can predict health changes and their effect on longevity. But someone who can work with you to determine overall income and the accumulation or depletion of assets for the foreseeable future clearly represents a welcome addition to the process.

With those thoughts in mind, read through the following with an open mind and your focus on your own situation. You may perceive what we deem an advantage or a disadvantage entirely differently. Of necessity, our views come from our own experience as secondhand observers. Neither of us has retired, probably to the growing irritation of our colleagues. We have spoken to many people in the retirement planning process, not just participants in TIAA-CREF. The concerns we have heard and situations that have arisen usually strike common chords. But they may not to you. No one is, strictly speaking, average.

Some participants want their retirement account to be invested and distributed over the lifetimes of the participant, spouse, and children. In those cases, the Minimum Distribution Option represents the only viable option. Even those who are not as single-minded ought to examine the MDO as an alternative to or as a companion to annuitization. You do not have to annuitize your entire accumulation, and you do not have to take that step on your Required Beginning Date. Remember, as you look at the numbers, that annuitization represents an irrevocable step, and you ought to be clear in your mind that the annuity you pick best suits your needs. Annuitizing in stages may work best for you. Assuming that your accumulation does not contract violently, the only cost of delay may result from a reduction in the permissible guaranteed period or term certain.

In the next chapters, we discuss the advantages and disadvantages of annuities generally. In this chapter, we focus on the pros and cons of the types of annuities available to you.

The Single Life Annuity

The single life annuity—or "One-Life Annuity," as it is called in TIAA-CREF's documentation—guarantees that you will have income for the rest of your life. Given the size of the monthly payment, it benefits those who have not had an opportunity to accumulate large retirement accounts and run the risk of outliving their assets. The one-life alternative seems obviously appropriate for single people who either do not wish or are not in a position to pass assets on to heirs or charity. They also do not have another person for whom they want to provide an income after their death.

In these cases, the value of an annuity comes to the fore. It guarantees that the payment stream that you have chosen will continue for the rest of your life. You will not, as noted above, outlive your assets. Combined with Social Security payments, a single life annuity, for those situated as above described, can provide the necessary income to be able to retire without fear.

If, however, you have a larger accumulation, say $750,000 or more, and you have other income-producing assets, you may find that an annuity is not the most advantageous choice. If you would like to be able to access funds as you need them (in addition to the minimum distribution, which must be taken out as a matter of law) and you would like to name heirs or a charity as your beneficiary, a single life annuity may not provide the right answer. You must face the trade-off between flexibility and security.

The Joint Life Annuities

If your annuity will provide the principal means of support for two people, you clearly need to take into account the fact that your consumption will exceed that for a single individual. Additionally, you must consider the effects of the different survivorship payment options. If you and your annuity partner are roughly the same age and are both in good health, you will probably choose full benefit to both participant and partner. That selection may reduce your monthly checks from inception, but it protects the survivor more fully than any of the alternatives. This seems appropriate where you have no way of knowing who will survive.

In some cases, perhaps if you or your annuity partner have sufficient or substantial assets outside of TIAA-CREF, you may feel that the half-benefit may be appropriate. The proposition that two can live as cheaply as one probably holds water only if one of the partners is an ascetic and remains healthy. On the other hand, in retirement the cost of two persons rarely amounts to twice the expense of one. Your costs will consist predominantly of fixed costs that will remain constant when one of the two of you passes away. Unless you move into smaller quarters, items such as real estate and car maintenance, state, local, and federal taxes will remain the main expense items. Food costs and possibly utility costs will decline, but they do not typically represent the big ticket items. No one can predict health costs.

Nonetheless, it seems unreasonable to us to assume that the survivor can live as well on half of what you enjoyed before. For that reason, you need assets outside of the TIAA-CREF accumulation to allow you or your partner to live comfortably with only a half annuity from TIAA-CREF. Assuming that you have provided for the drop in income for the survivor, you may feel that it is advantageous to take the larger monthly payments early while you are both alive to enjoy as much as possible together.

The third option within the joint annuity group is the "two-thirds benefit to survivor" option. In terms of income needs, this option may reflect the true cost of living alone versus the costs of two persons in retirement. Again, recognizing that each situation is unique, you may conclude that a 33% downward adjustment seems manageable. On the other hand, as compared to the other alternatives, the odds that this contraction of income will occur doubles. The death of either of you triggers the reduced annuity. You should look to the choice that you feel will give you and your annuity partner the optimal payment scheme during your remaining lifetimes.

Looking at the joint annuities as a class, you need to consider health issues, especially if one of you is ill. Is there a large age difference between the two of you? You should take such other factors into account as are appropriate to your circumstances. All of these considerations require a dispassionate forward look that tries to the fullest extent possible to predict the likeliest path that your lives will take and that also takes a worst-case scenario into account.

As with the single life annuity, you may also add a term certain, or guaranteed period, to a joint life annuity in case you both should die earlier than expected and you wish to insure that your assets give you, your annuity partner, and your beneficiary a full run for your money. You will have protected your heirs against the possibility that you do not live to your anticipated life expectancy. Conversely, should both of you live past the guaranteed date, then your beneficiary will receive nothing. Too bad; but from everybody else's point of view, leaving a beneficiary high and dry seems far preferable to dying young.

The decision as to whether to annuitize has several dimensions. It does provide the highly desirable lifetime income, thereby alleviating the risk that you will run out of money in old age. In effect, you will have your pension or annuity and Social Security, along with whatever other income your assets produce, to live on. If you husband those other income sources well, then you will have three legs to your stool and, one hopes, a satisfactory amount of income for the balance of your days. Obviously, if you elect a joint annuity and the same assumptions are made, your annuity partner will benefit as well.

The annuity choices and their consequences become more complex when viewed in context. To take the simplest dilemma first, if you elect a fixed annuity, you have made an implicit decision that you can tolerate the inflation that will occur during the remainder of your life and the resultant decline in the annuity's buying power. On the other hand, if you elect a variable annuity, then you are assuming that the long-term growth potential in the annuity will more than keep pace with inflation and that your annuity will have more buying power as the years proceed. You have also decided that you can bear the risk that your income may decline in any particular year because of adverse market conditions and investment experience. Again, you need to examine your other sources of income and the estimated level of expenses to determine if this choice is viable or presents an unacceptable risk.

There is no such thing as a risk-free retirement income. Fixed annuities run the risk of inflation. Variable annuities may counter that risk, but contain the very real possibility that, in any one- to three-year term, based on the worst case scenario of a sustained bear market that we witnessed from 1973 to 1975, your income will decline. To the extent that your other investments hedge against this risk, you can take the plunge. If no such fallback exists, then you may conclude that you want a fixed annuity and ought to consider the TIAA graded method rather than the TIAA standard method. Or you may decide to diversify your annuity and investment choices to provide a cushion against either market risk or inflation.

As you can see, the issues begin to grow in complexity and in some respects begin to resemble bets. TIAA-CREF can accommodate wagers on longevity because its risks are spread over a large insurance pool. You have only your life and your annuity partner's life to work with, and the trade-offs between a higher monthly payment in the early years versus lower payments after an annuitant or an annuity partner has died can prove difficult to puzzle out. If you are not single, the risks associated with a single life annuity will seem staggering. An untimely death will leave the survivor without any TIAA-CREF income. But to take a less extreme case, assuming that you and your spouse or other annuity partner are both in excellent health when you retire, how much should the survivor's benefit be as a percentage of the original monthly benefit?

If you knew not only how long you would live, but also how much of a gap there would be between the deaths of both of you, you would know the right decision. Thus, if you knew that you and your partner would die within months of one another, then a survivor's benefit of two-thirds would prove ideal, given the higher monthly payments that you will receive for almost all of your and your annuity partner's lifetimes. On the other hand, if you are wrong and one of you dies early under a survivor's benefit of two-thirds, irrespective of who dies first, the survivor may find that his or her income has fallen off a cliff. If you knew that the gap would only amount to fifteen minutes, then the otherwise unacceptable single life annuity would prove, against all odds, to be the best alternative.

At the other extreme, if one elects a full survivorship benefit, then one is betting that either you and your annuity partner will die early and the other comparatively late, so that the lower payments in the first years of the annuity will be more than offset by the greater flow during the years that the survivor lives alone. You are purchasing income assurance against an unexpectedly early death. Given the limited degree to which we can see into the future, this option becomes the default option and is by far the choice selected by the highest percentage of joint annuitants.

In looking at this range of choices, you are engaged in life insurance, but with at most two lives to work with and the potentially substantial costs of being wrong. These concepts tend not to come through when the average participant makes choices, but those are the consequences with which you will have to deal if your guess proves incorrect, often as a matter of dumb luck.

These factors also come into play when electing a guaranteed period. The longer the guaranteed period, the lower the monthly payment you will receive from TIAA-CREF. A guaranteed period represents a hedge against both you and your annuity partner's dying early. You assume that you will receive fewer monthly payments because you do not think that you will prove to be long-lived and you want the income stream to continue. If you knew that you were going to live twenty-five years beyond retirement, you would never accept a twenty-year guaranteed period. The payments are lower, and the guarantee holds no value for you. Your family history may comfort you in this respect, but one can never know to a certainty how these genetic factors will affect your life span.

The choice between a fixed and a variable annuity comes down to an economic decision about the future trends of inflation and financial market conditions. The other decisions boil down to educated guesses as to life expectancy, using that term in its usual, nontechnical meaning. Also, in electing a survivor's benefit, you may be influenced by the presence or the absence of other assets that will or will not produce additional income to act as a buffer.

Deciding whether to annuitize has one other dramatic consequence. If you annuitize your account and have chosen correctly, then you and your annuity partner, if any, will in all likelihood use up the account during your lifetime. Odds are that nothing will remain for heirs. The only exception would be the unexpired term of a guaranteed payment period, but those payments might generate an estate tax liability that might greatly reduce the benefit of the remaining payments. Any such payments would constitute income to your heirs.

TIAA-CREF does provide an alternative to annuitizing your account, the Minimum Distribution Option, that will be discussed in later chapters. What you need to bear in mind if you are deciding whether to annuitize are the factors listed above. No cookie cutter solution exists because every case will be unique. But the security of a lifetime income should not blind you to the fact that the type of annuity and the survivor's benefit you elect may have a profound effect (positive or negative) on your retirement lifestyle. You may reduce risk, perhaps even dramatically, but no choice can eliminate it.

29

Should You Have an Annuity Partner?

An annuity partner means an additional person whose life expectancy will be taken into account in determining the term over which payments will be made or the life expectancy upon which guaranteed periods will be computed.

For married couples, having an annuity partner represents a no-brainer, and the spouse makes the obvious annuity partner. For a single person, if you have some other person with whom you want to share the payment of your account, it makes sense to have that person as your annuity partner. Adding a second life will also permit the payment stream to continue over a longer period of time. On the other hand, it means that the monthly payments will stay lower than if you had elected a single life annuity. The issue comes down to values— your feelings about that other person versus your need for income. If you want that person to enjoy the income stream after you have died, then you should name that person as your annuity partner, keeping the income stream yourself for as long as you live.

TIAA-CREF and the Code also use two related concepts. The "calculation beneficiary" represents a term from the TIAA-CREF lexicon and comes into play if one does not annuitize. It means a person whose life expectancy will be taken into account to determine the time over which a payment stream will occur. That computation may only take the calculation beneficiary's life expectancy into account or it may take that term of years in conjunction with another's life expectancy to determine the applicable payment period.

The Code and the Treasury Regulations define the Designated Beneficiary (or "DB") in precise terms that will be elaborated upon in the discussion of estate planning. For present purposes, it equates to the concept of the Calculation Beneficiary. But you should keep in the back of your mind that the concept of the DB carries with it almost magical qualities under the Code. In addition to lengthening the applicable life expectancies over which payments will be received, having a DB can prove critical in a variety of circumstances.

First, if you die before your Required Beginning Date, your DB will receive the stream of payments over his life expectancy; if you do not name a DB, then as required by the Code, TIAA-CREF must compress the payments into a five-year term. If you die after your

RBD without having named a DB and without having started an annuity or taking minimum distributions, then the account will be paid out as a lump sum by December 31 of the year following your death. The best one can say about the last outcome turns out to be cold comfort. Your heirs can take the payments over two tax years and try to reduce the income tax liability by not swallowing the whole enchilada in a single gulp.

To anticipate the discussion in part V, the entire system is tilted toward your naming your spouse as your DB. You must have a DB by your RBD at the latest to preserve the value of your savings by lengthening the period over which the account will be paid out. If the account is paid out over five years, much of the accumulation's or annuity's value will disappear in income taxes and potentially in estate taxes. The results are about as poor for heirs who receive a lump sum. Anyway that you look at it, not having a DB will almost invariably prove to be a financial calamity.

30

What Should You Do if You Are Single?

A marriage penalty may still exist in the income tax portions of the Code when this book reaches you, but, generally speaking, the Code favors married couples, and most tax analyses presume that the readership will consist entirely of married couples. The gift and estate tax provisions of the Code in particular tilt heavily in favor of the married couple. Nonetheless, the fact remains that a great many people are single, either unmarried, divorced, or widowed, and their needs require attention, even if they are not blessed with various tax breaks under the Code.

For the single parent who has one or more children, naming children as Designated Beneficiaries makes eminent good sense. If you die before your Required Beginning Date and have not annuitized, your children may receive the payment of the account over their life expectancies. They will receive a lifetime income generated by compounding over a relatively long life expectancy. The size of that income stream will vary, depending on the value of your account as of the date of death. But one should not underestimate the value of that income, given the length of time over which compounding will occur.

Assuming that you have survived to your RBD and you decide to annuitize, should you name one of your children *as your annuity partner*? This issue brings you face-to-face with a familiar set of forks in the road. With an annuity partner who is a generation younger, the monthly payments will decrease, of course, as compared to a single life annuity because the term of the annuity will almost certainly be extended. They will not decrease as much as you might expect, because the Treasury Regulations that set out applicable life expectancies will treat your child as being only ten years younger than you.

The reason for that limitation appears in the Minimum Distribution Incidental Benefits rules (the "MDIB rules") that appear in the Internal Revenue Service Proposed Regulations. If you name a non-spousal beneficiary, the Code and the Proposed Regulations impose this ten-year rule, to insure that the plan's purpose remains the payment of retirement benefits, not the passage of wealth to the next generation. Whether you elect to annuitize or choose the Minimum Distribution Option, upon your death your child or children assume their actual ages. The payments to the surviving child or children will decline in accordance with the table shown in appendix C if you have annuitized; they will diminish under minimum distributions because the applicable life expectancy has increased dramatically. These issues are more fully discussed in part V. Only in Tax Land could a child have an assumed age as long as you live and then revert to her actual age thereafter, but it serves the prophylactic purpose of preventing a wealthy retiree from naming an infant and having payments continue for decades. One can achieve that result, but it requires use of the techniques discussed in part V. The result of the MDIB rules appear in the life expectancies set forth in appendix B.

Returning to the single parent-annuitant, upon your death, assuming that you predecease your offspring, your child or children will receive a reduced annuity based upon the difference in ages between you and your oldest child. The table set forth in appendix C shows the percentages of your annuity that your children will receive. In the statistically unlikely event that you survive your child or children, you will continue to receive annuity payments at the same rate until you too kick the bucket.

If you have other assets and/or can weather the decrease in payments that result from having a DB who is treated as being ten years younger than you are, the child as annuity partner may provide some estate planning benefits. Bear in mind, however, your estate will pay estate taxes on the discounted present value of the annuity upon your death, and if your child dies after you but before the expiration of the child's life expectancy, your estate may have overpaid the estate tax, the computed value of the annuity far exceeding its ultimate worth. Generally speaking, recognizing that some of the contingencies described above seem remote, the MDO probably remains the avenue of choice for those electing to pass their accounts on to their children rather than having the safety net of the annuity. You have to run the numbers, recognizing that you will have to make some assumptions about future rates of return, to find the better answer.

Assuming that you have not annuitized, TIAA-CREF and the Internal Revenue Service Proposed Regulations offer you a choice. You can either name your children individually as DBs, and your accumulation will be split to reflect your allocation among your children. If you elect this option, then TIAA-CREF will pay each child an income stream based on his or her individual life expectancy. On the other hand, if you name children individually, they have the power to accelerate the payout and to take, in the worst case, a lump sum distribution of their shares. Putting to one side the now anachronistic worst case of the child buying a motorcycle and taking off for Katmandu, the drawback to naming the children directly lies in their ability to defeat your planning for them to take their shares over their life expectancy, providing them with a measure of long-term financial security, increasing the total payments, and even furnishing indirect benefits to your grandchildren.

The other choice is to use a trust. You then interpose a trustee between your children and the account. Your children lose the ability to demand a lump sum distribution and a lump sum income tax liability that drains the account of much of its value. On the other hand, assuming that the trust is properly structured under the Internal Revenue Service Proposed Regulations and therefore the Service will look through the trust and treat it as having a life expectancy, an issue we deal in part V, the yardstick for determining the period over which payments must be made will be the shortest life expectancy, typically that of the oldest child. If you have children from more than one marriage or of very disparate ages, for example, you can create more than one trust and group children with relatively proximate birth dates together so that no child suffers an undue curtailment of the payment process. You could, if you only have a small number of children, create a trust for each one of them. At some point, the complexity of one trust per child outweighs the flexibility gained from using each child's life expectancy. Although the trust has some disadvantages, in some circumstances, it becomes the obvious choice. For example, if your children are minors, typically the situation prior to the Required Beginning Date, you really have no alternative but to name a trust. If one of your children will have trouble managing the money due to a disability or other problem, then the trust also seems the wiser option. If you fear that your children's creditors will have access to the account, usually as a result of divorce, then the trust may limit an ex-spouse's ability to benefit from the account to the amounts that are being slowly distributed over your child's life expectancy. The law of the applicable state will determine the extent to which the trust will shelter the account. Finally, some cases boil down to the degree to which a parent has faith in the child's financial prudence and feels comfortable in allowing the child direct control of the flow of funds.

Nonetheless, the trust labors under the following precept. *The gen-*

eral rule in this area, if you have not guessed it already, is that the Code and the Internal Revenue Service will look to the shortest life expectancy to measure the period over which payments must be taken. Thus, as noted above, if you name more than one beneficiary of the trust, then your oldest child becomes the measuring life. If you use a trust, instead of having one child receive all of the payments remaining after you die, the trust would divide them equally or however else you select.

You may have someone other than children to whom you are very close and want to leave an income stream should you predecease, and that person could serve as an annuity partner. Similar rules to those described above would obtain. On the other hand, you may very well feel that you want to derive as much income from the account as possible while you are alive and enjoy the best retirement you can. In that case, the single life annuity, which has the highest monthly annuity payment, may appeal to you. You may feel disquieted by the fact that you are not sharing, but the account is yours, the work that created it was yours, and the dollars in the account came from your paycheck and from your employer. You are harvesting what you reaped.

As usual, no cookie cutter plan exists, nor is there a cookbook recipe. The decision as to how you divide your account will reflect both your values and your circumstances. You may have a child, but he or she may be making money hand over fist. In that case, odds are that you will need that money before he or she does. But if you have a dependent in the tax meaning of the word who is actually dependent in the usual sense of the word, then you ought to consider carefully the part that your dependent plays in your retirement and estate planning. That other person will not enjoy the privileges that a surviving spouse does under the Code, but human values ought to prevail over tax considerations, especially when we are dealing with those whom we love. We cannot ignore economic realities, and taxes are one of them, but one should never lose sight of the importance of our relationships with others and how much more valuable they are than mere money.

Charitable donations form the subject of numerous treatises, and the entire range of issues therefore falls well beyond the scope of this book. However, some generalizations about the interaction of the TIAA-CREF account or the rollover IRA with the charitable deduction provisions of the Code deserve mention, in part because charitable gifts of retirement accounts have become a hot topic of late. They also represent an item of considerable interest to single individuals and to educational and other nonprofit institutions.

For the TIAA-CREF participant who annuitizes, the charitable gift seems at best a remote contingency. Passing the income tax issues discussed below, the participant who wants or needs to annuitize probably cannot afford to jeopardize future economic security, no matter how well intentioned he or she may be. The division of an account into two subaccounts, with one earmarked for charity, does not appear realistic for someone for whom that lifetime income has to be secured at as high a level as possible. Given the risks that we have identified in taking any form of retirement income, decreasing the pool of savings can only compound the problems that an annuitant may face years down the road. One can see that a single person who elects a guaranteed payment period might designate a charitable organization as the recipient of any payments remaining due upon the annuitant's early death, but this appears to be the only instance in which such a gift would come close to feasibility.

The income tax issue cuts across all of the other alternatives. The Code does not permit a direct transfer of a retirement account or an Individual Retirement Account to charity without incurring income tax. In other words, if you wanted to donate $100,000 from your TIAA-CREF account to, hypothetically, the American Red Cross, the Code regards the transaction as a distribution of $100,000 to you, followed by your donation of the money. Your income would receive a $100,000 jolt, and you would be eligible to deduct the gift up to 50% of your adjusted gross income (more or less) in the year of the gift. To the extent that $50,000 exceeded that figure, you would have a five-year period to use up the remainder. Looking at your tax return for the year of the gift, your income taxes will increase by as much as $40,000, but the likelihood that your charitable deduction would offset the entire tax would require that you have considerable other income in order to get the entire $100,000 up and over the 50% barrier. Congress has considered proposals to allow for such a direct transfer without the resultant tax penalty, but none of those proposals has been enacted into law.

The more usual scenario for making charitable gifts arises upon the death of the participant. Given the intersection of the estate and income taxes that can decimate a retirement plan upon the participant's death, an issue dealt with in the section on estate planning, some estate planners recommend avoiding the problem by giving what is left of the plan to charity. This gives rise to an estate tax charitable deduction, and the income tax does not come into play. The gift typically takes the form of a charitable remainder unitrust (a "CRUT") under which the income beneficiary, typically the surviving spouse or a child, receives lifetime income equal to a fixed percentage (at least 5%) of the fair market value of the trust, measured annually, and then the remainder vests in the charity upon the death of the income beneficiary. The estate tax deduction equals the value of the remainder interest, and the Internal Revenue Service has published regulations in the form of tables to compute the value of that remainder interest. The charitable interest must equal at least 10% of the initial fair market value of the trust in order for the CRUT to qualify for the charitable deduction.

Although the CRUT appears to solve the double whammy of the income and estate tax problem, it leaves open the question as to how to pay the estate tax on the retained interest, which does not qualify for the charitable deduction. Like all estate planning issues, this can be solved, but it will require advance planning. In addition, depending on the age of the income beneficiary and the discount rate in effect at the time of your death, the trust may not satisfy the 10% charitable remainder requirement. In most estate planning documents, you will need to have a formula clause so that the term of the CRUT can be adjusted to meet the statutory requirement to qualify for the charitable deduction. For example, if the income beneficiary is quite young, without some adjustment in the funding formula, the trust will not meet the statutory standard for a charitable deduction.

For those who are charitably inclined, obviously this option holds out a great deal of appeal. However, it should be borne in mind that the account will not remain a family asset but will pass to a charity.

In the nonretirement setting, one often encounters an estate plan where an insurance policy replaces the lost value of the asset, and the family comes out whole.

For those who are single, with perhaps a limited class of heirs, the testamentary charitable gift may also make sense. The heirs receive the assurance of lifetime income, and the estate tax complications of dying as the owner of a retirement account are largely avoided. With no dynastic sense driving you, the gift's advantages may far outweigh the cost of losing the asset.

Generally speaking, then, in certain circumstance, a charitable transfer at death may play a role in your estate planning. Until Congress changes the law, and a bill to that effect has made it almost all of the way through the legislative process on a number of occasions, one cannot during one's lifetime transfer a retirement account to charity without encountering what may prove unacceptable income tax costs.

Although TIAA-CREF is oriented toward annuities, one significant alternative to the annuity does exist within the TIAA-CREF universe. It will dominate much of the discussion in part V. Mandated by Congress and called the Minimum Distribution Option by TIAA-CREF, this payment method tracks the legal requirements contained in Section 401(a)(9) of the Code and the Proposed Regulations thereunder. The Internal Revenue Service has indicated that one can treat these regulations as though they were final, and they play a critical role in formulating an estate plan where a TIAA-CREF and/or any other types of retirement account (treating multiple plans as though they were one) constitute the largest asset.

Although the purpose of this book is not to convert readers into pension specialists, a fate arguably worse than death and a feat impossible to achieve merely by reading as entertaining and informative a book as this one, you need to understand certain basic concepts in order to comprehend how the MDO operates. For our sakes, as well as for yours, we will try to keep the description brief and nontechnical.

Basically, the minimum distribution rules seek to carry out the congressional purpose that retirement accumulations be used for that purpose and not become perpetual safe harbors from income taxation. These rules spell out the minimum amount that must be withdrawn from a retirement account after the Required Beginning Date in order to avoid a 50% penalty for underdistributions. For a qualified plan like TIAA-CREF, the RBD means the later of (1) the date when you turn $70^{1}/_{2}$ (actually the April 1 following, but everyone tends to use $70^{1}/_{2}$ because it is simpler and avoids having to receive two distributions in the same year) or (2) the date on which you actually retire. An Individual Retirement Account does not meet the statutory definition of a qualified plan, and distributions must begin when the holder reaches $70^{1}/_{2}$.

The Code mandates that, at a minimum, the retirement plan must annually distribute an amount equal to (1) the fair market value of the account as of the last day of the preceding year divided by (2) the life expectancy of the participant and, if the participant has named a Designated Beneficiary, over the joint life expectancy of the participant and the DB. TIAA-CREF calls such a DB a "calculation beneficiary."

We have previously discussed the necessity of having a DB at all times. We discuss the issue of how to measure life expectancy in part V in detail. Here we only cover the matter in brief, its importance stemming from the fact that it is the one factor in the equation as to which you can make a choice. The size of your account will depend on a multitude of factors, some of them outside of your control.

As noted before, if you die before or after the RBD, having named a surviving DB, then the DB can receive payment of the account over the DB's life expectancy. If your DB does not survive you and payments on your account have begun, the RBD having passed, then, upon your subsequent death, the account will, according to the Code, have to be paid out at least as rapidly as it was prior to your demise. However, you presumably took advantage of the joint life expectancy measured by your and your DB's ages, and the payment stream's duration will depend on when you died relative to the beginning of the calculated term based on that joint life expectancy.

If your DB predeceases you, you can name another DB. If this occurs after the RBD, you can name a new DB, but you cannot lengthen the payment period. You can only shorten the period by naming an older DB.

What happens if you survive the DB? As indicated below, we recommend using a calculation of life expectancy that will stretch out payments as long as possible. The hybrid method, which we recommend for married couples in particular and discuss below, will provide protection from the untimely death of the DB and stretch out your life expectancy as long as possible. According to the Internal Revenue Service tables, when you are 115 years old, you will still have 1.8 years of life expectancy. The tables do not venture beyond that point.

Upon your death, the balance will be paid out over the remaining life expectancy or in a lump sum (1) if you outlived your spouse's and your own life expectancy, or (2) if you outlived your spouse's life expectancy and used the hybrid method of calculating your own life expectancy. If some life expectancy remains, then the payments will continue over that term of years.

To postpone income taxes and to make the account go further, if one can afford this strategy, the value of having a DB as of the RBD now comes into sharper focus. If the account is being paid out over the joint life expectancy of the participant and the DB, the surviving DB can enjoy the benefits of the stretch in payments.

If, however, the spouse is named as the DB, then none of the rules above described applies. A surviving spouse may stop, reset, recalibrate, or even get a fresh start on the payment clock. Most significantly, the spouse can make the account the spouse's own and name a new set of DBs. The surviving spouse enjoys rights under the Code not available to any other DB, and they can produce enormous economic returns.

The DB needs to be an individual because only individuals have life expectancies. Entities—such as estates, trusts (with one exception), charities, and so forth—have zero life expectancies. Even the oldest institutions in Western civilization have zero life expectancies. The Roman Catholic Church, to take an example, which will outlive all of us, has a zero life expectancy.

For all intents and purposes, as noted above, the tax rules always look to the shortest life expectancy over which to measure the payment period. For example, unless one has subdivided a retirement account, naming an entity with a zero life expectancy for even $1 of the account equates to having named no DB, the shortest life expectancy being zero in that hypothetical. In such a case, the account will be paid out at death as a lump sum.

The DB serves, then, a critical function in the event of a premature death before payments begin and otherwise when payments begin. A joint life expectancy is invariably longer than one life expectancy, and more will be distributed net of taxes the longer one can stretch the payment period. If you can afford it, you will want to extend the payment period for as long as possible. That stretching process increases the time over which tax-free accumulation is occurring inside of the account and deferring the day on which distributions must be made and income tax paid.

One final burst of technical stuff and then we are done: how are life expectancies computed?

The first method takes a snapshot of the life expectancy per the Internal Revenue Service tables as of the RBD, and one elects that as a term certain. This method also goes under the "subtract one" label, so named because life expectancy is reduced by one year as each year passes. For these purposes, irrespective of method, the IRS uses a table based on the 1980 census, and given the progress made by organized medicine since that date, the life expectancy is probably understated. That speeds up the payout, the distribution of taxable income, and the payment of income taxes. It seems inadvisable to hold your breath until the IRS decides to issue a more modern table with longer life expectancies.

By way of a textual footnote, the Internal Revenue Service issued new tables in the spring of 1999 based on 1990 census figures. In Section 7520(c)(3) of the Code, Congress mandated that, beginning in 1989, the service amend the tables at least once every ten years to take into account the most recent mortality experience for valuing remainder interests, annuities, and income terms. Section 7520 did not include minimum distribution requirements under Section 401(a)(9) within the aegis of the required revisions. Currently, then, we have the curious situation of the Internal Revenue Service's using two mortality tables to value, in effect, the same thing. The 1999 change occurred within months of the year-end deadline that Congress imposed.

The second method takes advantage of the fact that your life expectancy does not decline by a year for every year that you live. Your life expectancy may only decrease by two-thirds of a year. This method goes by the charming sobriquet of the "recalculation method." Annually, one literally recalculates one's life expectancy. The older you get, the older you are likely to be when you die.

This sounds pretty neat, if you want the longest time period. However, when someone dies, their life expectancy, recalculated annually, dwindles naturally enough to zero. If the DB predeceases the participant, then the remaining payment period will become the single life expectancy of the survivor. The pace of payments will permanently accelerate.

At the risk of repetitiveness, once you have passed your RBD, *you can name another DB, but you cannot lengthen the applicable payment period. As of the RBD, it becomes fixed, ready or not.* You must name a DB by the RBD at the latest. In addition, to avoid the five-year rule in the event of death before the RBD, you should have a DB at all times. Your employer's plan may treat your spouse, if any, as your default DB, but check in any event to make sure that you have named a DB, even if you are 25 and in the best of health.

The literature on which method, recalculation or term certain, is more advantageous has also taken on monstrous proportions. Being safety minded, and not just perverse, we prefer the third method, the hybrid method, for married couples. Under this option, we recommend that the DB's life expectancy be measured by a term certain, safeguarding the participant against the DB's early death. Where the spouse is the DB, one can then place the participant on recalculation. If the participant dies, then the spouse inherits the account, no tax is due, and various other good things can happen, as described in part V. If the spouse predeceases, then the term over which the payments will be made does not contract to a single life expectancy. Upon the participant's death, the at-least-as-rapidly rule will apply to a longer period of time.

The same logic applies to most situations involving single individuals. If, however, the ultimate beneficiary will be charity, then the use of the recalculation method will prolong the payment stream for as long as possible because one never actually runs out of life expectancy using recalculation, and the estate tax consequences disappear because the estate tax charitable deduction will shelter the remainder of the account from taxes if one donates the remaining balance to charity.

If you read and understood this chapter to this point, you deserve a break and probably a medal because you have mastered the essential rules of pension distribution and taxation. You will know enough to make your own plans (with further help from your well-intentioned authors and estate-planning professionals). We remind you, however, of the old adage about the dangers of a little knowledge. The likelihood that you will be able to apply this smattering of information to dazzle someone at some cocktail party or other social function remains small, and our goal remains more modest than improving your social interactions. We want to inform you sufficiently so that you can ask the right questions and distinguish among the answers.

Returning from this detour (which lawyers distinguish from a frolic) to the world of TIAA-CREF, the importance of the MDO stems from the fact that it is the only option that prevents your account from being paid as a large premium to an insurance company, irrevocably committing you to receive an annuity. The account remains your own asset, and you can vary the amount that you take out in any year through the use of Systematic Withdrawals, *but only if your employer's plan permits,* so long as it does not fall below the statutory minimum. *The MDO represents the floor, not the ceiling.* The MDO also provides the only mechanism for passing the account on to your children, with results that will described later.

If you are going to elect the MDO, then you need to select a DB, pick the method of computing life expectancy, and run the numbers to see if your account is large enough to keep you and your calculation beneficiary in comfort. You do not receive any guarantee with the MDO, and the larger the account, the further it will take you. In addition, you need to see how well the account will stand up to the test of time, namely the possibility that you will live well past your anticipated life expectancy. And you need to gauge whether your account warrants passing on to your children. All of these issues will receive ample coverage in future chapters, thereby keeping you riveted to the edge of your seat, but the critical concepts are behind us.

What Are the Pros and Cons
of the Minimum Distribution Option?

33

We now need to look at the implications that the choice of the MDO will have upon you and your Designated Beneficiary. To start with the obvious negatives, the MDO does not offer the security of an annuity. You do not obtain the assurance of a lifetime stream of income, and everything depends on the size of your account and how you manage it. If your accumulation is large you may have to live to 100 and a little bit longer to reduce the MDO to a pittance; or if your account is not large, you may find yourself in trouble at 80 using the MDO. Most of us would take our chances if confronted with the former because so few human beings live to be 100. If the latter seems likely rather than remotely improbable, it strongly suggests that, other things being equal, you should not elect the MDO.

One needs to bear in mind that the government tables upon which the MDO is calculated have, as noted above, themselves become long in the tooth, being now almost twenty years old. Given that you will likely enjoy a longer lifetime than the tables project, the tables are distorted by relying on obsolete numbers and thereby accelerate the payment stream.

Again, depending on the size of your account, you may find that you will have to exceed the MDO in order to make ends meet or to live in the retirement style to which you would like to become and stay accustomed. Depleting the account in this fashion only hastens the day when the account's distributions will not suffice for your purposes. You need to have the discipline (one might almost say the iron discipline) not to take any excess unless absolutely called for in the circumstances.

If you elect the MDO, then TIAA-CREF will pay you only that amount, but you can use Systematic Withdrawals to increase your annual take if that is permitted by your employer's plan. You need to know whether this critical feature appears in your employer's plan; if not, you are locked into a rigid mathematical computation of your annual income. Here you and your calculation beneficiary need to make some hard decisions about your future lifestyle, your personalities, and your spending habits. Also you should have some other assets to provide a cushion and some leeway because not all of the reasons why one would want to exceed the MDO originate with a desire to increase consumption. Medical costs not covered by Medicare or even a Medicare supplement may necessitate withdrawing more than the MDO in any one year or for a more extended period.

On the other hand, the MDO provides flexibility, allowing you to manage your money after retirement and, depending on investment performance, probably affording you a better hedge against inflation than an annuity. You can move your account among the TIAA-CREF investment options if you are still within the TIAA-CREF universe, or you, a full-time money manager, or an investment professional can manage your own IRA. In either scenario, the account still belongs to you, and you can decide whether this is finally the year that you travel to Australia. If your account experiences steady growth, your income will not quickly peak, but will increase annually at a rate that should keep you even and possibly ahead of inflation. Again, assuming steady, single-digit growth and a normal life span, you will in the long run receive more income than you would have had you annuitized. Market risk will still exist for you, as it will for someone with a variable annuity, but you will be the master of your destiny.

Finally, as mentioned above, the MDO remains the only avenue for estate planning for a TIAA-CREF accumulation and turning it into a source of wealth for you, your partner, and your children. With extended payment streams and assuming a long-term growth rate of 7%, the MDO can allow a family to realize 400 to 500% of the retirement balance by the time that the payments have run their course.

As always, you come down to the interplay between risk and reward. The MDO holds out the most reward, but you will be assuming different and perhaps steeper risks than the annuitant. Your values, the size of your account, and your self-assessment will determine whether the MDO comports with your goals.

If Your Employer's Plan Allows, Should You Withdraw Your Money from TIAA-CREF When You Retire?

34

In our experience, most employers allow their TIAA-CREF participants when they retire to withdraw all or a part of their accumulations from the employer's plan and to roll over it over into an Individual Retirement Account. The Supplemental Retirement Annuity, consisting of the employee's own funds and the earnings thereon, does not labor under any restriction on withdrawal that we have encountered. The question that is often posed to us is whether you should withdraw all or some of your funds from TIAA-CREF to whatever extent your employer allows.

Once again, the answer will depend on your values and your economic situation. If annuitization appears the sensible choice, then the question answers itself. Stay with TIAA-CREF. To withdraw funds, put them into an IRA, and then annuitize the IRA involves three steps that are unlikely to yield much advantage over sticking with TIAA-CREF. You may find that other annuity providers will claim that they can provide higher income from the same amount of premium paid, but if so, you must undertake due diligence to determine whether these claims are warranted and whether the investment experience of the alternative provider would lead you to believe that the promised results will materialize. Generally, TIAA-CREF's expense ratio ranks among the lowest in the industry, and that works to your advantage. It earned its stars from the rating services based on the factors that are attractive to an annuitant. Finally, you must assess the risk-reward ratio as between TIAA-CREF and the other provider.

The key determinant will prove, across the board, to be future investment performance. Here you have to retain your common sense and not be impressed by the sheer number of investment choices that another company or mutual fund family can offer. Not too many TIAA-CREF participants regret, as of this writing, the absence of a TIAA-CREF Russia, Indonesia, Thailand, Brazil, or whatever-third-world-country-is-in-economic-spasm Fund. No one, except possibly the mining companies, has shed too many tears in recent years over the absence of a TIAA-CREF Gold Fund.

The TIAA-CREF stable of investment choices may only number ten entrants, but each is clearly defined, comprehensible (with the possible exception of the Bond Market Fund described earlier), and diversified. If you believe that you will secure better investment performance elsewhere, then it behooves you to move, but you ought to know why you are making the move. You may find that some of the rigidity attributed to TIAA-CREF originates instead in your employer's choice of plan options, and that, viewed solely as an investment advisor, TIAA-CREF's performance holds up pretty well to the competition. It also carries an eighty-year history of paying annuities through TIAA, and CREF is the oldest variable annuity company in the United States.

The second difference that comes from withdrawing from TIAA-CREF is intangible. If you move your account from TIAA-CREF to a smaller organization or one with more local offices, you gain a measure of personal contact and attention that you may find attractive and beneficial. If you stick with TIAA-CREF, then you will almost always be dealing with someone at the other end of an 800 number. If you roll out part of your accumulation into an IRA that is being managed by a local or more accessible provider, you may or may not get better investment performance, but you will probably get more individualized attention. As of this writing, TIAA-CREF has formed a trust company to deal with some of these issues, but it is difficult to see how a start-up organization with potentially two million customers will provide the same level of service that can be obtained from a brokerage house, bank, or other financial institution with multiple offices and local contacts. Those institutions make service their goal, however maddening and inadequate it may seem from time to time, and you may feel that your needs are being better served. In this instance, TIAA-CREF faces the uphill fight and lacks the decades of experience that the alternate providers have.

You also obtain greater freedom from the bureaucratized style that an organization as large as TIAA-CREF has had to adopt. For example, if you have an IRA locally and you want to make a withdrawal, a phone call will produce a check on the same or the next day. By contrast, going through the Systematic Withdrawal process can take a few weeks. The importance of these factors depends on your values, whether you have a trusted investment advisor, and how comfortable you feel working with TIAA-CREF.

For those who can withdraw everything, the issue in our minds boils down to investment performance. The amounts that you will receive over your retirement will depend largely on how good and reliable a return the money manager can provide. The other considerations mentioned above do play a role, but they become secondary, if not tertiary, compared to the critical issue of what happens to your money. As we have said before, retirement does not represent the finish line, but rather the point at which contributions end and your income stream depends entirely or in large part on what your account produces. Again, you need to go through your personal calculations of risk, time, and money. These issues continue unabated in importance this side of the grave. Any choice involves risk; whether staying with TIAA-CREF or not, whether you or your spouse is making the choice.

Underlying this discussion is the assumption that your account does not consist entirely or substantially all of traditional TIAA. If it does, then this discussion is academic. Aside from the TIAA component in your SRA, you have locked yourself into a position where it will take ten years for you to regain complete freedom of choice. This aspect of the TIAA-CREF institutional arrangement should always remain part of your planning, recognizing that the idea of safety may appear to make the TIAA option more attractive as you age. It bears repeating that you do want to minimize risk so that you can meet your basic needs, but you have to recognize that the cost of meeting those needs will change over time and you need to have structured your account so that you do not become a victim of inflation after you retire or a victim of unacceptably slow growth as your accumulate your account and try to make it grow for the long haul.

It also bears repeating that the choices you made years before will bear fruit years later. The investment process can never revert to a formula or become static. The decision as to where you park your money during retirement will hinge in large part on what you did before the momentous day when you end your career. Unfair as it may seem, them as has, gits. In this field, that translates into the truism that the larger your account, the greater freedom of choice you will enjoy and the more fun you will have during your retirement if good health and consistently good investment performance can be maintained.

Estate Planning for a TIAA-CREF Account

35

What Are We Talking About?

Up until now, all of the chapter titles have consisted of questions that you would theoretically ask yourself. This one poses a question from you to us, and we think that you are entitled to an answer as to the subject matter of this section of the book. We begin with the background against which our thinking has been formulated and our experience formed.

Increasingly, we have found that many clients' TIAA-CREF accounts constitute their largest and most important asset. This parallels the national trend toward the growing importance of Individual Retirement Accounts and qualified retirement plans as a percentage of net worth. It appears that a greater number of Americans are becoming pension millionaires. The working couple, who were regarded as an anomaly two decades ago, now represent a sizable minority of the work force. With two incomes providing a dual opportunity to defer income and save for retirement, the buildup of pension assets has accelerated.

Over almost two decades, the stock market has proven to be a powerful catalyst for the increase in wealth represented by pension plans. The interplay between the stock market and retirement funds has proven to be a virtuous cycle. The constant inflow of new funds into retirement plans of one kind or another has added liquidity to the market and provided a continuous source of demand for common stock. Meanwhile, as a result of mergers, stock buybacks, and (to a lesser extent this decade than last) transactions bringing companies back into private hands, the supply of investment-grade stock has decreased. Although we live in an economy as healthy as it has been in decades, this imbalance of supply and demand means that more dollars are chasing fewer shares. Inevitably, that drives up prices.

Estate planning for a TIAA-CREF account or, for that matter, any sizable accumulation of pension assets involves taking such steps as may be necessary to allow the retiree and spouse to pass their pension accounts down to their children. If you want to, are willing to take the necessary steps, and have the means to do so, a pension account represents a source of wealth that can benefit two or three generations. These are the issues that will be addressed in this part. Although Congress is hostile to the concept of the retirement account as a mechanism for wealth transfer, the Code and the Internal Revenue Service Regulations provide the means to achieve this goal, all of it legal and aboveboard.

In many instances, the estate planner faces what amounts to a two-asset estate: (1) a house and miscellaneous other assets, and (2) an amalgam that consists of an outsized TIAA-CREF or other pension account and/or one or more IRAs. The size of that retirement accumulation makes the prospect of exhausting it during the lifetimes of the retirees improbable and, in some cases, barring reckless extravagance or longevity unknown since the days of the biblical patriarchs, almost impossible. For those who have the resources, either inside or outside of TIAA-CREF, to enjoy a comfortable retirement, passing this large and precious asset down to children becomes highly desirable. In effect, you are giving your family the benefit of what equates to your life's savings.

The value to your heirs, whether your children or someone else, stems from the same factors that make the qualified retirement plan attractive to you. The assets grow free of income tax, and they are taxed only when distributions are made. If you can substitute a younger generation of beneficiaries, you can extend the period of time over which that payment stream will continue. This maximizes the tax-free compounding, postpones the income tax for as long as the law allows, and, using a 7% rate of return over the long haul, can result in the TIAA-CREF or other pension account distributing 400 to 500% of the balance in your account as of the date of retirement to you, your spouse, and your children. To be sure, these represent pre–income tax dollars, and no one can tell how much purchasing power will be lost through decades of inflation. But, at the worst, you may be funding your grandchildren's educations, in whole or in part, and providing a supplemental source of income that will last through your children's lifetime. You may never have considered yourself as the fountainhead of so much wealth, but it can happen.

In the preface, we wrote about the time value of money issues that underlie the entire retirement accumulation process and beyond. For those who can afford to and choose to pass their accounts on to their heirs, these issues assume paramount importance. One of the sub-agendas of this book is to bring this option to your attention and tell you how to achieve this result. The earlier that you decide to use your account for more than retirement income, the easier a transfer of wealth will become.

The decision has numerous repercussions. It will affect your financial planning, require you to think through how and to create the means by which federal estate and state transfer taxes will be paid, and compel you to confront issues of asset preservation and growth. From a familial perspective, it can and usually does raise a myriad of other issues. How much do you trust your children? How much of your retirement accumulation will you want to spend and how much will you want to leave behind for your loved ones?

Given the nature of the Minimum Distribution Option, electing to pass on your account also requires that you keep close tabs on your retirement income and expenses and that you have enough by way of reserves to live comfortably even if you outlive your life expectancy.

We can only alert you to the issues and give you solutions to the problems. The all-important implementation of the plan depends on you. But if you can see well before retirement age, that this option is feasible, getting started on putting the building blocks in place to make this happen as quickly as possible will increase the odds that everything will work as you planned with the least amount of disruption to your lifestyle and at the lowest cost.

For example, it may become necessary to purchase second-to-die life insurance for the reasons we will explain later. The table contained in chapter 41 shows how the cost of that insurance increases as one ages. At the extreme, the couple in their forties will pay aggregate premiums over ten years for the same amount of insurance as the couple in their seventies will pay in the first year of a similar ten-year program.

We have two clients who allowed us to calculate the cost of delay. Both are physicians. One postponed his estate planning for a quarter of a century and got down to business when he was 80. The other is 55, the age at which the other client should have started. They both have substantial estates and bought the same amount of second-to-die life insurance. As a result of an impending sale of a corporate division, the older man lucked out and got a cheap policy, all things considered. His premium is six times larger than his colleague's. The delay cost 50% of the face amount of the policy, in this case $1.5 million. Your numbers may not reach that magnitude. Our example only underlines what the table indicates: delay can become very expensive. You and time do not want to maintain an adversarial relationship.

Remember Shakespeare's Richard II, "I wasted time, and now doth time waste me." Used judiciously, time can prove an invaluable ally; ignored or, worse, squandered, it becomes an implacable foe. To quote another literary source from our century, W. H. Auden, "O let not time deceive you/You cannot conquer time."

Once your career is well launched and your future path pretty well set, you can begin to calculate whether and how you can attain this goal. The rewards are significant to you in terms of financial independence and flexibility, to your children in terms of increased income and wealth, and even to your grandchildren, whose educational costs and other needs can be underwritten by your TIAA-CREF account. How important your account proves to be to your children will depend, in large measure, as noted above, on the amount of inflation that the economy experiences between today and days well after tomorrow.

Estate planning for the TIAA-CREF account relies heavily on the use of the MDO. You should bear in mind that the minimum is exactly that—the least that the Code requires that you withdraw from your plan without incurring a 50% penalty for any shortfall. If that proves insufficient for your needs and wants, then you ought to take more. The concept is not that you should scrimp by in retirement so that your kids can live on velvet. We only go around once, under the Western approach to metaphysics, and you should enjoy your retirement, especially in the early years when travel and other leisure activities are least likely to be constrained by issues of health and physical well-being. In all likelihood you have done more for your children than your parents ever did for you, but somewhere one has to draw the line. For some of you, you will be able to achieve both: first, a comfortable retirement that you earned through decades of hard work and shrewd investing, and second, the passage of that wealth to your heirs so that the family realizes the maximum economic value of what you have created.

For those readers who are starting out or are in midcareer, you should understand that the seven-figure account is not an historical fluke, confined to the generation just ahead of the baby boomers. The remarkable stock market over the past fifteen years and an economy that has not been this healthy since the early 1960s have accelerated the appearance of the seven-figure account and compensated for years of low salaries and underperformance by stocks.

Nonetheless, if you are just starting out on your career, it seems virtually inevitable that you will have a seven-figure account when you retire. A math teacher at a boarding school in Connecticut brought this home to us. He posited a teacher who begins his career at age 25, earning $20,000 annually. His salary never changes until retirement at age 65. He contributes 5% of his salary to his TIAA-CREF account, and the school doubles that contribution. The school where this teacher worked used this formula, and it does not represent a fiction. If one assumes a long-term rate of appreciation of 8.95% (the historical return on equities being about 11.5% annually), that teacher will retire with a $1 million TIAA-CREF account. That teacher's first year MDO will amount to about $50,000, using today's life expectancies. He will receive a 250% raise by not working.

The moral of the story is that younger participants can reasonably count on something very similar happening to their accounts, if and only if they begin to save when they are young and stay the course. To be sure, the purchasing power of that account will have eroded between now and then, but the odds are high that your TIAA-CREF accumulation will make you a pension millionaire. Amidst all of the strains of meeting your current obligations, you have to adjust your thinking to take that into account. Based on our experience working with clients, the transition from a modest lifestyle to the realization that they are people with wealth or substance, to use the Victorian term, necessitates a major change in their frame of reference. Again, if you have this likelihood in mind from the beginning of your career, or at least from the point where your career path has become predictable, the cost of switching gears will lower to everyone's benefit.

The story of how to make that mental changeover and to take the right steps will unfold in the following chapters.

The tools with which we will be working are the ones described in the estate planning primer: the annual exclusion from gift tax of $10,000 per donee, the estate and gift tax exemption, currently at $750,000, and the unlimited marital deduction. We will add some bells and whistles, but those three fundamental building blocks provide the underlying foundation.

Although we are not painting castles in Spain, you should not overlook one final point that lurks barely hidden behind these projections. Put bluntly, a million bucks ain't what it used to be. Invested today, early in 2000, in the S&P 500, it would yield a dividend income of roughly $20–25,000. Invested in 8% bonds, it yields an income of $80,000. The first figure will not cut it, and the second will take care of most, perhaps all, of life's necessities, but you will not live "like a millionaire." Or more accurately, you will, because one needs more than a million dollars to achieve long-term financial security and to enjoy the lifestyle that one associates, historically, with being a millionaire. The odds look pretty good that you will have a large account if you have the discipline to save and invest for the long term. It will not turn out to be as easy as rolling off a log or writing about what a snap it will be, but it can be and has been done.

What Are the Benefits of Estate Planning for Your Retirement Account?

The only way to pass a TIAA-CREF account beyond the current generation requires that you elect not to annuitize. You must instead elect the Minimum Distribution Option, because that avoids the conversion of the account into a premium. The first benefit, assuming that this comports with your values and resources, is that you will have responsibility for your own financial destiny. To underline the point, you have rejected the safety net of a lifetime annuity and have chosen instead to take distributions at your own pace, subject to the governmentally prescribed minimum. You cannot decrease the amount of the MDO; but you can increase it, either through Systematic Withdrawals from your TIAA-CREF account, if allowed by your employer's plan, or by hitting other retirement or nonretirement assets.

If you are not disciplined or possessed of a large amount of assets in the seven figures, you do run the risk of outliving your assets. Everyone choosing the MDO should be setting something aside in case that one or both of you, whether married or not, enjoys extraordinary longevity. If you have not saved against that eventuality, the MDO may reduce you to poverty in your extreme old age. The MDO carries that risk, and you will have to manage your finances accordingly.

The flexibility afforded by the MDO has, on the other hand, a number of advantages. If one assumes a modest amount of growth in your account, say 7% annually, then the amount of the MDO will increase every year. For the first several years of retirement, assuming a married couple, each aged 70, your account will grow because you are taking out less than 7% of the account's value annually. The MDO is calculated by dividing the size of your account annually by the applicable period of life expectancy. If you have twenty years of life expectancy, then the minimum distribution rules only mandate that you received a 5% distribution. If we posit a 7% long-term growth rate, the account will grow. In fact, the numerator, the size of your account, will increase until, using 7% as a benchmark, your remaining life expectancy falls below fourteen years. The magic of fourteen years stems from the mathematical fact that you will then begin drawing slightly more than 7% of your account out every year.

That percentage will increase over time, but there are strategies for slowing that outflow. Your income will, as a matter of law, increase and enable you to keep pace with inflation more easily than if you were, for example, on a fixed annuity. If you retain a portion of your account in CREF investments, your account and therefore your income have the potential to grow significantly. If the market retreats in any year, your income may decrease, depending on how large the downward movement has been and whether you have other assets to tide you over.

You need to monitor your spending to take into account the certainty of a market decline. The stock market does not rise every year, the experience of the last few years notwithstanding. And assuming double-digit returns for the indefinite future, as a retirement planner for one of our clients did, borders on the reckless and irresponsible. Happily, in this case, the clients agreed. Whatever the right number may be, you should err on the side of conservatism and caution. Any

Table 36.1a

Minimum Distributions

John and Jane Doe

Assumptions	
Year of First Required Distribution	2000
Beginning Account Balance	$1,000,000
Client's Ages	71
Beneficiary's Age	70
Type of Beneficiary (Spouse = 0, Nonspouse = 1)	0
Year of Client's Death	2013
Year of Beneficiary's Death	2017
Account Growth Rate	7.0%

Recalculate Client							
Year	Client's Age	Beneficiary's Age	Beginning Balance ($)	Divisor	Minimum Distribution ($)	Growth 7.0% ($)	Ending Balance ($)
2000	71	70	1,000,000	20.2	49,505	66,535	1,017,030
2001	72	71	1,017,030	18.9	53,811	67,425	1,030,644
2002	73	72	1,030,644	18.1	50,042	68,159	1,041,861
2003	74	73	1,041,861	16.9	61,649	68,615	1,048,828
2004	75	74	1,048,828	16.1	65,145	68,858	1,052,541
2005	76	75	1,052,541	15.0	70,169	68,766	1,051,138
2006	77	76	1,051,138	14.3	73,506	68,434	1,046,066
2007	78	77	1,046,066	13.2	79,247	67,677	1,034,496
2008	79	78	1,034,496	12.3	84,105	68,527	1,016,918
2009	80	79	1,016,918	11.4	89,203	64,940	992,654
2010	81	80	992,654	10.4	95,448	62,804	960,011
2011	82	81	960,011	9.s	100,001	60,201	920,211
2012	83	82	920,211	8.7	105,771	57,011	871,450
2013	84	83	871,450	8.0	108,931	53,376	815,895

return over your projection will prove a pleasant surprise. That beats overestimating your return and having to suffer the consequences later on.

The critical point remains that you have control over your destiny by changing the mix of investments and electing how much income to take each year. If you are able to live comfortably on the MDO alone, subject to the caveat that one is supposed to enjoy, not endure, retirement, the economic benefit will reach its maximum potential. We have set forth three hypothetical fact patterns, all assuming that a couple retires at age 70, and then showing the payout for an account of $500,000, $1 million, and $1.5 million. The math always works out the same in terms of the total paid versus the retirement benefit. The

Table 36.1b

Minimum Distributions

John and Jane Doe

Assumptions	
Year of First Required Distribution	2000
Beginning Account Balance	$500,000
Client's Ages	71
Beneficiary's Age	70
Type of Beneficiary (Spouse = 0, Nonspouse = 1)	0
Year of Client's Death	2013
Year of Beneficiary's Death	2017
Account Growth Rate	7.0%

Recalculate Client							
Year	Client's Age	Beneficiary's Age	Beginning Balance ($)	Divisor	Minimum Distribution ($)	Growth 7.0% ($)	Ending Balance ($)
2000	71	70	500,000	20.2	24,752	33,267	508,515
2001	72	71	508,515	18.9	26,906	33,713	515,322
2002	73	72	515,322	18.1	28,471	34,080	520,931
2003	74	73	520,931	16.9	30,824	34,307	524,414
2004	75	74	524,414	16.1	32,572	34,429	526,270
2005	76	75	526,270	15.0	35,085	34,383	525,509
2006	77	76	525,509	14.3	36,753	34,217	523,033
2007	78	77	523,033	13.2	39,624	33,839	517,248
2008	89	78	517,248	12.3	42,053	33,264	508,489
2009	80	79	508,459	11.4	44,602	32,470	496,327
2010	81	80	496,327	10.4	47,724	31,402	480,006
2011	82	81	480,006	9.6	50,001	30,100	460,105
2012	83	82	460,105	8.7	52,886	28,505	435,725
2013	84	83	435,725	8.0	54,466	26,688	407,948

difference arises from the obvious fact that one can live more easily on an income three times the size of the baseline example of $500,000.

But even if you only have a TIAA-CREF account of $500,000, use of the MDO may remain feasible. Your spouse may have a retirement accumulation as well, you and/or your spouse may continue working in a part-time capacity, or you may have other income-producing assets that will make up any shortfall between needs and means. Then, too, one may have a modest lifestyle and no debt. You have paid for the house, tuition payments may, thank goodness, only be a distant memory, and you are content to live quietly and not incur the expenses of incessant travel. Such people do exist, and we have worked with them. To take a case that comes to mind, the couple had $600,000 in

Table 36.1c
Minimum Distributions
John and Jane Doe

Assumptions	
Year of First Required Distribution	2000
Beginning Account Balance	$1,500,000
Client's Ages	71
Beneficiary's Age	70
Type of Beneficiary (Spouse = 0, Nonspouse = 1)	0
Year of Client's Death	2013
Year of Beneficiary's Death	2017
Account Growth Rate	7.0%

Recalculate Client						
Year	Client's Age	Beneficiary's Age	Beginning Balance ($)	Divisor	Minimum Distribution ($)	Growth 7.0% ($)	Ending Balance ($)
---	---	---	---	---	---	---	---
2000	71	70	1,500,000	20.2	74,257	99,802	1,525,545
2001	72	71	1,525,545	18.9	80,717	101,138	1,545,966
2002	73	72	1,545,966	18.1	85,412	102,239	1,562,792
2003	74	73	1,562,792	16.9	92,473	102,922	1,573,242
2004	75	74	1,573,242	16.1	97,717	103,287	1,578,811
2005	76	75	1,578,811	15.0	105,254	103,149	1,576,706
2006	77	76	1,576,706	14.3	110,259	102,651	1,569,098
2007	78	77	1,569,098	13.2	118,871	101,516	1,551,743
2008	79	78	1,551,743	12.3	126,158	99,791	1,525,376
2009	80	79	1,525,376	11.4	133,805	97,410	1,488,981
2010	81	80	1,488,981	10.4	143,171	94,207	1,440,017
2011	82	81	1,440,017	9.6	150,002	90,301	1,380,316
2012	83	82	1,380,316	8.7	158,657	85,516	1,307,175
2013	84	83	1,307,175	8.0	163,397	80,064	1,223,843

TIAA-CREF, the slightly younger wife was still working, their house was paid for, and the wife had $200,000 or so in Individual Retirement Accounts. The husband had retired at age 65, was working part-time, and was letting the account grow until he reached age 70 and his wife had also retired. For them, a first-year distribution of $40,000 as a worst case made economic sense, given their lifestyle and pattern of spending. They wanted their children to realize estimated benefits of roughly $2 million.

Some number exists below which estate planning for a TIAA-CREF account becomes unrealistic. What that floor equals we do not know. Obviously, the smaller the account, the lower the odds that the MDO will work to provide enough income for a couple or even a single retiree to live comfortably, and the first priority in any financial planning has to be a sufficient income stream to provide for you and your spouse or partner.

If, on the other hand, one survives the cut, so to speak, then the account can work its tax-deferred magic for the benefit of two and possibly three generations. As will be discussed later, attendant costs arising out of the federal estate tax will require attention and funding.

Finally, being able to pass on one's TIAA-CREF account to one's family produces enormous satisfaction for those who pursue this alternative. Your work and sacrifice have unexpectedly led to financial security and well-being for your family. Your children and grandchildren will have a range of career and other options that might otherwise have proven unavailable. And all because you planned and took the right steps at the right time.

This may appear an utterly redundant chapter, considering that we covered some of the issues earlier. Admittedly, you will find some overlap, but the designation of a beneficiary in the estate planning process differs from the general run-of-the-mill rules that we discussed before. We will undertake a more focused discussion because if you are estate planning, the choice of the DB can make a difference of potentially millions of dollars. These are distinctions that amount to a difference. The choice of your DBs, primary and contingent, also serves as the foundation of the estate plan, and you simply have to get it right.

In any event, to avoid later confusion, we thought a quick review of some basic concepts should be injected here so that you do not become lost later on. Some of this information appeared in earlier chapters, and we will review it at the gallop. Rather than reduce you to despair with one overdose, we will deal with the various tax issues in several chapters rather than in one chapter of overwhelming length, complexity, and prolixity. A book is not written to be the equivalent of fraternity hazing. "We endured this torture and so must you" does not seem a sensible solution when you are writing a book intended to be useful and, on occasion, actually read. If you need to refresh your recollection of the three basic rules of the estate planning universe, mark this page, skim the primer, and return to the discussion at hand.

Nonetheless, no matter how well versed you feel you may be, you will have to think through the estate and retirement planning process in stages, and no one would describe this material as commonsensical. We have learned this stuff through repetition and rote and by living with it professionally. But we need to gather the threads together. We have eliminated as much of the technical detail as possible; with effort, concepts contained or implicit in the Code can be expressed in comprehensible English. Although we still discuss rules, you should know that questions do remain about their interpretation in unusual circumstances. But if all kinds of estate planning professionals can understand this stuff, we are not talking about differential equations, or 11-dimensional space, or even humble rocket science.

We begin with a speedy overview of the DB question.

Having a Designated Beneficiary

We covered this point before, and we cannot overemphasize the importance of having a DB. Without one or with the wrong one, TIAA-CREF or any other provider will pay out your account after your death within one or five years, depending on whether you die before or after taking distributions. Putting to one side the personal tragedy represented by an early death, not having a DB amounts to a financial catastrophe because of the bunching of income that occurs. You can figure that 40% of your account will wind up in the hands of the Internal Revenue Service in the form of income taxes and your heirs will have lost the benefit of tax-free compounding for the balance. They may also have to pay estate tax based on the size of the account as of the date of death, unreduced by income taxes.

Who are the right DBs? They must be individuals because the critical function of a DB is to furnish a measuring life over which payments will be made and only people have life expectancies. An estate does not have a life expectancy. Charities do not have life expectancies. Trusts, with the single exception to be discussed later, do not have a life expectancy. Naming any of these entities equates to having no DB, and the disasters pictured so vividly in the previous paragraph will then occur.

The invariable rule in this area boils down to this: the Code will look to the shortest life expectancy to measure the time over which distributions will be made. If you elect a DB without a life expectancy—in effect, a zero life expectancy—you might as well have selected no DB because the rapid payments described above will occur by operation of law.

At the very latest, you must have selected a DB when distributions begin. That does not argue for waiting until the eleventh hour. You always need a DB so that your account will be paid out over the DB's life expectancy rather than over five years, the statutory default, should you die before you begin taking distributions. **Get the TIAA-CREF form, fill it out, file it with your school's benefits office or with TIAA-CREF directly if you have not already done so, and keep a copy.** We are deadly serious about this.

A footnote to this discussion: many retirement plan providers, including TIAA-CREF, do not use the term "Designated Beneficiary" on their forms. They may substitute the term "Primary Beneficiary" or some variant on that phrase. That person is, for tax and other related purposes, your DB.

The importance of having a DB by your Required Beginning Date is that your choice will determine the period over which the TIAA-CREF account, retirement plan, or Individual Retirement Account will be paid. As of the RBD, that term is cast in cement. If you have selected a DB, then the payment stream will occur over your joint life expectancies, computed as described earlier.

One more rule related to DBs: once you have begun receiving distributions, you can change your DB as often as you like. What you cannot do is lengthen the period over which distributions will be made. If your DB dies, you do not get a second chance to pick a younger person or have some other form of do-over. By picking the wrong DB after distribution has begun, namely someone older than your original choice, you can only shorten the distribution period. You cannot extend it. It is a one-way street.

You may wonder why you should not pick an infant or a grandchild as your DB if you want to prolong the payment period and extend the tax-free compounding that occurs within your retirement plan. The Internal Revenue Service and Congress anticipated that move. Unless your DB is your spouse, in which case actual age will be used, a non-spousal DB will be treated as being at most ten years younger than you are for as long as you are alive. This set of postulates falls, as you may remember, under the elegant title of the Minimum Distribution Incidental Beneficiary rules. If you are 71, the Code will treat your infant grandchild as being 61 years of age for purposes of computing the applicable life expectancies. Only if you realize the abuse that the Code and Congress were trying to thwart do these odd rules make any sense. After you have died, your DB resumes his or her actual age for these purposes. We are not talking common sense; we are discussing tax law.

The Spouse as the Ideal Designated Beneficiary

Of all of the universe of possible DBs, the most favored by the Code remains, of course, the spouse. More likely than not, if you are married, you will have chosen your spouse to be the other measuring life for the payment of your account. In TIAA-CREF parlance, your spouse has become your "calculation beneficiary." Many plans will treat the spouse as the default DB even if you do not file any paperwork. Do not assume that to be the case. File the necessary paperwork. It takes about 5 to 10 minutes.

If you name your spouse as your DB, your spouse, and your spouse alone, has numerous options that inure to no other DB. We assume, for this discussion, that your spouse will survive you.

To begin with, the spouse's most powerful privilege under the Code is to roll over your account into your spouse's name upon your death. If your spouse can, under your employer's plan, roll your account out of TIAA-CREF, your spouse can establish an IRA or add to an existing IRA. If your spouse elects to remain within TIAA-CREF, then the accumulation will flow into an account called an Individual Retirement Annuity. For estate planning purposes, the name represents a label only because the account will not be annuitized. In this respect, it resembles the RA and the SRA, both called annuity accounts, that you are not, by hypothesis, annuitizing.

If your spouse is working, then your spouse can add to an existing IRA or the Individual Retirement Annuity account, if one already exists. The account belongs to your spouse, *and your spouse has the right to name new DBs for the new or augmented account.* In effect, your spouse can reset the clock by which the payment schedule is measured. Again, no other DB has that right. If you die before the RBD, only the spouse can halt distributions from commencing upon your death if your spouse so elects, effects a rollover into his own IRA, and is under the age of $70^1/_2$. Your spouse can defer distributions until he reaches age $70^1/_2$ or until the date you would have turned $70^1/_2$ had you lived longer. No five-year payout and not even the commencement of payments over the life expectancy of your DB occurs if you name your spouse, and your spouse has not individually passed the RBD.

If your spouse has passed the RBD and has a retirement plan or IRAs of his or her own that names you as the DB, the distribution period as to those accounts has become frozen. Your spouse should, therefore, not add your TIAA-CREF accumulation and any other retirement accounts standing in your name to an existing account. Instead, the spouse should create a new account or accounts and name appropriate DBs, typically children. Your spouse will enjoy a longer payment period, subject to the MDIB rules. This will slow the outflow of funds and preserve more for the next generation, subject always to the rigid axiom that the financial needs of the current generation come first.

The ability of the spouse to name new DBs sets the stage for the passage of the account down to the next generation. Children make the natural choice as the new DBs for your spouse. Thus, you have put into position the *possibility* of moving the account down to the next generation. Your account has some hurdles to overcome before it reaches the promised land. But your spouse can stop the clock, reset the DBs, and have the flow out of the TIAA-CREF account confined to a new and narrower channel.

Parenthetically, if you have a very large account, instead of naming your spouse as the sole DB, you could name your children as the DBs of a fractional share of your account equal to the then prevailing estate and gift tax exemption. That amount is $675,000 in 2000 and 2001, and will rise to $1 million in 2006. One needs a large account to take advantage of this opportunity because you want to make sure that your spouse will have enough to live on despite the diversion of part of your account to children.

After 2006, when the estate tax exemption and the generation-skipping tax will both equal $1 million, it will become feasible to name grandchildren as DBs without tax consequences, again assuming the requisite size account. What you are doing, if your account is so large that the diversion of a portion to children or grandchildren will not impinge on your spouse's standard of living, is a direct jump from one generation to another, with the balance to be transferred when your spouse dies. For those so situated, unless they have other assets that are sure to appreciate rapidly, using the exemption in this way becomes highly beneficial to your descendants and is tax-efficient, utilizing the exemption to transfer a valuable asset.

Your spouse has other advantages. If your spouse postpones taking distributions until the time that you would have turned $70^1/_2$ or the spouse turns $70^1/_2$, either of these options will permit further accumulation to occur and increase the size of the account. In addition, having named children as DBs, the second measuring life for withdrawals can become a child's. Now your spouse faces the MDIB rules. That means that if your spouse is 68 and your oldest child is 38, the MDIB rules will transform your child (solely for these purposes) into a 58-year-old, and life expectancies will be computed accordingly. Or to take the postponement route, your spouse will be 71 and your oldest child will be deemed to be 61, at least until your spouse dies.

By way of a sidebar, we have found that one of the disturbing side effects of immersing one self in these rules is that their *Through the Looking Glass*—or plain nutty quality—so obvious at first becomes dimmer with the passage of time. In this instance, familiarity breeds a loss of contempt. Legal fictions abound around us, but it still does evoke a sense of wonder that a system can exist (and be treated as rational) in which a 38-year-old is deemed to be a 58-year-old. This unnatural state of affairs ceases when the spouse dies, and the child reverts to actual age for future computational purposes.

The Contingent Designated Beneficiary

What happens if your spouse does not survive you? *The effect will vary enormously depending on whether you have passed the RBD.* First, assuming you have not passed the RBD, you provide for this possibility by naming one or more contingent beneficiaries. According to its literature, TIAA-CREF does not accept more than one beneficiary per contract. If you want to achieve a two-generational payment and have more than one child or heir to whom you wish to pass the account, TIAA-CREF requires that you either (A) split your account into as many MDO contracts as your contingent beneficiaries, typically your children, or (B) you name a trust as the DB.

The choice between naming your children individually as your contingent DBs or naming a trust amounts to more than an election between simplicity and what appears to be an additional layer of complexity. You have to exercise your judgment about your children, assuming that they are all of legal age as of the RBD, and weigh a number of factors. We dealt with these issues in chapter 30 when we discussed the single parent and the naming of one or more DBs, and you should consult that exposition of the relevant factors before making your election.

Having read that an entity has a zero life expectancy, you might reasonably conclude that naming a trust would a calamity. However, the Internal Revenue Service's Proposed Regulations provide the four conditions under which the Service will regard the trust as transparent or disregard it entirely. Instead, the Service will look through the trust to the applicable beneficiaries and measure payouts by the shortest life expectancy among the beneficiaries. In their original, pristine form, the four requirements were these:

1. The trust must be valid under state law. For your lawyer's sake, it better be.
2. The beneficiaries and their interests must be ascertainable. You

can name a fixed or closed class, such as your children living at the time of your death, but you cannot name your descendants or your grandchildren if your children are still of child-bearing age. TIAA-CREF or any administrator will have no way of knowing who may be born, and so forth, and the identities and interests of the beneficiaries will be unascertainable.

3. The trust must be irrevocable.

4. A copy of the trust must be provided to the administrator of the plan.

The last requirement proved to be, as you can imagine, a trap for the unwary because all of these requirements had to be met by the time distributions began and sending a copy of the plan was a detail often overlooked.

Recognizing this problem, the Internal Revenue Service amended the Proposed Regulations late in 1997 to allow for revocable trusts and for an executor or trustee to provide information about the beneficiaries as late as nine months after the applicable date of death. With ruthless logic, the Service inserted the requirement that the trust be irrevocable when one dies. It seems impossible for it to be otherwise, but the cautious draftsman will insert this tautology into the trust to avoid disqualification. After a while, based on firsthand experience, you stop feeling stupid stating the self-evident.

As often happens, what the Service gives with one hand, it takes away with the other. The liberalization carries with it a major drawback, namely that if a revocable trust is named and the trust is amended, the administrator must be informed of the change and the different interests of the beneficiaries under the amended agreement. Failure to furnish that information can disqualify the trust, subject to the nine month absolute deadline after death.

In our opinion, the odds of flunking the last test seem formidable. This boils down to a matter of personal preference, but we stick with the old rules, sending a change of beneficiary form and the irrevocable trust to TIAA-CREF by certified mail, return receipt requested. If you change your mind about whom you want as your beneficiaries, we file a new change of beneficiary form and a new irrevocable trust with TIAA-CREF, and the old irrevocable trust becomes so much paper. It never will be funded. In this way, one knows, when the papers are signed, that the rules have been complied with, and one also knows the ropes for making a change of beneficiary at some later point. You also know that TIAA-CREF is on notice of the identity of your beneficiaries.

Whether one sticks to the old rules or uses the new ones, the result turns out to the same—the life expectancy of the oldest beneficiary will determine the time over which the payments will be made.

To return, then, to where we left off, if your spouse predeceases you, then the trust becomes the primary beneficiary and the account passes to the next generation directly from you.

Second, assume you have passed the RBD and your spouse predeceases you. The benefit to the next generation does not approach what it would have been if your spouse survived you. Assuming that your spouse was your DB as of the RBD, then you have irrevocably determined the period over which payment will be made. Upon your death, the Code requires that the balance in the account be paid over the "at least as rapidly" method. That means the payments will occur over the period you selected as of the RBD. This resembles the choice of a guaranteed period with a one-or-two life annuity. Whatever the unexpired balance of the payment period may be when you die, and it may be zero as discussed later, that will determine the term over which your children will receive the balance in the account and the earnings thereon. No surviving spouse exists who can reset the clock by naming the children as DBs, and the payment period set as of the RBD will have to run its course.

If your spouse dies before the RBD, then naming your children as your DBs avoids this result and permits the payment stream to continue over two generations. Note, however, that the computation of the MDO will be based upon the regulatory fiction that your child is only ten years younger than you are. If you remain within TIAA-CREF, then the monthly payments that you will receive under the MDO will be lower than they would have been had your spouse lived past the RBD, assuming that your spouse was less than ten years younger than you are. Paradoxically, if your spouse was more than ten years younger, your payments will be larger if you name a child or children as your DBs. Of course, in that instance, the odds are pretty good that your spouse will survive you, but untimely deaths do occur. You should also bear another detail in mind if you name children as your DBs. Unless your employer's plan allows you to take Systematic Withdrawals from your account after retirement, TIAA-CREF will pay you the amount of the MDO and no more. If your employer's plan does not provide that flexibility but permits a partial or total withdrawal of your retirement account from TIAA-CREF as of the date you retire, you ought to consider the implications of that choice prior to the RBD and whether you can make a withdrawal thereafter.

There may be a way to place your bets to beat the odds. It requires a warm and loving family, especially your children. It also requires that your children be financially responsible and that their personal lives be stable. If you are not sure which of you or your spouse will die first, the following may solve the problem. Name your children as your DBs, noting the impact on your distributions and making any necessary allowances to keep your income at an acceptable level if the MDO is going to be too low. Name your spouse as your contingent beneficiary. If your spouse predeceases you, then the children will benefit from the additional time over which the account will be paid, bearing in mind that they revert to their true ages for purposes of calculating their life expectancies after you die. If, however, you predecease your spouse, you must rely on your children to disclaim their interest in the account, thereby making the contingent beneficiary, your spouse, the owner of the account. Your spouse can then name your children as your spouse's DBs, and everything will then be back on track. Although this technique should work under existing law, no direct precedent from the Internal Revenue Service exists as of the date of this writing and you should consult a qualified estate planning lawyer before you attempt to use this suggested approach. You will quickly realize, no doubt, that you and your spouse are placing a great deal of trust in your children and are also assuming that they will not face bankruptcy, divorce, or other financial constraints that may interfere with their ability to make the disclaimers.

One final issue merits your attention. Whether you are dealing with an IRA provider, be it a bank, brokerage house, or other financial institution, or with TIAA-CREF, you need to check beforehand as to whether the holder of your retirement account will respect your designation of your beneficiaries.

This cuts across the board with almost all retirement plan providers. They do not have the forms and staff in place to deal with a complex designation, of a DB, even a trust. *With any IRA in particular, you must check to make sure that the planning and the complex DB description will work, given the bureaucratic structure of the IRA provider or custodian.*

To review, the basic steps that must be taken in your planning, if you are married with children, to pass your account down to the next generation are these:

1. Do not annuitize your account, but elect the Minimum Distribution Option.
2. Name your spouse, if any, as your Designated Beneficiary. If you are not married or are the surviving spouse, follow the second sentence of point 4 if your account is still in TIAA-CREF or name your children as your DBs.
3. Use the hybrid method for calculating life expectancies.
4. Name your children or a trust that satisfies the Internal Revenue Service Proposed Regulations as your contingent DB if your spouse is still living. At your death, the contingent DB becomes your primary beneficiary.
5. If your spouse survives and the account is still with TIAA-CREF, your spouse would name your children or the same trust as primary DB or the children if the account is no longer with TIAA-CREF.
6. If you change your mind about your intended beneficiaries, file a change of beneficiary form with TIAA-CREF and name other individual beneficiaries (or amend their shares of the pie) or another irrevocable trust as your contingent or primary DB, depending on the circumstances when the choice is made. In the alternative, use a revocable trust and make sure that every change of beneficiaries within the trust is filed with TIAA-CREF.
7. Bear in mind, however, that this planning will not achieve optimal results if you named your spouse as your DB as of the RDB, and your spouse predeceases you. The clock cannot be reset, and the payout period is fixed. It will never take your children's life expectancies into account.

For single individuals, as noted above, the strategy they should follow amounts to a variation on the same theme. If they have children, they or a trust with them as beneficiaries should become DBs.

If there are no family members to whom you want to leave your account, then a charitable donation may become the option of choice.

You will note that nowhere in this list of items do we mention your will and the balance of your property. As we said in the primer, like life insurance, the TIAA-CREF account, any other type of qualified plan, or an Individual Retirement Account passes outside of the will through the designation of a beneficiary, that is, in effect, by contract between you and TIAA-CREF or any other provider of retirement benefits. We will explore the issues as to how this part of your estate planning should be integrated with your planning for the balance of your assets in future chapters.

In this and the preceding chapters, we intended to introduce the concepts and mechanisms that make the transfer of the TIAA-CREF account to the next generation a reality. If this all seems to be too good to be true, it is, because we have not touched upon the really tough problems that must be overcome to effect the results described above. Aside from your spouse's mortality risk, there is always a catch, and, in this instance, the federal estate tax and its state counterparts now loom as the largest obstacles to achieving your goals.

How Does the Federal Estate Tax Affect This Plan?

An Overview of the Issues

All good things must come to an end, and the same rule that governs our lives applies with equal force to retirement plans. They enjoy such tax-favored treatment under the income tax that it comes as a surprise to see how they can be savaged by the federal estate tax. Ironically, their vulnerability flows inexorably from their preferential treatment under the income tax provisions of the Code. In a sense, what is given with one hand may, if you do not plan, be taken away with the other.

With some explanation from your helpful guides, you will find that, again, the basic concepts do not require abstruse reasoning. You may find that a quick glance at the primer or the glossary may be required from time to time just so that you remain familiar with the legal patois. You have already covered the basic principles of estate planning: now you get to see them in action.

You have to understand the fundamental difference, *for estate tax purposes*, between a retirement plan of any stripe and almost every asset you can imagine accumulating. *The critical distinction flows from the fact that your retirement account consists entirely of untaxed income.* You deducted on your Form 1040 the contributions that you made to your retirement account (other than any set-aside of after-tax dollars to buy a Teacher's Personal Annuity or other tax-deferred annuity). You did not have to include your employer's contribution into your taxable income over all those decades. And your account grew inside the plan without having to pay any income taxes on dividend or interest income or capital gains on any realized appreciation. These qualities make the qualified plan so beloved by so many Americans.

So what, you may think. Consider the following hypothetical. Suppose for a moment that you have two assets, each worth $1 million, and that each asset generates an estate tax at the highest marginal rate of 55%. The first of these assets consists of a portfolio of marketable securities, real estate, and other comparable assets. The second represents your TIAA-CREF account. If you pay the estate tax on the first asset, you will have $450,000 left ($1 million minus $550,000). Outrageous, if not confiscatory, considering that the underlying income that created the asset was taxed once already. Bad as this result may be, it seems positively benign compared to what happens to the retirement plan.

If you want to come up with the same amount of cash to pay the tax liability on the TIAA-CREF account, you face a double tax burden. Your executor must take a distribution from TIAA-CREF to pay the tax. Suppose he takes the full $1 million, because, as you will see, your executor will need it. That will generate a federal income tax of $400,000. If you live in a state with its own income tax, that will also have to be paid. Out of the balance comes the $550,000 due the Internal Revenue Service for federal estate tax and payment due your state for state taxes. You will receive an income tax deduction for the federal estate tax (but not for the state tax) paid under an esoteric tax concept called "income in respect of a decedent." The value of the income tax deduction of about $400,000, assuming the existence of any income against which it can be offset, increases the amount left to your estate from $50,000, a 95% wipeout, to about $210,000. Approximately 80% of your accumulation has disappeared to pay taxes. Compared to the other assets, it takes two dollars of retirement plan money to pay one dollar of estate tax.

In effect, the double whammy of estate and income taxes wrings out the income tax shelter you have enjoyed over the years. When you die, all of the chickens, so to speak, come home to roost. The Code views the plan stereoscopically. On the one hand, it treats the plan balance as though it were principal or after-tax dollars like the hypothetical first mix of assets described above. The Code calculates the tax on the balance in the account as though it were $1 million like any other. On the other hand, the Code regards the plan as a treasure trove of untaxed income to be walloped as soon as a sizable distribution is made. In effect, your estate will have taken a lump sum distribution, but, rather than leave the balance to your loved ones, your executor must snatch it from them and send it to the Internal Revenue Service. Not good.

Unless your assets fall below $1 million, this dilemma will affect the portion of your retirement plan that will pass to your children, for reasons to be discussed later. Avoiding the draconian results described above marks the point at which serious planning begins. This issue should remain in the forefront of your mind because the earlier you plan your way around it, the cheaper and easier it becomes to cope. You may only pay a fraction of the estate tax illustrated above and the cash will come from other sources, but avoiding Scylla and Charybdis requires more planning and forethought on your and your estate planner's part than even Odysseus employed.

For most people, this treatment comes as a rude awakening. Some despair of solving the problem, and one often sees the suggestion that one give the remainder of the plan to charity, for which one receives an estate tax charitable deduction, as the only way to avoid the double taxation described above. Solutions do exist, but they will cost you or your estate money, either after you die or, preferably, far less before you do. If you leave the problem to your estate, the solution will cost more than if you had dealt with it head-on while you were alive, but the problem can be solved. It will involve the use of time, which can be your friend or your enemy, depending on how you use it.

Another Continental Divide

Hey, you may be thinking, what about the increase in the estate tax exemption and the unlimited marital deduction and some of the other features of the federal estate tax? Don't they provide shelters and solutions? The answer is yes and no. It depends on your values and your economic circumstances.

To summarize the next few pages, you face the following choice:

you (or preferably someone else) can pay more tax and leave more to your family, or,

you can try to minimize taxes and leave less to your family.

This sounds paradoxical or counterintuitive, and it is. It makes up the first of many paradoxes that we have encountered in planning for estates with large retirement accounts.

If you want to leave your family with the maximal benefit from your retirement plan, then as suggested earlier, you will name your spouse as your Designated Beneficiary and your spouse will name your children as the spouse's DBs. This scenario assumes that you die first. If the order of deaths is reversed and your spouse dies before RBD, then you name your children as your DBs after your spouse has died. We have discussed possible solutions for solving the spouse who dies after the RBD problem.

This set of moves has a number of repercussions. Assume for the moment that you have a typical two-asset estate—the first set of assets consisting of a house, some savings, and assorted other items and the second, the outsized TIAA-CREF accumulation and perhaps some Individual Retirement Accounts. To put some numbers on this hypothetical, let's say the asset situation looks like this:

Table 39.1

Asset	Husband	Wife
House	$0.00	$300,000
Stocks, savings, etc.	$175,000	$175,000
TIAA-CREF account	$1,200,000	
Totals	$1,375,000	$475,000

Let's assume that we are in 2000, the estate tax exemption is $675,000, and the husband dies first.

The first commandment of conventional estate planning reads, "Thou shalt use thy exemptions to the fullest." Upon the death of the husband, that would, to simplify, result in creating a trust that would hold the $175,000 of savings, and so forth, in his name, and the TIAA-CREF account would be divided into two parts. The first would equal the value of the unused exemption, here $500,000, and the balance of $700,000 would become part of the marital share, in this case passing by a formula contained in the designation of beneficiary form filed with TIAA-CREF.

Assuming that the survivor dies after 2006, the survivor's estate will probably incur about $82,000 of federal and state estate taxes, assuming that the other assets do not appreciate and the TIAA-CREF accumulation owned by the wife does not skyrocket in value.

However, this result contains a hidden cost. The $500,000 in the credit shelter trust cannot qualify for multigenerational treatment, that is, payment over the lifetimes of the participant and spouse and their children, and the spouse as the beneficiary with the shortest life expectancy becomes the measuring life. Each distribution will obviously generate income taxes, and the account will slowly, then rapidly, diminish with only one measuring life. The children may receive something if the survivor dies before the end of his or her life expectancy, but it will take the form of either a lump sum payment if the survivor elected recalculation or payments over the balance, if any, of the spouse's life expectancy under the subtract one method. In the latter case, the payout will still be relatively swift and be partially consumed by income taxes. If the wife is 70 when the husband dies and assuming a 7% return, the trust will generate about $805,000 over fifteen years and then be exhausted (see table 39.2). Had the trust been left outright to the spouse, and the spouse had survived and named children as DBs, the ultimate return would be on the order of $1.8 to 2.5 million, assuming the same 7% long-term rate of appreciation. However, the estate taxes would increase by about $250,000.

Generally speaking, a retirement plan makes a poor choice for an asset to place into a credit shelter trust. Ideally, one wants an asset that will appreciate, with the increased value passing to the children free of estate tax. All of the appreciation that accrues to the credit shelter

Table 39.2 **Credit Shelter Trust Analysis**
Minimum Distributions   Recalculate None
Jane Doe

Assumptions	
Year of First Required Distribution	2000
Beginning Account Balance	$475,000
Client's Age	71
Beneficiary's Age	70
Type of Beneficiary	Nonspouse
Year of Client's Death	2,15
Year of Beneficiary's Death	0
Account Growth Rate	7.0%

Results						Recalculate None
Year	Client's Age	Beginning Balance ($)	Divisor	Minimum Distribution ($)	Growth 7.0% ($)	Ending Balance ($)
2000	71	475,000	15.3	31,046	31,077	475,031
2001	72	475,031	14.3	33,219	30,927	472,739
2002	73	472,739	13.3	35,544	30,604	467,798
2003	74	467,798	12.3	38,032	30,084	459,850
2004	75	459,850	11.3	40,695	29,341	448,496
2005	76	448,496	10.3	43,543	28,347	433,299
2006	77	433,299	9.3	46,591	27,070	413,777
2007	78	413,777	8.3	49,853	25,475	389,399
2008	79	389,399	7.3	53,342	23,524	359,581
2009	80	359,581	6.3	57,076	21,175	323,680
2010	81	323,680	5.3	51,072	18,383	280,991
2011	82	280,991	4.3	65,347	15,095	230,739
2012	83	230,739	3.3	69,921	11,257	172,076
2013	84	172,076	2.3	74,815	6,808	104,068
2014	85	104,068	1.3	80,053	1,681	25,697
2015	86	25,697	1.0	25,697	—	—
Total Distributions				**$805,846**		

trust can pass to the remaindermen, usually children, free of estate or gift tax. The children may have to pay a 20% capital gains tax when they sell assets, but that beats an estate tax rate that ranges from 37% up to 55%.

The retirement plan, in this context, represents a wasting asset, with a relatively quick paydown and income tax on every distribution. In effect, there will be no principal, and the trust will hold nothing but untaxed income. The income tax will diminish any appreciation that occurred over the duration of the credit shelter trust. The remainder cannot pass free of ordinary income taxes, and it will not receive the benefit of lower capital gains taxes.

Although we recommend some strategies for circumventing the burden of the estate tax, they assume that you will either have sufficient cash flow or other assets to carry the load. If you do not have a comparable situation, then you ought to consider setting up your designation of beneficiary in the following manner. *Name your spouse as your primary DB, but provide that if your spouse disclaims all or any part of the TIAA-CREF account, the disclaimed portion will pass to the credit shelter or bypass trust.* This will reduce taxes by funding the credit shelter trust. It will also allow your spouse to make a choice years down the road, one hopes, as to what makes good economic and tax sense given the facts at that time. Generally speaking, we always insert this provision into the designations we draft, on the not implausible theory that we do not possess the foresight to know what the circumstances will be when a choice has to be made. Use this option to build in flexibility. The survivor may never use the disclaimer, but it will be available if circumstances dictate that it would be advantageous.

For example, suppose you have a $1.5 million TIAA-CREF account, and you leave your spouse as the primary DB, making provision for a disclaimer to the credit shelter trust. You die in 2000, when the exemption amount is $675,000, and we can safely assume that the surviving spouse will survive until 2006, when the exemption amount will be $1 million. If your spouse wants to minimize taxes, the disclaimer should be $675,000. If your spouse wants to maximize the return to the family and save on taxes to a lesser degree, the disclaimer would amount to only $500,000. However, the risk of the latter strategy is that the account may grow to beyond $1 million, giving rise to some federal estate tax. If the larger disclaimer is used, then the remainder amounts to only $825,000 and the account and the spouse's IRA and other assets have $175,000 room to grow and not have the spouse's estate incur any estate tax. The survivor can also make gifts, if the economics warrant, during the balance of the spouse's lifetime to reduce the size of the ultimate estate and the taxes that it will generate.

This example illustrates the interplay between the exemption amount in the year that you die and the exemption that will prevail when the survivor dies. The conventional approach emphasizes maximization of the existing exemption, and that clearly represents the safer choice. It may lead to the result that the spouse's estate will not fully utilize the higher exemption down the road. As a consequence, more of the account will be distributed over the life expectancy of the survivor than needed to be, and less will be distributed over the life expectancy of children. As usual, no hard-and-fast rule exists because various factors, such as the health of your spouse, the size of the account, the mix between TIAA assets and CREF assets, and expected investment performance, will affect the ultimate outcome. Whatever one chooses, the flexibility will be there.

On the marital side, one must also avoid conventional thinking. Most marital trusts now take the form of a "QTIP," a qualified terminable interest property trust, to give it its full moniker. The popularity of this type of trust stems from the ability of the deceased spouse to dictate what happens to the principal of the trust after the death of the surviving spouse. Such a trust protects the corpus of the trust from second marriages, the mental incompetence of the spouse, or financial imprudence on the part of the surviving spouse.

As applied to the retirement plan, the QTIP accentuates the negative. In order to qualify for QTIP treatment, the trust instrument or agreement must provide that all of the trust's income be distributed to the surviving spouse at least annually. With the spouse as the only permissible beneficiary, the spouse's life expectancy will provide the measuring life. The income, at least in the early years, may exceed the Minimum Distribution Options. Under trusts drafted over the last ten years, it cannot be accumulated, but must be distributed. The Internal Revenue Service ruled in 1989 that the spouse is entitled to the greater of the plan income or the minimum distributions. This ruling accelerates the outflow of funds from the plan because undistributed income cannot be reinvested. If the spouse is long lived, it becomes more likely that the spouse will outlive the assets in the trust or that they will prove insufficient to maintain the spouse's lifestyle in the twilight years.

Early in 2000, the Internal Revenue Service reversed its position, holding that the spouse may elect to receive only the minimum distribution requirement. This may improve the economic return from a QTIP, but it depends on two factors. First, if as every existing trust now provides, the trustee must demand the higher of actual income or minimum distributions, then the undistributed income will accumulate in the trust. The trust income tax rates that would apply to the undistributed income make that alternative unattractive. Trusts will require amendment so that the excess remains in the plan, increasing the odds that the income will continue for a longer period of time and can grow

Table 39.3   **Marital Trust Analysis**

Minimum Distributions   **Recalculate None**

Jane Doe

Assumptions	
Year of First Required Distribution	2000
Beginning Account Balance	$500,000
Client's Age	71
Beneficiary's Age	70
Type of Beneficiary	Nonspouse
Year of Client's Death	2015
Year of Beneficiary's Death	0
Account Growth Rate	7.0%

Results						Recalculate None
Year	Client's Age	Beneficiary's Age	Beginning Balance ($)	Divisor	Minimum Distribution ($)	Growth 7.0% ($)	Ending Balance ($)
2000	71	0	725,000	15.3	47,386	47,433	725,047
2001	72		725,047	14.3	50,703	47,204	725,049
2002	73		721,549	13.3	54,252	46,711	714,008
2003	74		714,008	12.3	58,049	45,917	701,876
2004	75		701,876	11.3	62,113	44,783	684,546
2005	76		684,546	10.3	66,461	43,266	661,351
2006	77		661,351	9.3	71,113	41,317	$631,555
2007	78		631,555	8.3	76,091	38,882	594,346
2008	79		594,346	7.3	81,417	35,905	548,834
2009	80		548,834	6.3	87,117	32,320	494,038
2010	81		494,038	5.3	93,215	28,058	428,881
2011	82		428,881	4.3	99,740	23,040	352,181
2012	83		352,181	3.3	106,721	17,182	262,642
2013	84		262,642	2.3	114,192	10,391	158,041
2014	85		158,841	1.3	122,185	2,566	39,222
2015	86		39,222	1.0	39,222	—	—
Total Distributions					**$1,229,976**		

in the tax-sheltered plan environment. Second, estate planners will have to cope with a technical problem. If the spouse does not take all of the income, which the trust must still allow, has the spouse made a gift to the children who will probably receive the trust remainder when the spouse dies? Estate planners have fashioned drafting fixes to avoid potentially disastrous gift tax results, but it will take time before all of the applicable trust instruments conform to the new Internal Revenue Service ruling and all of its implications have been fully understood. In any event, the undistributed income will become part of the survivor's estate, reviving the risk of substantial estate taxes down the road.

Again, as with the credit shelter trust, the spouse cannot name new DBs because the account belongs to the trust and not to the spouse. As with the credit shelter trust, one has minimized estate taxes, subject to the caveat above, accelerated income taxes, and eliminated any chance of passing the account on to the next generation. And, at least theoretically, one has increased the odds that the retirement accumulation will not see the surviving spouse through unless the spouse saves against that eventuality, remarries, or has other assets (see table 39.3).

From an economic point of view, you achieve a better result by designating the spouse as the DB of the entire account. That will allow him or her to name children as DBs. However, this gambit will increase the size of the survivor's estate by slowing the outflow of funds. From an economic viewpoint, this provides a positive result, but again it entails the payment of more estate tax.

In addition, if the entire account passes to the surviving spouse, it no longer becomes available to fund the credit shelter trust, except through the disclaimer technique. Assuming that the disclaimer remains unused, then depending on the mixture and ownership of assets, this may well result in overfunding the marital share and underfunding the exemption. Using the example above, the account will eventually pay out approximately $5 to 6 million (assuming a 7% long-term growth rate), but the surviving spouse's estate will face an estate tax of about $432,000. The total return has increased, the federal estate tax bill has grown, and we have knowingly and voluntarily violated the first commandment of conventional estate planning.

However, when one weighs the increased tax against the increased economic return, the tax appears, in the long run, to be a relative pittance against the background of two generations of payments with

Table 39.4a   **Lifetime Income**

Joint Lifetime Income Projection						
Year	John	Jane	Life Expectancy	Earnings ($)	MDO ($)	Balance ($)
1999						1,200,000
1999	69	69		0	0	1,200,000
2000	70	70	20.60	84,000	58,252	1,225,748
2001	71	71	19.80	85,802	61,906	1,249,644
2002	72	72	18.90	87,475	66,119	1,271,000
2003	73	73	18.10	88,970	70,221	1,289,749
2004	74	74	17.30	90,282	74,552	1,305,479
2005	75	75	16.50	91,384	79,120	1,317,743
2006	76	76	15.70	92,242	83,933	1,326,052
2007	77	77	15.00	92,824	88,403	1,330,473
2008	78	78	14.20	93,133	93,695	1,329,911
2009	79	79	13.50	93,094	98,512	1,324,493
2010	80	80	12.80	92,715	103,476	1,313,732
2011	81	81	12.10	91,961	108,573	1,297,120
2012	82	82	11.50	90,798	112,793	1,275,125
2013	83	83	10.80	89,259	118,067	1,246,317

Surviving Spouse Projections						
Year	Spouse	Oldest Child	Life Expectancy	Earnings ($)	MDO ($)	Balance ($)
2014						1,246,317
2014	84	55	14.50	87,242	85,953	1,247,606
2015	85	56	13.80	87,332	90,406	1,244,532
2016	86	57	13.10	87,117	95,002	1,236,647
2017	87	58	12.40	86,565	99,730	1,223,482

potential for benefit, albeit indirectly, to the third generation. That represents the global view. In the shorter term, one must have the dough to pay the tax to realize the economic benefits. In effect, this equates to the inability to come up with the down payment on an otherwise advantageous deal or investment. The future cash flow will not become available to meet the immediate obstacle.

For these reasons, if one wants to maximize the value of the TIAA-CREF account to the family, then one must operate with a different logic than conventional estate planning would dictate. You must think outside of the box. Upon the death of the participant, the TIAA-CREF account will pass to the surviving spouse tax-free through the unlimited marital deduction. *It bears repeating: this means that the participant's exemption will deliberately not receive full funding (unless there are other assets available for the purpose and in our hypothetical and most cases there aren't), and the marital share will exceed what normal estate planning practices would dictate.*

Table 39.4b   **Distributions to the Children**

Adam

Year	Age	Life Expectancy	Earnings ($)	MDO ($)	Balance ($)
2018					611,741
2018	59	24.60	42,822	24,868	629,695
2019	60	23.60	44,079	26,682	647,092
2020	61	22.60	45,296	28,632	663,756
2021	62	21.60	46,463	30,729	679,490
2022	63	20.60	47,564	32,985	694,069
2023	64	19.60	48,585	35,412	707,242
2024	65	18.60	49,507	38,024	718,725
2025	66	17.60	50,311	40,837	728,199
2026	67	16.60	50,974	43,867	735,306
2027	68	15.60	51,471	47,135	739,642
2028	69	14.60	51,775	50,660	740,757
2029	70	13.60	51,853	54,467	738,143
2030	71	12.60	51,670	58,583	731,230
2031	72	11.60	51,186	63,037	719,379
2032	73	10.60	50,357	67,866	701,870
2033	74	9.60	49,131	73,111	677,890
2034	75	8.60	47,452	78,824	646,518
2035	76	7.60	45,256	85,068	606,706
2036	77	6.60	42,469	91,925	557,250
2037	78	5.60	39,008	99,509	496,749
2038	79	4.60	34,772	107,989	423,532
2039	80	3.60	29,647	117,648	335,531
2040	81	2.60	23,487	129,050	229,968
2041	82	1.60	16,098	143,730	102,336
2042	83	0.60	7,164	109,500	0.00

Eve

Year	Age	Life Expectancy	Earnings ($)	MDO ($)	Balance ($)
2018					611,741
2018	57	24.60	42,822	24,868	629,695
2019	58	23.60	44,079	26,682	647,092
2020	59	22.60	45,296	28,632	663,756
2021	60	21.60	46,463	30,729	679,490
2022	61	20.60	47,564	32,985	694,069
2023	62	19.60	48,585	35,412	707,242
2024	63	18.60	49,567	38,024	718,725
2025	64	17.60	50,311	40,837	728,199
2026	65	16.60	50,974	43,867	735,306
2027	66	15.60	51,471	47,135	739,642
2028	67	14.60	51,775	50,660	740,757
2029	68	13.60	51,853	54,467	738,143
2030	69	12.60	51,670	58,583	731,230
2031	70	11.60	51,186	63,037	719,379
2032	71	10.60	50,357	67,866	701,870
2033	72	9.60	49,131	73,111	677,890
2034	73	8.60	47,452	78,824	646,518
2035	74	7.60	45,256	85,068	606,706
2036	75	6.60	42,469	91,925	557,250
2037	76	5.60	39,008	99,509	496,749
2038	77	4.60	34,772	107,989	423,532
2039	78	3.60	29,647	117,648	335,531
2040	79	2.60	23,487	129,050	229,968
2041	80	1.60	16,098	143,730	102,336
2042	81	0.60	7,164	109,500	0.00

Table 39.4c   **Multigenerational Analysis Summary**

Client Name	John Doe		
Client Birth Date	01/01/1930		
Distributions Through Age	83		
Spouse Name	Mary Doe		
Spouse Birth Date	01/02/1930		
Distributions Through Age	87		
Children			
Adam	Birth Date 01/01/1959		Share 50%
Eve	Birth Date 01/01/1961		Share 50%
Total Joint Lifetime Income Distributions	$1,217,622		
Total Distributions to Surviving Spouse	$371,091		
Total Distributions to Participant and Spouse	$1,588,713		
Total Distributions to Children			
	Adam	$1,680,138	
	Eve	$1,680,138	
Total Distributions to Family	$4,948,989		

Upon the death of the surviving spouse, the entire remaining balance of the plan will become available to the children, rather than just a fractional share. By naming children as new DBs, the surviving spouse has extended the payment period during the spouse's lifetime and thereafter, and the balance in the account will exceed what it would have been had the account been lodged in a QTIP. This can only occur if the surviving spouse owns the entire TIAA-CREF accumulation or other retirement account. For that reason, the entire account will become part of the survivor's estate.

As an inevitable consequence, the survivor's estate will be larger than it would have been under conventional estate planning. More estate tax will be owing as a result. However, if one can preserve the plan through the taxation process, the overall return to the family will exceed that achieved under conventional planning. All of the plan survived, and longer life expectancies have succeeded to the surviving spouse's. Hence one arrives at the paradoxical result that one pays more tax, but the family receives more money. We have tried to make this more concrete in Table 39.4a–c to show the differences in outcomes.

Even with all of that in mind, if there are no other assets to pay the federal estate tax and the other techniques for reducing the size of one's estate and paying the federal estate tax are either not feasible or seem prohibitively expensive, you can hedge your bets. As we mentioned before, name the spouse as the DB. Provide in both the designation of beneficiary forms filed with TIAA-CREF that if your surviving spouse disclaims all or a part of the account, it will pass into a credit shelter trust. Obviously, you need to create such a trust, the usual form being a revocable living trust separate from the will. Under the Code, a beneficiary can disclaim all or part of an inheritance within nine months after the event that gave rise to the property's passing into the disclaimant's name, and the consequent transfer will not be treated as a taxable gift. Most states have statutes that lay out the formalities that must be observed if the disclaimer will be treated as valid for state and therefore for federal estate tax purposes. This needs to be done through a professional, and you should not try to do this at home.

Even for those who intend to maximize the overall return to the family, this approach merits consideration because circumstances may change in unforeseen ways and the chance to revisit decisions made years before may produce a better result.

One must look, therefore, at other techniques for reducing the size of the taxable estates and saving estate taxes. The conventional wisdom will not produce the optimal economic result. If one knew, of course, which spouse was going to die first, one would load that spouse up with ownership of all of the assets other than the retirement account. In this way, one would utilize the estate tax exemption to the full extent permitted by the mix of assets. For better or for worse, human beings do not possess that foresight, and the Code and the Internal Revenue Service have disincentives to your making deathbed gifts when the identity of the survivor is obvious to even the meanest intelligence.

Again, to maximize the family's return from the TIAA-CREF account, one must accept the increase in the survivor's estate and the accompanying taxes. One must look for other methods to reduce taxes and to pay them, preferably at a discount.

Having eschewed the yellow brick road in terms of the division of the estate between the marital share and the credit shelter trust, we need to look elsewhere to find techniques to reduce the size of your taxable estate. Again, this involves a profound mental and psychological switch. Up until now, you probably never thought that your net worth amounted to a hill of beans or that your estate planning would prove as challenging as it is turning out to be. But you have, through your own efforts, managed to accumulate wealth, and that means your estate planning can no longer stick to plain vanilla. Your estate planning needs more flavors, and you need to use more than the credit shelter trust and the estate tax exemption to minimize taxes. If you can make the transition from a person trying to make ends meet and having something left over for a reasonable level of comfort to someone who really owns something and needs to plan accordingly, you will readily appreciate that the dilemmas that you face compare favorably to the alternative of not having enough. For most of your life, you probably expected that the alternative would prove your lot, and now you must make the difficult adjustments to having more than you had expected.

As you can imagine, there exists a substantial literature on how to go about reducing the size of your taxable estate. Some techniques are not well settled, if not downright controversial, and others pertain to truly large estates within very wealthy families. The discussion that follows assumes two parameters: (1) the steps recommended are legal (in fact they appear in the Code); and (2) they will not adversely affect your financial security. To repeat, the latter factor should always assume primacy. Estate taxes are, after all, someone else's problem. Providing for your needs for the rest of your life is yours. Estate taxes represent the tail, your financial and living needs the dog, and one does not allow the tail to wag the dog, at least not in a rational universe or estate plan.

The other axiom we follow is that you are not interested in leaving a legacy of litigation entitled *Estate of [insert your name]* v. *Commissioner*. From experience, we know that such litigation is expensive and time-consuming. From your heirs' point of view, this bequest equates to your leaving them a poison pill, and we want optimal results.

Outsized costs of estate administration takes part of your estate out of your heirs' hands and into the hands of lawyers, witnesses, and the Internal Revenue Service. We do not regard that as acceptable, and we will stick to well-accepted methods of reducing the taxable estate.

In a nutshell, you can best reduce the size of your taxable estate by making gifts. We will look at a gamut of gift techniques, from the most prosaic to the more cost-effective, bearing our two tenets above in mind.

Starting with the outright gift, you need to examine your financial situation to see how much you can afford to give away without infringing on your economic security. If you are satisfied that you have the means to make annual gifts to children and other family members of $10,000 each ($20,000 if both spouses consent), then that hoary and simple technique deserves the fullest use you can make of that statutory safe harbor.

The next technique may involve unwinding some of your holdings. You should not own property as joint tenants with right of survivorship or as tenants by the entireties. The names vary depending on the state, but the concept remains the same. Joint ownership of this kind represents a trap for the unwary. Once one of the spouses dies, the survivor inherits the entire property. The asset passes outside of the will, simply because that is the nature of the ownership. In effect, you have a contract between spouses. This creates two major problems. It prevents the use of the property to fund the $675,000 and growing estate tax exemption, and it swells the size of the survivor's estate. The latter being the problem that we are trying to overcome, joint tenancies work the exact opposite of what we want to accomplish from a tax point of view.

If you own most, if not all, of your assets, other than retirement accounts, in joint name, you have company. Lots of it. Many couples own virtually all of their assets in joint name, a throwback to the days when having two nickels to rub together seemed unlikely. Joint ownership seemed easiest, it reflected economic reality, and it had no discernible tax consequences. That bit of youthful innocence needs to be unwound. For real estate, that means a quitclaim deed from one spouse to another and, in some cases, use of the technique described below.

Dividing bank accounts or holdings of securities involves considerably less effort. It means creating two accounts where one had existed and moving the money on paper. On a lighter note, if you are splitting an investment account, we recommend one of two methods: the meat cleaver and the sporting. The first approach divides each holding in half and involves very little time, thought, or effort. This may cause you to place your securities in street name with a reputable brokerage firm, a major convenience and no longer a risk with SIPC insurance of $500,000 per customer, in addition to which most reputable brokerage firms add their own insurance for in excess of $10 million per account. The larger firms provide even higher limits. The sporting technique allows for a couple to pick who gets which block of stock or mutual fund shares and allows you to find out, over time, which of the two of you is a savvier or luckier investor. Chivalry dictates that the wife gets first pick, the husband second, and so on. Whichever method suits your fancy, get your assets into individual names. The only general exception to that rule relates to out-of-state real estate, where jointly owned property avoids ancillary administration, or in colloquial terms, probate proceedings in the other state. One other limited exception will arise to that rule later on, but the general axiom applies.

Most of the other gift techniques involve our constant companion, the time value of money. For many TIAA-CREF participants, the home usually represents the second largest asset. Not knowing which spouse is going to die first, picking the right spouse to own the residence involves a crap shoot. A better alternative removes the house (and a second principal residence, as opposed to an investment property) from both estates. It does so without affecting your lifestyle, subject to one caveat.

The technique leaps, metaphorically speaking, out of the Code and is called the "qualified personal residence trust." Lawyers need acronyms for everything, and this one is the "QPRT," pronounced phonetically despite the absence of vowels. The QPRT works as follows. You give your house to your children, not today but some number of years down the road. For the sake of argument, let's say that the transfer will occur fifteen years from now.

The Internal Revenue Service allows you to discount that gift by a monthly rate that fluctuates with market interest rates. The gift is treated as the remainder interest after fifteen years have passed. If the discount rate is 8.0% (as it is in February 2000), the value of the gift will equal about 27% of the current fair market value of the house.

Right off the bat, using the time value of money, your gift has received a 73% discount. Unless you have made significant gifts in the past, this gift will reduce your estate and gift tax exemption, but it will not cause you to have to pay any federal gift tax.

If the house appreciates by 4% annually, then fifteen years from now, it will be worth roughly twice its current fair market value. You will have used some of your gift/estate credit, but each dollar you used took about $8 out of your estate, as compared to holding on the house. The $8 estimate assumes you die one day after the QPRT ends. More likely, you will live longer, the house will continue to appreciate and the estate tax savings will also grow. By comparison, and this is why time value of money concepts are so powerful, holding on to that credit until you die will only shelter $1 of assets for each $1 of exemption you have preserved. You have begun to leverage that exemption, and that seems a lot more exciting and is a lot more effective than a dollar-for-dollar approach. In terms of estate tax savings, recognizing that a number of factors can affect this outcome, you will save about $3.50 of tax for each $1 of exemption used. This assumes that your estate is in the 50% bracket, applicable to estates over $2 million, and as noted above, you die the day after the QPRT ends. Had you held on to the exemption, each $1 of exemption would have saved $.50 of tax.

With the QPRT, if you sell the house and buy a replacement house, the trust rolls over to the new house. If you do not use all of the proceeds of sale in your repurchase, or you do not buy a new house, then you will receive an annuity for the balance of the trust term from the excess cash. You want the annuity to be as low a percentage as possible so that any appreciation will inure to your children and pass to them free of estate and gift tax. The same transfer of the appreciation will occur if you remain in the house. True, your children will take over your original cost basis for the house when they sell it, but a 20% capital gains tax seems more appealing than an estate tax that, as of 2006, will start at 41% and rise to 55%.

Okay, the fifteen years have passed and the children now own the house. You have protected yourself in the trust by allowing yourself to remain in the house as long as you like by paying a fair market value rental. Your children or a trustee for the children cannot evict you from your own house. This will allow you to reduce your estate by paying your children rent. That will represent taxable income to them, but you will have a means of shoving liquidity out to them and out of your estates.

What's the rub? Three things, none of which should be treated lightly. First, you need liquid assets or, at the least, other assets with which to pay the rent. We wrote elsewhere that it is not considered effective estate planning to save estate taxes if the client ends up as a homeless person. If that occurs, your estate planner has looked through the wrong end of the telescope.

Second, the grantor or creator of the trust must survive the term of the trust. If not, the structure collapses, and you end up where you started with the house back in your estate. Thus, on the one hand, the longer the term of the trust, the greater the economic benefits will prove. On the other hand, one cannot ignore actuarial realities, and it is desirable that the trust work as intended. If you are around 65 to 70 years of age or older, to hedge our bets, we occasionally recommend putting the house in joint name. In this way if either you or your spouse lives out the term, the trust will have fulfilled part of its purpose, subject to the considerations contained in the next paragraph. Once again, you are using a joint life expectancy instead of a single life. This situation represents the one of three exceptions to the joint property rule. (The other is the household checking account, but this typically does not amount to a sizable sum, and out-of-state real estate, mentioned earlier, to avoid probate.)

In designing a QPRT, one can of course use a single grantor who may be younger or healthier. If you use the joint QPRT, then you have two choices that will depend on your financial circumstances.

The first option is to provide that if either of you dies during the retained term, the decedent's interest reverts to his or her estate, and a disposition can be made that satisfies the marital deduction rules. In this way, the early death will not produce any tax, if that is an issue. However, half of the house will become part of the survivor's estate, more likely than not, and you will at least have postponed the day of reckoning. The decedent's will could give the survivor the half outright, and the survivor may be able to try a second QPRT on the lapsed half. In any event, half of the house passed via a QPRT, and a half a loaf....

The other alternative is to permit the survivor to live in the house for the balance of the term. This is not a disposition that meets the marital deduction tests, and it can only be sheltered from tax by the estate tax exemption. If no other assets appear on the horizon to fund the exemption, then this may become preferable, and the entire house will pass to the donees, typically children or a trust for their benefit. In this case, the QPRT has worked with regard to the whole house, again assuming that the survivor can meet the rental obligation. This is a matter of individual choice and circumstances.

The third consideration came to light in connection with QPRTs of houses in Greenwich and Darien, Connecticut, and in Southampton, New York. If you live in an area where house rentals have soared, then you do not want to risk the possibility that you may not be able to live in your own home because its value has outstripped your ability to occupy it as a tenant. If you are still young (say in your fifties) when you first contemplate a QPRT, time will probably remain for a second look in a few years when you may have more assets and a better chance of being able to afford your own home.

From an income tax point of view, the trust does not have an independent existence. Thus, you will still pay the property taxes and deduct them on your Form 1040. A deed will have to be recorded to transfer the property into the trust, and the trustees will receive the tax bills if you do not have a mortgage or taxes are not added to the escrow created under the mortgage. Tell the trustees what to expect. Instruct them to forward the tax bills to you for payment lest they have heart failure upon receipt. This suggestion reflects some actual experience, where children-trustees received a tax bill and called in a panic. You do not want to shorten their actual or actuarial life expectancies.

If there is a mortgage on the property, check with the mortgagee bank or whoever currently holds the mortgage to make sure that the transfer does not accelerate the mortgage and the underlying note. You may find that a bank will not want to have the QPRT created at the outset if you are buying a new house. The bank may not consent because your mortgage will be pooled with other mortgages and sold in the secondary market to institutional investors. They set standards for pooled mortgages, and they are not looking for deviations from the norm or complexity.

The existence of a mortgage does pose a theoretical problem. One school of thought holds that the gift at the time that the QPRT is created consists only of your equity in the house and that each payment of principal on the mortgage becomes, then, a separate and later gift.

In effect, you are adding to the equity, and that should be regarded as a separate addition. Administratively, this poses a pain in the neck. It means filing a gift tax return for each year of the QPRT's existence. Also, each of the later gifts will carry a smaller discount, because the end of the trust is so much closer, and the economic benefit will decrease.

The second school of thought holds that you can avoid this issue because you and/or your spouse will agree to indemnify the trustees against the mortgage liability. You can then claim the fair market value of the house as the basis for computing the gift from the outset. Adding this indemnification represents the accepted wisdom in estate planning circles, but it seems like belt and suspenders to agree to pay a liability for which you are already liable and evidenced by a mortgage, subject to which the trust takes title. Oh, well. We advise clients to take the second approach and file a gift tax return accordingly. The Internal Revenue Service has three years to object, and this has not occurred in our experience. From the Internal Revenue Service's point of view, the game hardly seems worth the candle.

Under either theory, you will still pay and deduct the mortgage interest for income tax purposes. And you will still pay and deduct the property taxes, either directly or through a mortgage escrow.

We have used this technique a great deal, and it merits serious consideration. It allows for the time value of money to work for you in three ways: the gift is discounted, the appreciation passes to children free of gift or estate tax, and the rent you pay will reflect the appreciation and move more assets out of your estates.

As is true with all of these time value of money techniques, the younger you are when you use them, the better the result you can achieve because you will have more time with which to work. Assuming that the QPRT based on a fifteen-year trust in the example above could instead run safely for twenty-five years, the gift would equal 9.5% of the house's fair market value, the house would have appreciated to almost triple its value (assuming the same 4% annual increase), and the estate taxes saved would equal $13 for each dollar of exemption used. With younger grantors of the QPRT, one can risk the longer term, the actuarial risks having shifted in your favor.

Other techniques exist for reducing the size of your estates, and the most successful are rooted in the time value of money. They involve splitting assets, like the house in the QPRT, retaining an income interest, with the remainder to your children. You are not giving away the whole asset, and you should not imperil your financial security. Realistically, your ability to take advantage of these techniques, all of them described in the Code and lovingly expanded in the Internal Revenue Service Regulations, will depend on your economic circumstances. The more you can afford to give away without affecting your financial well-being, the better, and better still if you make gifts early rather than later. Some of these options typically interest what financial institutions refer to as "the high net worth individual." They merit exploring if you have liquid or income-producing assets, want to keep the income, and kick the assets out to your kids at a reduced gift tax cost. Again, each dollar of credit or exemption used will move a multiple out of your estate, and that makes more sense than hanging on to the exemption until your executor has to file the federal estate tax return.

Whatever your economic situation, be aware that a substantial number of charlatans abound with various schemes that promise to reduce your taxes to zero. Given the stakes involved and the general antipathy to paying taxes of any kind, some of the advice out on the street will not merely get you in financial trouble, but quite possibly in the slammer. You can still rely on your common sense, and if any proposition sounds too good to be true, then it is. You are legally entitled to reduce or avoid taxes; you risk criminal penalties if you evade them.

For example, the latest casualty in the continuing guerilla warfare between the Internal Revenue Service and taxpayers suffering apparently from the tax equivalent of road rage focuses on charitable gifts to buy life insurance on the donor's life. Having had one of these schemes outlined to us in all seriousness, it clearly did not pass the smell test, or for that matter, any other test. About two months later, the Internal Revenue Service pulled the plug. Curiously, the guy who was promoting the charitable life insurance wheeze has resurfaced with some new surefire way to beat the system. We keep tabs on him to remain informed of what the lunatic fringe or those on the bleeding edge of the law are concocting on a current basis. His visit (usually preceded by a series of annoying phone calls from his executive assistant) promises to be an intellectual treat, a chance to show why the new perpetual motion machine will not work either.

No rational person, in our opinion, would choose this approach. Nor will anyone with half a brain opt for the constitutional trust or its variants, all of which claim to get all of your income and assets out of the federal tax system. The nuttiest arguments against paying income taxes claim that the Sixteenth Amendment to the Constitution, which made the income tax permissible, is itself unconstitutional.

Finally, it has become quite expensive to be wrong in making one's tax decisions. Interest and multitiered penalties, along with legal fees, will have you walking the floor at night. Whatever else you do in this area, do not sin in haste and repent at leisure. Use reputable professionals and stay within the white area of the law. Your reward will not occur in heaven, but in sparing yourself a living hell and in sparing your beneficiaries a hell of a mess. No legal work has proven to be less rewarding from any point of view than trying to extricate new clients from these catastrophes at the lowest cost. At that point, they have become lose, lose propositions. The sight of a grown man, woman, or couple banging their individual or collective heads against the wall probably remains one of the least edifying aspects of tax practice.

How Should Your Estate Plan Deal With the Estate Tax?

Assuming that you want to preserve retirement plans for your family, how do you pay the resultant estate tax? As we have seen, using the plan itself to pay the tax literally compounds the problem by creating two taxes where only one had existed beforehand. You will need $2 of retirement plan assets to pay $1 of estate taxes. As much as 80% of your plan can disappear up the flue.

If one rules out tapping into the retirement accumulation, only two options remain. The first involves selling or liquidating other assets to pay the freight. In most instances, this proves to be impossible because the assets do not exist in the requisite amount. Or the assets may lack the necessary liquidity. A federal estate tax return is due nine months after the date of death, and relying on real estate, unless your property can be mortgaged and your executor is prepared to take the risks that a mortgage may entail, may prove impractical, depending on interest rates and all of the other factors that affect the real estate market generally and your real estate specifically. In addition, your estate will need the liquidity to service the mortgage until the property can be sold.

You may also find the idea of having your other assets liquidated abhorrent. True, it will occur in a good cause, but if you saved and built a terrific stock portfolio, a lovely home, a vacation retreat that you wanted to keep in the family, and so forth, the thought of jettisoning these items or selling those assets under duress to satisfy the Internal Revenue Service could reasonably appear repulsive. You may have some friends who bought a house or something else really cheaply from an estate; if so, you may well remember their delight at acquiring whatever asset they bought at such a bargain price. Somewhere, down the road, the shoe will be on the other foot, and your executors may find themselves between the same rock and a hard place that resulted in the forced sales from which your friends profited.

Having to liquidate a beautifully crafted stock and bond portfolio, based on personal experience with clients' estates, usually proves agonizing to the family, although you may think that you could live with this problem (no pun intended) if such a portfolio could somehow magically appear on your balance sheet. Put differently, the thought that assets that you built up, on which one tax has already been levied and on which the government now has the effrontery to levy a second, must be liquidated to pay the Internal Revenue Service can seem like pouring salt into the wound or adding insult to injury.

However, if the assets are there, you should plan to minimize the tax and then reconcile yourself to the inevitability of death and taxes. Variants on the qualified personal residence trust exist to reduce the bill. Something will be saved from the wreckage, and in all likelihood, you will leave your children and the other objects of your bounty more than anyone saw fit to give to you. But we do not mean to minimize the pain of having to sell assets to pay the tax or the problems that are created when those assets do not exist in the first place. One way or the other, the taxes need to be paid. Despite the efforts to create or picture a kinder, gentler Internal Revenue Service, it makes for a dreadful creditor that is protected under a variety of federal statutes, including the Bankruptcy Code.

There is an alternative, and in all likelihood, it comes as a stranger to most of our readers. For all of the reasons articulated movingly above, you should at least consider the purchase of second-to-die life insurance as an alternative.

At the outset, we should state that we do not have any financial interest in any insurance agency or company except possibly through a minute holding of some New York Stock Exchange stock that, unknown to either of us, has a life insurance subsidiary that, also unknown to us, offers second-to-die life insurance. Neither of us recommends insurance as an investment vehicle. It obviously has a role to play if you are concerned about dying young and replacing your income stream. This is the stuff of advertisements, and it can provide considerable financial protection if the unlikely early death does occur.

We also recognize that, for many of you, the only form of life insurance you may have encountered is the group term policy available through your employer. TIAA-CREF also offers life insurance, which, given the nature of its underlying business, seems appropriate, and you may have purchased some term policies through TIAA-CREF. But based upon our experiences working with clients, many have never bought life insurance of any sort and find the notion foreign and in some cases unappealing. We all receive unsolicited invitations to buy insurance in the mail, television advertisements run the gamut from sentimentality to hucksterism of the worst sort, and the whole process seems morbid and sordid.

Whatever your feelings about life insurance in general and however limited your experience may be, you need to sit back and think through the issues as objectively as possible. You are looking at a decision that could affect the well-being of those you love and possibly unborn descendants.

We need to explain what this insurance product is and why it bears close scrutiny. Second-to-die life insurance policies are offered by only a few life insurance companies, and one can quickly find the pick of the litter. By the time this book appears, TIAA-CREF itself may offer second-to-die life insurance because of its integral role in estate planning for TIAA-CREF accumulations.

Putting to one side your preconceived notions about insurance and insurance salesmen, we are talking about a profoundly different product than the garden variety protection of the family policies that make up the great bulk of policies sold. Second-to-die life insurance is designed with the federal estate tax in mind. Second-to-die life insurance remains an ideal product for the limited purpose of paying transfer taxes and getting assets down to the next generation at minimal cost.

We need to begin with a definition. A second-to-die life insurance policy is a single policy typically taken out on the lives of husband and wife. The insurer pays the proceeds upon the death of the surviving spouse. That, as we have seen, happens to be the point at which the federal estate tax needs to be paid. The insurance proceeds become available when they are most needed.

In its purest form, a second-to-die policy represents insurance being used for an unusual purpose—to pay a liability to shelter other assets from taxation.

For younger participants, it may make more sense to buy two policies, one of conventional insurance on the life of the principal breadwinner and the other second-to-die life insurance. In lieu of conventional life insurance upon the death of the principal breadwinner, one can buy first-to-die term insurance. One tends to focus on income as the principal flow of cash that needs to replacement. Assuming that the other spouse stays at home, the cost of providing professional child care, homemaking services, and so forth amounts to a fair chunk of expense, and one should insure against those hitherto overlooked items of expense. A nonworking spouse has enormous economic benefit, and one ignores that at one's peril. The second policy would come into play upon the death of the surviving spouse.

From what was left from the first payment, the income from which has been paying necessary family expenses over the years, and the second payment, the family could pay or at least make a substantial dent in the federal estate tax. In any event, the first policy, if suitably large and the proceeds well managed, will do double duty, and for younger participants, this may prove the most economical and sensible alternative, especially if one starts early and young children are part of the overall picture.

Second-to-die life insurance policies have a number of advantages. First, because two lives are being insured, the premium will almost invariably prove lower than it would be on an individual's life. Second, in almost every case, you will find a policy even if one of the insureds is uninsurable. It may not come cheaply, but it should be available. Third, as is always the case, you need to take the time value of money into account. The second-to-die life insurance policy exemplifies this brand of estate planning.

The time value of money enters into the picture in a number of ways. First, as Table 41.1 shows, the earlier that you begin to pay for this insurance, the cheaper it becomes. Each of the premiums quoted assumes that they will only be paid for ten years, and then the policy becomes fully paid, no further premiums being necessary. These figures assume that the anticipated returns to the insurance company will not change drastically, and therefore the policy will be fully paid after ten years have passed. The couple in their forties will pay as much over the ten-year period required to make this policy fully paid as the couple in their seventies will pay in the first year.

Table 41.1 **Estimated Costs of Second-to-Die Insurance**
($1,000,000 Insurance)

Ages of Both Spouses	10 Payments ($)	15 Payments ($)	20 Payments ($)
40	4,016	3,141	2,743
45	5,761	4,503	3,932
50	8,288	6,483	5,663
55	11,820	9,242	8,070
60	16,717	13,077	11,428
65	23,331	18,260	16,034
70	31,772	24,967	22,186
75	41,857	33,294	33,302

Source: Northwestern Mutual Life, Select Issue, Current Northwestern Mutual Life Dividend Scale, as of December 1999.

Minimum amount of whole life/maximum term insurance. The number of payments is dependent upon dividend performance and may increase or decrease.

Second, you want to gain as much leverage as you can. You want to pay as little for the policy as possible, and you want the multiplier effect of your premiums to be as high as possible. The couple in their forties who pays $41,000 for a $1 million policy will know that their children will benefit as the investment rises twenty-five times; the couple in their seventies will see theirs rise 2.5 times. Obviously, this comes about because the life insurance company gets the use of the money for a considerably longer time with younger policyholders.

Third, what you have done is prepaid your federal estate tax and, using the example above of the couple in their forties, you will have paid four cents on the dollar. Even the much older couple will pay forty cents on the dollar. The value of the policy is building tax-free for the day when it is needed. The Internal Revenue Code contains provisions as favorable to insurance companies as they are to any other industry, the most important being the tax-free buildup of value in the policy to the policyholders and to the insurance company. In effect, the same compounding, free of income taxes, occurs within the life insurance policy as occurred in your TIAA-CREF account or other retirement assets.

If you purchase a second-to-die life insurance policy early, you will have found someone else to pay the tax and, from your point of view, to pay it at a discount.

One can, however, exaggerate the investment desirability of second-to-die life insurance. One of our clients asked whether the full amount of the policy would be paid if she and her husband died after making just one premium payment. Yes, we said, that is how life insurance works. "Wow," she exclaimed, "what a fantastic rate of return!" Cheered momentarily by her ability to see the silver lining inside of what appeared to us to be the blackest thundercloud, one of us rejoined, "Wow, what a calamity! But if you want to focus on the bright side of this disaster, more power to you." On balance, we believe that most individuals will prefer to survive to the day when the policy becomes fully paid and then some and settle for a somewhat less spectacular rate of return rather than die young, smiling, if possible, at the thought of how brilliant one's estate planning had proven to be.

On the other side of the coin, we worked with a couple whose distaste for life insurance may prove tragic. The husband was 70 and had Type II diabetes, and his wife was 66. The annual premium for a ten-payment $1 million policy amounted to $27,000. We will never know what they found so distasteful, but the articulated rationale was the thought that they would be long lived and the insurance company would therefore earn a profit on the transaction.

They proposed instead to create their own fund and contribute $20,000 annually to pay the eventual transfer taxes. We ran a spreadsheet that showed that they would have to earn 9% after taxes on their money, year after year, and that funding the trust would take twenty-three years. The total cost would amount to $460,000, approximately 80% more than using the insurance company. Unfortunately, they did not buy the concept. In the interim, the husband suffered a severe heart attack, and their financial situation is now clouded for a number of reasons. The moral of the story is that it is hard to beat a tax-free investor, as you learned from the growth of your TIAA-CREF accumulation, and how hard it is to beat a company that specializes in a particular line of business.

We recommend to clients that they pick a policy that is projected to be fully paid up after ten or at most fifteen years. No matter which company writes the insurance, they will have to make projections as to the investment returns it will earn over the payment period. The stronger the insurance company, the less likely it will be that you will have to pay additional premiums if earnings do not pan out as planned. You do not want to pay life insurance premiums for the rest of your lives, and you will soon find better uses for the money. If you can't, there should prove to be plenty of individuals around you who will. If you still can't, then, to borrow a line from *Car Talk*, write your dilemma on the back of a twenty-dollar bill, send it to us in care of our publisher, and your authors will help solve this vexing and unusual problem. More seriously, ending the phase of premium payments frees up your funds for other payments.

On the downside, putting affordability off to one side for the moment, if you wait to take out a second-to-die life insurance policy until you are in your sixties, some of the payments will occur after you have retired. Depending on a number of factors, but mainly your retirement income, this may necessitate the postponement of travel or other activities best taken advantage of while you are still relatively young and healthy. Unquestionably, this poses a dilemma, and again, your choice will depend on your value system, the number of payments that will extend into your retirement, and the state of your health and finances. The answer is not obvious, but those represent the factors that you will have to keep in mind in making your choices. Very few TIAA-CREF participants to date have realized the need for a second-to-die life insurance before they reach retirement or, only a few years before that they have to consider the directions into which they want their income to flow.

On the other hand, if you plan ahead and foresee the issues and opportunities that a large retirement account creates, you can solve the problem of the federal estate tax relatively cheaply. In addition, you will be applying for and obtaining insurance while you are both probably healthy, and this will reduce the size of the premium. In too many cases, we have had clients apply for second-to-die life insurance in their late sixties, get hung up in their decision making, during which time one of the pair suffers a deterioration of health. But, in most instances, the foremost concern remains finding a way to pay for the second-to-die life insurance policy, and we turn to that in the next chapter.

The issue of affordability, especially after one's income declines after retirement, constantly arises. It probably represents the largest barrier to purchasing second-to-die life insurance that we have encountered. For starters, the premiums represent an unanticipated and unwanted expense, in much the same way that the estate tax problems inherent in having an estate consisting primarily of retirement assets come as a shock and a surprise.

We turn now to the issue of paying for the policy. We assume that the case has been made for obtaining the policy. On the other side of the coin, you need to be able to afford the policy, however nifty the long-term goals that it serves. To some extent, this boils down to a value choice and a decision as to how your savings can most effectively be used. Often we counsel clients who are going to be paying premiums during their retirement years. If the accumulation is large enough, we advise clients to take the necessary funds out of their TIAA-CREF accounts under the Minimum Distribution Option's upward flexibility.

Alternatively, if the premiums are going to be paid after age 55 but before retirement, we recommend use of the Interest Payment Retirement Option or Systematic Withdrawals from one's TIAA accumulation or CREF accumulation, as the case may be. Under either scenario, you are tapping into your TIAA-CREF account for the ultimate benefit of your children. However, this assumes that the employer's plan allows this use of those TIAA-CREF options for these purposes and in these circumstances. Some plans may not. If they are available, then of the two, the IPRO seems more appropriate. The TIAA's growth potential is lower than CREF's, and the loss of a dollar early will cause less of a negative compounding effect over the years. Again, make sure that you have quantified the impact of drawing down your accumulation on the current generation. Your needs represent necessities; the goals of estate planning only represent targets.

Whatever option you choose to fund the policy, you have to understand that, sure, it may decrease what the kids will get years down the road, but without the policy, the haircut would ultimately be far more severe. It might qualify as a scalping. Recognizing that fact, the children of a few of our clients pay the premiums or a portion themselves.

Nowhere is it written that you must pay all of the bills, especially in those instances where the children have not pursued an academic career and are better able to afford the outlay. Sharing the burden will not have an adverse estate tax consequence. Universally, we have found that when a parent or parents explain what is going on, the children are appreciative and, on occasion, financially helpful when they can be.

Paying the premiums may require some ingenuity and some sacrifice, but the second-to-die life insurance policy remains for most people the only option to pay the federal estate tax and not have their accounts decimated by the combined federal income and estate taxes.

The other piece of advice is to try to start early. None of us can predict the future, but by the time you are in your fifties, you can begin to make projections as to where your TIAA-CREF account is going. Assume a reasonable rate of return, recognize that the double-digit returns we have seen in the stock market over the last few years do not represent the norm, and then make your best estimate of your compensation, contributions, and the level of contributions by your employer. If you get started early and find that you have undershot, it will prove far cheaper to increase a policy's amount when you are ten or twenty years older than it would have been had you started at the higher figure later. If you do start young, you should look at the blend of first-to-die and second-to-die life insurance that we mentioned above.

All of that said, this aspect of the estate planning proves to be the most troublesome. It obviously means a present cost is incurred to create a future benefit that you will not live to see. Typically, you have to come up with the money, and oftentimes that is not easy. The realization of the size of the account and its potential may not occur until late in your career, and that means that the policies, which have to be paid for with after-tax dollars, may prove a strain.

In terms of your children's and your own thinking, you should recognize that second-to-die life insurance has two paradoxical aspects, both of which benefit the children and should serve as further inducements to contribute to the cost.

We tend to think of insurance as protection against someone's dying young and preserving income or assets. Second-to-die life insurance has the opposite effect. It protects your heirs against your or your spouse's having an extended life span that runs down the balance in the retirement account. If that occurs, your heirs will clearly need less of the insurance to pay taxes, and the balance will be distributed to them, free of estate tax as we will shortly discuss. They may not be able to invest as advantageously through tax-free growth as they would have if the plan had remained larger, but the insurance proceeds will help them cope with the disappointment.

It serves the same function if you or your spouse decide to spend down more of the plan than originally planned. After all, whose money is it? Again, the taxes will decrease, and the second-to-die life insurance policy will provide an alternative source of wealth to replace the one you and/or your spouse cheerfully and rightfully enjoyed during your lifetimes.

The paradox is that the second-to-die life insurance protects against someone's dying too old, the opposite of the premise on which 95% or more of life insurance is sold. It partially compensates your children for the fact that the runout of the account will not prove as large as the model had suggested. It also gives you more freedom to enjoy your retirement, having provided a backstop to your TIAA-CREF account for the benefit of your children.

The second paradoxical aspect is that it protects the children against the wrong parent dying first. The discussion several chapters back spoke about the different results that follow if the participant survives or if the nonparticipant spouse survives. If the former, then the balance in the account must be paid over the "as rapidly as" method, which may produce a lump sum payment or a continuation of the payment stream over the comparatively few years of remaining life expectancy. The payments under this alternative pale next to the potential if the spouse survives, names the children as Designated Beneficiaries, and so forth.

Second-to-die life insurance protects the children by providing them with capital to replace the economic opportunity lost because the spouse did not survive. The full amount of the insurance will not be required to pay the Internal Revenue Service, and the children will inherit the proceeds of the policy instead.

Dealing with life insurance for many will, we know, prove a new experience. Your employer probably provides you with a term insurance that is related by some complex algorithm to your compensation. You probably relied on that to serve your purposes and have never had to shop for additional insurance. Ask for recommendations, do some shopping and some research, and you will probably find an excellent carrier with competitive rates. Parenthetically, you may find, as we suspect is often the case, that your employer's term policy falls short of your true needs, and the mix of types of policies will make sense even if you are at the apex of your career. Remember that the proceeds from your employer's plan will need to be invested, and even $1 million is no longer what it used to be.

You also need to consider the type of policy that you buy. Generally speaking, the least expensive policy will pass the risks on to you. Not everyone agrees with the following bit of advice, but we believe in it firmly. By way of further disclaimer, neither of us is an insurance expert. Nevertheless, if you hadn't noticed, we do hold opinions, and this being our book, we feel free to express them. In our view, the second-to-die life insurance policy has to work on a hell-or-high-water basis. It forms the linchpin of the estate plan. Consequently, we do not recommend that our clients use a variable or universal life policy, where the length of time over which premiums are paid and the amount of the death benefit will depend on your or someone else's investment acumen. The premiums will probably appear lower, but they typically presume consistently high returns. Over the last few years, if one picked the right stocks, this type of policy probably represented a home run to its holders, but we think that one ought to take risk in one's investments and not with the economic future of your family. Or put another way, one ought to place only so much faith in the equity markets and in your ability to pick winners when you deal with issues that have ramifications for two and possibly three generations.

The universal policy typically costs the least because the insurer usually makes fewer, if any, guarantees. The whole life policy falls at the other extreme, with a term policy somewhere in between. Unlike either term or universal life, the whole life policy does provide a cash buildup within the policy. The guaranteed rate may not be something to write home about, but the leading companies have far better investment experience and you can reasonably expect that, at worst, you will have to pay premiums for an eleventh year.

Most of our clients buy a blend of term and whole life. As the cash value grows inside the latter, the proportion of term decreases, reaching zero at the end of the payment period. From that time forward, the earnings on the internal growth of cash fund the future premiums. At worst, in our experience, the insurer will exact an extra year's premium to reflect actual investment experience. Universal life does not make any such guarantees, and often the projected rate of return seems unrealistic to us. Again, this remains a issue of opinion, but we think that this is one area in which conservatism plays a valuable role. The cheapest policy does not necessarily represent the best choice. If investment experience falls short of what was projected, then the payments of premiums can continue for an unspecified period.

In this area, as in so many others, buyer beware. If you find that you are confused or undecided, use your lawyer or some other disinterested third party, who will not receive a commission depending on which policy you buy, to guide you through the maze.

Next, you want to make sure that the insurance company is a recipient of the highest ratings from the applicable companies or agencies and that it insures lots of lives. Typically, such a company will offer competitive rates, and you will rest easy knowing that the company will not fold between the time you paid your premiums and the day when the insurance proceeds are needed pronto.

By the time that this book appears, TIAA-CREF may offer second-to-die life insurance. Bear in mind that the new insurance company will probably form a free-standing corporation, it will virtually represent a start-up operation, and its policies may not receive the full faith and credit backing of TIAA-CREF parent. No one can know what the rates will be, but as one would expect from a new company, it will not be insuring a great many lives at the outset. The new TIAA-CREF insurer and its products need to be viewed with the same critical and objective detachment that you want to bring to the table irrespective of who the insurer may be.

43 How Do You Preserve the Insurance Policy from Estate Taxation?

Now, you may be thinking, this all sounds pretty neat, but won't there be an estate tax on the insurance policy that will cut its effectiveness in half? In the previous chapter, we talked about your children inheriting the second-to-die life insurance policy as though the estate tax did not exist.

To paraphrase *Macbeth*, we are not keeping the word of promise to your ear and breaking it to your hope. Under current law, you can structure your estate plan so that the policy is not part of either your taxable estate or the taxable estate of your spouse. This does not involve estate planning arcana, the device having been around since 1968 and been blessed by innumerable Internal Revenue Service rulings. President Clinton proposed eliminating the technique described below in his 1998 budget proposal, although there would have been work-arounds. Upon the proposal's reception on Capitol Hill, Congress proclaimed it dead on arrival, and legislation was never drafted to implement this idea. The idea did not reappear in the president's 1999 budget proposal, although some other controversial ideas (including a repeal of the qualified personal residence trust, which did not survive the 1998 trip down Pennsylvania Avenue), did resurface. For at least as long as the Republicans control Congress, it seems unlikely that change will occur in this area or with regard to the QPRT.

The technique for removing the second-to-die life insurance policy from both estates involves the use of an irrevocable trust. Using a new policy for simplicity's sake, the trustee applies for the insurance, the trustee is the owner and the trust the beneficiary of the policy, and neither you nor your spouse retains any rights in the policy at all. This takes the policy out of both of your estates under Section 2042 of the Code because you have retained none of the "incidents of ownership," to use the Code's surprisingly elegant phrase, over the policy. You cannot borrow against the policy, you cannot change the beneficiary, and you receive none of the cash buildup in the policy, among other typical benefits of owning a life insurance policy.

What about the payments of premiums? Here we have to take a momentary diversion. As you may remember, you can give $10,000 annually to any number of recipients, and each gift will fall under the annual exclusion from gift taxation. If you and your spouse split the gift, you can give $20,000 to a donee without gift tax consequences. Now, the annual exclusion only applies to a *present* interest in property. That means that the recipient can get his mitts on the property currently and use it for whatever purpose.

The payment of a premium on a life insurance policy constitutes a *future* interest. You are paying money today in order for your heirs to get a lot more money years, one hopes, down the road. Thus, giving your children money that is earmarked to pay the life insurance premium would not qualify for the annual exclusion.

Enter a family from northern California in the late 1960s called the Crummeys. Their lawyers devised a clever twist that has earned the Crummeys immortality (at least for the last thirty years) among estate planners and their clients. The parents gave the trustee the money with which to pay the premium on the policy in their irrevocable life insurance trust, after which the trustee turned around and notified each of the beneficiaries of the addition to the trust. Each of the beneficiaries had thirty days to withdraw his or her share of the addition. If anyone failed to exercise the power, the trust provided that it was presumed that the power would not be exercised. At the end of the thirty-day waiting period (or earlier if all of the beneficiaries sent back replies indicating that they would not be exercising their power of withdrawal), the trustee could turn around and pay the premium to the life insurance company.

The withdrawal power achieves the delightful effect of transforming a future interest into a present interest, and the gifts then qualify for the annual exclusion. Thus, the gifts made by the Crummeys qualified for the annual exclusion, and the result was no gift taxation and no reduction in the donors' gift or estate tax exemption. And that is how it is done to this day.

From the time value of money point of view, these gifts pack far more punch than outright transfers. First, it enables the children to fund the payment source for the federal and state estate taxes that will be due upon the death of the surviving parent. Second, it allows the children to inherit the TIAA-CREF or retirement account (or IRA) without having to pay the double whammy of income and estate taxes. As a result, they will receive an income stream of significant size over their lifetimes. In the alternative, they will inherit the policy, largely undiminished by taxes because of the existence of the second-to-die life insurance policy and the Crummey trust.

When one considers the cumulative time effect of money from the tax-free buildup of value in the policy, the estate tax–free transfer for the benefit of children, and the increased payments that the children can receive by extending the payment period and allowing for additional tax-deferred compounding within the retirement plan, the multiplier effect of making these gifts becomes enormous. One would be hard pressed to come up with a more economically beneficial use of the annual exclusion, recognizing that, in all likelihood, the premium divided by the number of children will not soak up the entire annual exclusion.

That presumes a number of children. What if you only have one? One annual exclusion of $10,000 or $20,000 may not cover the premium, depending on the size of the policy and the ages of the insureds. The question of who can be a holder of withdrawal right or power holder remains the subject of ongoing controversy between the Internal Revenue Service and taxpayers. The Internal Revenue Service takes the position that a power holder must have more than a contingent interest in the trust and, therefore, one cannot name holders who will only inherit if some intervening lives end in untimely fashion. Again, we stick to the tried and true. If you need another power holder, then give that person some portion of the proceeds of the insurance policy and sidestep the issue. The amount can be modest, though not piddling, and that will make the holder a direct beneficiary of the trust. Let someone else duke it out with the Internal Revenue Service; you have better uses of your time and money.

So far, so good. But that still leaves one practical estate planning problem to solve. Assuming that we are dealing with the typical two-asset estate, how do we get the money from the trust that is holding the insurance proceeds to the executor of the estate, who is legally charged with paying the estate tax? You cannot provide that the insurance proceeds are available to pay estate taxes. That will result in the policy proceeds being included in the survivor's estate by virtue of their being available to pay the survivor's debts.

Normally, one of these trusts states that the trustee can buy assets from the decedent's estate or lend money to the executor to facilitate the administration of the estate. But in the typical two-asset estate, there is nothing to buy and nothing against which to collateralize a loan.

Here is where one departs again from the yellow brick road of normal estate-plan drafting. Most wills provide that taxes are paid from the residue of the estate. The residue means what's left after bequests have been paid, debts settled, and other obligations (aside from taxes) dealt with. In the situation that we have posited, the normal tax clause will not cut the mustard because the estate couldn't pay the estate tax generated by the retirement account on the best day of its life.

Instead, one provides that the taxes become the obligations of the beneficiaries of the estate in proportion to the benefit they receive from the estate. Terrific, and where do the beneficiaries get the money to meet this monstrous obligation? Well, they are also beneficiaries of the trust, and the trust provides the trustee discretion to distribute funds to satisfy the beneficiaries' legal obligations. If the funds are needed, the trustee makes a distribution to that extent on behalf of the beneficiaries to the executor of the amount of federal and state transfer taxes, and the executor now has the wherewithal to write the necessary checks. That closes the circle, the money now having a legal path to follow from the trust to the executor of the estate.

You may be wondering, with good reason, how one calculates the amount of second-to-die life insurance to purchase. Here judgment and projections come into play. No one can know for certain what the right number will prove to be until the event occurs. We try to project what the TIAA-CREF accumulation will be worth and what the resultant tax bill will be. This obviously involves a lot of assumptions, especially if one is projecting three or four decades into the future. One must presume no changes in tax law or rates, project growth rates for the TIAA-CREF accumulation and other significant assets, subtract payments to be made out of the account under the Minimum Distribution Option, and assign approximate dates of death. Your assumptions may be crystalline, you may use sophisticated software, but the process is largely judgmental. However flawed one may view the creation of this model, it beats inaction, passivity, or guesswork. As long as one does not mistake model for reality, you should come out reasonably close to the target.

Bear in mind that you should be monitoring the size of your TIAA-CREF accumulation and other assets and meeting from time to time with your estate planning advisors. If adjustments need to be made, time will remain to do so, probably up until the Required Beginning Date. You may need to add more insurance if the growth of your account proves a pleasant surprise, but nothing substitutes for vigilance on your part as to what is happening to your assets.

In general, one should err, if one can afford it, on the high side. If one has too little, then the precious plan may become the only source of meaningful liquidity. If one buys too much, the worst that happens is that the children receive the excess free of estate tax, pocketing it themselves instead of having to send it off to the nearest Internal Revenue Service Service Center. Hardly a tragedy.

Well, that is it. These windy chapters have told you how to circumvent the estate tax and preserve your retirement account for your children instead of accumulating for the ultimate benefit of the government. You will need a lawyer and life insurance agent who know what they are doing, but finding them should not prove impossible. You may have to buy them a copy of this book or, better yet, tell them to buy one themselves (tell them it is deductible if they do) if they want to understand the mechanics of beating the system.

We say this mindful of the fact that for many participants, the second-to-die life insurance policy may mark their first foray into life insurance. The premium cost represents the downside, the liability side, of achieving the goal of passing the TIAA-CREF account or similar retirement account down to children or the next generation. You can finance the premium cost, in whole or in part, through either the Interest Payment Retirement Option or Systematic Withdrawals if that is allowed by your employer's plan. Or you can take more with the MDO than you might have planned on in order to preserve the integrity of the plan upon the death of the surviving spouse or upon your death if you are single. Or you can use other income or assets. Again, the earlier you start, the cheaper the plan will be. You might look at a straight ordinary life insurance policy. The premiums are guaranteed and therefore the policies are more expensive. However, because the death benefit keeps growing, you may choose to start with a policy with a smaller face amount than you ultimately want and rely on time and increasing death benefits to lead you to your goal.

However you choose to deal with this matter, you will need to find a funding mechanism other than your plan to pay the federal estate tax or there will be no plan worth sneezing at or passing on to the next generation.

What Effect Does Your or Your Spouse's Not Being an American Citizen Have on Your Estate Plan?

44

Up until this point, we have not differentiated between American citizens and noncitizens and their estate planning. And until 1988, neither did Congress. But for the last twelve years, the treatment of noncitizens for estate tax purposes has changed dramatically. You may find these rules to be, at the very least, discriminatory; in our minds, they border on the punitive.

Surprisingly, given the large number of noncitizens working in university and hospital settings in particular, in our experience information about this difference in treatment has not become popular knowledge. If you or your spouse (or a friend) is not an American citizen, you need to know the rules, obtain the specialized estate planning that your status necessitates, and then consider how these rules affect the planning for your TIAA-CREF and other retirement accounts. In order to underscore the differences, let's start with the rules applicable to Americans and contrast them with those applicable to a couple in which at least one of the spouses—by hypothesis, the survivor— is not an American citizen.

Quickly, the major rules applicable to married individuals who are American citizens run as follows:

1. For both gift and estate tax purposes, they enjoy an unlimited marital deduction. This means that they can transfer assets freely from one to another during their lifetimes without incurring any gift tax, and the federal estate tax will only hit upon the death of the surviving spouse. In effect, no tax occurs until a transfer to another generation takes place.
2. Both of the spouses have a gift and estate tax exclusion that will rise to $1 million in 2006 under current law. They can, if they plan their estates and structure their assets properly, pass at least $2 million to the next generation free of estate tax.
3. A marital transfer at death can take a multitude of forms and still qualify for the marital deduction.

None of these rules applies to the non-American spouse. For the sake of simplicity, let's assume the one spouse with assets is an American and the other, without assets, is not.

First, an American spouse can only transfer $100,000 annually to a noncitizen spouse without adverse gift tax consequences. The American spouse will incur either a decrease in the size of the remaining exclusion or, the exclusion having been exhausted, some gift tax if more is transferred in any year.

Second, again for simplicity's sake, let's assume that the American spouse dies first. To the extent that the exclusion still remains, the estate can fund a credit shelter trust. However, the only way in which property can pass to the noncitizen spouse and qualify for the marital deduction requires that the property be transferred to a Qualified Domestic Trust (a "QDOT"). To simplify, that is defined as a marital trust with at least one American trustee, formed under the laws of one of the states, and whose assets are reachable by the Internal Revenue Service.

This requirement has far-reaching consequences. If the family home is owned in the usual joint tenancy with right of survivorship, the deceased spouse's interest cannot pass directly to the noncitizen spouse and qualify for the marital deduction. Instead, the noncitizen spouse must transfer it to the QDOT. That creates the somewhat awkward title arrangement under which the QDOT trustee owns an undivided one-half interest and the noncitizen spouse owns the other. The same rule applies to all other property held in joint name.

Moreover, for over fifteen years, American married couples have been presumed to own jointly held property fifty-fifty. Formerly, the law required that one establish which spouse contributed how much to the jointly held property, and the property was then allocated to each's estate proportionately to each's contribution. This represented a major pain in the neck, and Congress repealed this requirement in 1976. If one spouse is a noncitizen spouse, then the old rules will apply, and one must track down the relative contributions made by both spouses to determine the percentage of ownership. For houses in particular, this rule can easily become an accounting nightmare, which is why Congress changed the law for Americans. To summarize the obvious, noncitizen spouses should not hold assets as joint tenants with right of survivorship.

Turning to the QDOT, if the noncitizen spouse receives a distribution of principal after the death of the American spouse, then the trustee must withhold and pay to the Internal Revenue Service an estate tax on that distribution. You determine the amount of the estate tax by adding the distribution to the taxable estate of the predeceased spouse. This obviously has two adverse consequences: you are pre-paying the estate tax, possibly decades in advance, and you are effec-tively reducing the amount of principal that the noncitizen spouse will net from the distribution. For an American survivor, the distribution of principal typically has no tax ramifications.

Upon the death of the surviving noncitizen spouse, the value of the QDOT as of the date of death is *added back to the estate of the deceased American spouse*, and the estate tax is computed accordingly. This treatment obviously carries with it substantial disadvantages. First, the QDOT does not receive any shelter from the noncitizen spouse's exclusion. It has become in effect part of the American spouse's estate. Second, one must reopen the estate of the deceased American spouse and add to it the value of the QDOT at its fair market value as of the noncitizen spouse's date of death. If those assets have appreciated, and the prepayment of estate taxes discourages the distributions of principal during the noncitizen spouse's lifetime, the tax could amount to a substantial amount of money. In almost every case, the federal estate tax due upon the death of the surviving noncitizen spouse will exceed the tax that would have been payable had the surviving spouse been an American citizen. Finally, if the QDOT exceeds $2 million in value, if a bank is not one of the trustees the trust must post a letter of credit or bond in favor of the Internal Revenue Service to insure the collection of the estate tax that will ultimately be owing.

Unlike most major changes in the Code, this set of changes became effective immediately. As a result, Congress inserted a number of pro-visions designed to alleviate hardship. One can avoid this set of puni-tive rules by becoming an American citizen before the estate tax return is filed. Or the noncitizen spouse can assign the marital bequest to the QDOT. Or, most flexible of all, the noncitizen spouse can create a QDOT and transfer property to it and satisfy the Code in that way.

This book cannot delve into the fascinating question as to whether Congress overreacted to the theoretical possibility that a noncitizen spouse would inherit under the unlimited marital deduction, would then leave American soil, taking all of the inherited assets along, and thereby avoid any American estate taxation. Right or wrong, we take the Code as we find it, and couples in this situation need to consult counsel promptly to arrange their ownership of assets to avoid some of the dra-conian results described above. Joint tenancies need severing, the noncitizen spouse needs to have assets owned individually to fund his or her exclusion amount, the marital bequest not being eligible, and the QDOT ought to be in place. Waiting until someone dies means undue delay, and a couple with at least one noncitizen spouse needs to attend to the matter with dispatch. Relying, for example, on the relief provision that one can become a naturalized citizen before the estate tax return is due may not work, as we learned when the Immigration and Naturalization Service lost our client's application. The return is due nine months after the date of death, and usually the Internal Revenue Service will only give one six-month extension. Depending on the nationality of the noncitizen spouse and the INS backlog, the change in citizenship may not occur within the proscribed time period.

For our purposes, we can narrow the issues to what makes the most sense when one is dealing with a TIAA-CREF or other retirement account. Despite the yawning differences in the rules, the choice of solutions, oddly enough, does not differ greatly from that available to American citizens. The American citizen spouse, here assumed to be the TIAA-CREF participant, can create a QDOT and, for that matter, a credit shelter trust that will pay out the benefit measured by the noncitizen spouse's life expectancy. That may prove to be the most tax-efficient approach, but as discussed earlier, it does not produce the optimal results that one obtains from a multigenerational approach.

To obtain that benefit, one must designate the noncitizen spouse as the Designated Beneficiary, and the noncitizen spouse can then create a QDOT-Individual Retirement Account to which the TIAA-CREF benefits are irrevocably assigned. Those steps allow the noncitizen spouse to name new DBs, presumably the children, and will produce the same results in terms of overall economic return. The estate tax problem is exacerbated, however, because the surviving spouse does not have an exclusion to cushion the tax. The QDOT-IRA will become part of the estate of the first spouse to die. Consequently, the noncitizen's exclusion must be funded with other assets. To preserve the retirement account, the need for and the amount of second-to-die life insurance needed to satisfy the estate tax both increase, unless the noncitizen spouse owns additional assets with which to pay the tax. In this case, ordinary estate planning may again be stood on its head, and it will make better sense to move the nonretirement assets into the name of the spouse likely to die second or to the noncitizen spouse.

One neat question that the law currently leaves open to question concerns the meaning of the term "principal" when applied to distributions from a qualified plan to a noncitizen spouse. Does it mean anything distributed in any year that exceeds that year's income, even if that excess will be taxed as income? Does it mean anything in excess of the Minimum Distribution Option? The Internal Revenue Service has offered precious little guidance on this point, but it does create a potential problem for the noncitizen spouse. Ironically, if part of the TIAA-CREF or other retirement account also funds the credit shelter trust, the same types or amounts of distributions would clearly fall under the heading of income and be taxed as such. On the marital side, if placed into a conventional marital trust, it could receive principal status and generate an estate tax.

The absurdity of having the same type of distribution be given utterly different treatment in the case of the noncitizen spouse illustrates the ill-conceived nature of the remedy that Congress chose when it enacted this legislation in 1988. In any event, the moral is clear: a noncitizen spouse needs special planning that will be fact driven and no solution will function like a cookbook recipe. This area is a tangle, and the best solution may seem somewhat less than ideal.

For the reasons expressed earlier about the importance of having a DB at all times, the estate planning and the moving parts for the noncitizen spouse should be in place as early as possible to prevent an unfortunate outcome.

We have only given a brief overview of the issues. Anyone reading this book who is not an American citizen or whose spouse is not an American citizen needs to see a qualified estate planning lawyer immediately if the issues discussed in this chapter have not previously been addressed.

As the figures plainly indicate, the multigenerational approach can produce potentially enormous returns for a family. Unless your economic situation clearly precludes this alternative, you should consider this option and see if it works for you.

In examining your options, you will begin, of course, at the fundamental fork in the road between annuitization and the Minimum Distribution Option. Your choice will depend on the size of your accumulation and other factors that affect your financial security. Any estate planner worth his salt will set as his first goal the lifelong financial well-being of the older generation. Estate taxes represent someone else's problems, and the paramount issue remains that the reasonably foreseeable income needs of the retiree and spouse, if any, will be met.

Assuming that one gets over that hurdle, the next issue you must face will also prove virtually arithmetic. Will the MDO prove sufficient to let you live comfortably and how long will it hold out? That means taking your courage into your hands, assuming that your accumulation is not huge ($3 million or more), and making some assumptions about the extent to which your account will grow over time. Once you get over, say, $3 million, the TIAA-CREF account has grown to the point that the MDO becomes generous and the risk of running out of money has become minute.

But if you are not in that comfort zone, and the vast majority is not, you need to be brutally honest with yourself. Do you have the necessary financial discipline to stay the course and have your assets do the same? Do you have the fortitude to withstand periods of stock market turbulence? Do you really want to control your financial destiny or would you prefer the greater security of an annuity? On the other hand, how different is a CREF annuity from the MDO, given your accumulation and likely life expectancy? Recognizing that no retirement choice is risk free, does the MDO exceed your threshold of acceptable risk?

If one feels comfortable with that projection, the next issue becomes intensely practical. How will you pay the federal estate tax? Will you need second-to-die life insurance or do you have other suitable assets? If you elect second-to-die life insurance, will the premiums come from current income or will you have to tap your TIAA-CREF accumulation or other assets? If the former, does the plan adopted by your employer permit this use of your accumulation? Can you make use of the Interest Payment Retirement Option or, somewhat less desirable, the Systematic Withdrawal? If you can make use of these mechanisms, then you need to make your best-informed estimate of the effect that diverting some of your accumulation or the income on it to this purpose will have on your future income.

In the end, you come back to the time value of money and how to harness it most effectively. You need to do your retirement and estate planning informed by this concept and determine what will result in the optimal result for you and your family, both during your lifetime and thereafter. We will not see 16% returns in the equity markets year after year, but for those who rode the coattails of the great bull market of 1982–99, the opportunity now exists to achieve spectacular financial goals through far-sighted estate planning in an era when markets will not, at least for a time, duplicate the experience of the last seventeen years.

For those who do not have to face retirement immediately, these issues should remain equally salient. Your planning will depend more heavily on projections, but you have the opportunity to achieve similarly splendid results if you start the processes of saving and planning early. Decades of time will inexorably work the same result that the bull market produced in a decade and a half.

Finally, you need to think about the legacy that you want to leave your children. For most TIAA-CREF participants, their accounts represent their largest asset and the equivalent of their life's savings. The American dream assumes that each generation will be better off than its predecessors. Simply because you chose the less lucrative (in money or money's worth, to use the language of the Code) path into academic pursuits does not entail that you cannot accomplish this goal. In this respect, TIAA-CREF participants are in the same boat with many other Americans in other professions who have accumulated substantial retirement accounts that now represent their largest assets.

The only differences between the professor and the physician may lie in the size of the accumulation, the spaciousness of the house, and the horsepower of the family's cars. Conceptually, both must deal with the same dilemmas of the two-asset estate, and they both require the same type of planning. The unfortunate fact remains that those in the nonprofit sector typically learn somewhat later than their counterparts in other professions that they can accomplish the same goals, and this makes the successful achievement of the identical ends more expensive. But it can be done, and for many it will seem the best, most logical, and most loving solution for their families.

Conclusion

Based upon our experiences working with dozens of participants, TIAA-CREF remains a lifelong mystery that they feel that they cannot solve. In this book, we have taken the same course that you would have, had the problem been posed in your area of expertise. First, we and you have teased apart the various aspects of TIAA-CREF, making each of them more comprehensible in the process. Second, we have tried to provide background information where needed. Most of the difficulty that our clients talk about when they describe the TIAA-CREF literature springs, in our opinion, from the assumption that the reader has the necessary legal and estate planning knowledge to assimilate what is written. You can test this theory by rereading some of the material that you previously found impenetrable.

Although we are not educators, this book focuses on education. Much of what you learned concerned the nuts and bolts aspects of TIAA-CREF's operations. Much of what you need to learn will appear in your employer's plan documents.

The more profound issues involve values and how you feel about your family, the remaining years of your career and your life, others about whom you deeply care, and your personal needs and interests. That voyage of discovery will occur inside of you and not in the pages of this book.

Finally, this book has drummed into you the relationship between time, money, and risk. What may have seemed static, such as your investment choices or estate planning, should now appear fluid and dynamic. As we wrote this book, we realized that no retirement plan is free of risk. Unless you are independently wealthy or your accumulation is very large, you will have to cope with market risk and inflation for the rest of your life. That is the human condition, at least in the United States at the beginning of the twenty-first century.

TIAA-CREF began at the beginning of the twentieth century, when pension plans for teachers and others in the nonprofit sector did not exist. This book attests to the success it has achieved in fulfilling the needs which gave rise to its formation. The conundrums that we leave you with are ones that your predecessors could not have imagined. We welcome your comments, and we wish every one of our readers long-term success and, if possible to attain in this vale of tears, happiness and contentment. You worked long and hard for what you have saved, and we hope that it becomes and remains a source of financial comfort and emotional satisfaction.

Appendix A

Contribution Limitations Under Section 403(b) of the Code and Related Sections

The Code contains several separate limitations on how much an employee can contribute or have contributed to his Section 403(b) account, whether held by TIAA-CREF or in a custodial account. The different limitations apply in different circumstances, and they are generally mutually exclusive. Some of them are designed to increase the contributions during the last years of employment.

1. The overarching lifetime limitation on the exclusion from income is 20% of the employee's compensation multiplied by the years of service. This figure may eventually be reached, but not frequently. It is limited by the annual limitations on contributions described below.
2. Most employee contributions are made through salary deferral agreements and so they fall under the familiar rules applicable to Section 401(k) plans laid out in Section 402(g), namely the greater of $9,500 or $7,000 indexed for post-1988 inflation. The limitation is $10,000 in 1999. This limitation applies to all of the salary reduction plans in which an employee participates.
3. Section 415 contains another overarching limitation, this one on annual contributions, The combination of employee and employer contributions may not exceed the lesser of (i) 25% of the employee's compensation or (ii) $30,000.
4. For employees with at least fifteen years of service, the Code provides a special catch-up limitation in Section 402(g)(8). Subject to the Section 415 limitations, the employee can increase his contribution by the least of.

   i. $3,000;
   ii. $15,000 less prior amounts contributed under this election; or
   iii. $5,000 times years of service minus prior salary reduction contributions made to the plan.

5. If the employee elects, the fourth limitation applies to the year in which the employee separates from service from an educational or-

ganization, a hospital and other health-related organizations, or a church. In that case, the employee may use the lifetime formula, assuming however that he has only ten years of service, or make an annual contribution treating the annuity plan as if it were a defined contribution plan. The Section 415 limitations would not apply. This represents an irrevocable one-time election that must be duly filed with the Internal Revenue Service

6. The fifth limitation is a provision to allow the employee to increase the size of his or her accumulation before retirement. Like the fourth limitation, it requires a timely election by the employee. The employee can contribute the least of:

    i.   25% of compensation plus $4,000;
    ii. any shortfall against the lifetime exclusion; or
    iii. $15,000.

These rules appear in Section 415(c)(4) of the Code.

These elections under numbers 4 to 6 are mutually exclusive and can be made only once, They are irrevocable.

Distributions from Section 403(b) plans are not eligible for lump-sum distribution and income-averaging treatment. Section 402(d)(4) defines an eligible lump sum distribution in terms of plans under Section 403(a) only.

Appendix B

The Internal Revenue Service Mortality Table
Upon Which Life Expectancies
Are Computed for the MDIB Rules

Age of Employee	Maximum Period Certain	Age of Employee	Maximum Period Certain
70	26.2	93	8.8
71	25.3	94	8.3
72	24.4	95	7.8
73	23.5	96	7.3
74	22.7	97	6.9
75	21.8	98	6.5
76	20.9	99	6.1
77	20.1	100	5.7
78	19.2	101	5.3
79	18.4	102	5.0
80	17.6	103	4.7
81	16.8	104	4.4
82	16.0	105	4.1
83	15.3	106	3.8
84	14.5	107	3.6
85	13.8	108	3.3
86	13.1	109	3.1
87	12.4	110	2.8
88	11.8	111	2.6
89	11.1	112	2.4
90	10.5	113	2.2
91	9.9	114	2.0
92	9.4	115 and older	1.8

Source: Prop. Reg. Section 1.401(a)(9)-2, Q-4 (July 27, 1987).

For those interested in the recalculation method, note how life expectancy does not decrease one year for each year lived. Interestingly, the decrease in life expectancy for each year lived declines with advancing age. At first, the decrease almost equals a year, but then it falls off to .2 years or 2.4 months when one has lived to be 110.

Appendix C

Table Under the MDIB Rules for the Percentage of the Participant's Annuity That Can Be Paid to an Annuity Partner Who Is not a Spouse Depending on Age Difference

Excess of Age of Employee Over of Beneficiary	Applicable Percentage
10 years or less	100
11	96
12	93
13	90
14	87
15	84
16	82
17	79
18	77
19	75
20	73
21	72
22	70
23	68
24	67
25	66
26	64
27	63
28	62
29	61
30	60
31	59
32	59
33	58
34	57
35	56
36	56
37	55
38	55
39	54
40	54
41	53
42	53
43	53
44 and greater	52

Source: Prop. Reg. Section 1.409(a)(1)-2, Q-6(b)

The IRS illustrated these rules by the following example:

Distributions commence on January 1, 1993, to an employee (Z), born March 1, 1927, after Z's retirement at age 65. Z's granddaughter (Y), born February 5, 1967, is Z's beneficiary. The distributions are in the form of a joint and survivor annuity for the lives of Z and Y with payments of $500 a month to Z and upon Z's death of $500 a month to Y, i.e., the projected monthly payment to Y is 100% of the monthly amount payable to Z. There is no provision under the option for a change in the projected payments to Y as of April 1, 1998, Z's required beginning date. Consequently, as of January 1, 1993, the date annuity distributions commence, the plan does not satisfy the Minimum Distribution Incidental Benefits rules' requirement in operation because the distribution option provides that, as of Z's required beginning date, the monthly payment to Y upon Z's death will exceed 54% of Z's monthly payment (the maximum percentage for a difference of ages of 40).

Appendix D

Accumulation of Retirement Assets

Years until retirement:	25
Annual tax deferred contributions:	$10,000
Rate of Return:	7%
Inflation:	3%
Tax Rate:	28%

Balances shown are net of accumulated deferred taxes, i.e. after tax disposable income.

Annual savings are increased each year with inflation.

Nominal (Actual) Dollars shown.

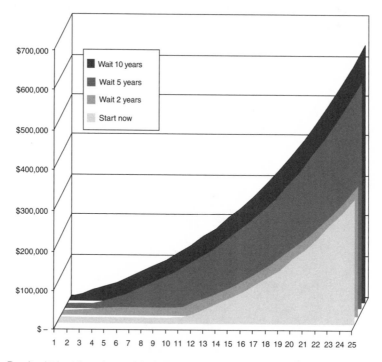

Appendix E

Delay Is Costly

Desired Retirement Nest Egg:	$1,000,000
Years Until Retirement:	30
Rate of Return:	7%
Inflation:	0%
Tax Rate:	28%

The amounts noted represent the tax-deferred amount to be put aside each year in order to acquire an after-tax retirement nest egg of $1,000,000 for retirement in 30 years, starting at different times along the way.

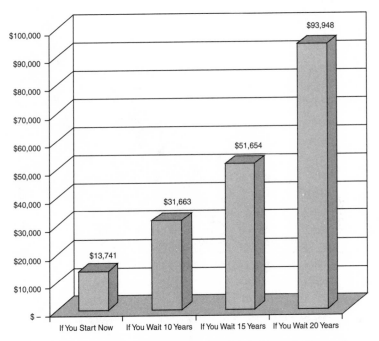

Results obtained through used of the Investment Growth Calculator on fidelity.com. ©
Copyright 1998-2000 FMR Corp. and published with the permission of Fidelity Investments.

Appendix F

Investment Growth
(Tax-Deferred Account, Non Inflation Adjusted)

Years of Investing:	25
Initial Balance:	$50,000
Annual Investment:	$0
Rate of Return:	7%
Inflation:	0%
Tax Rate:	0%

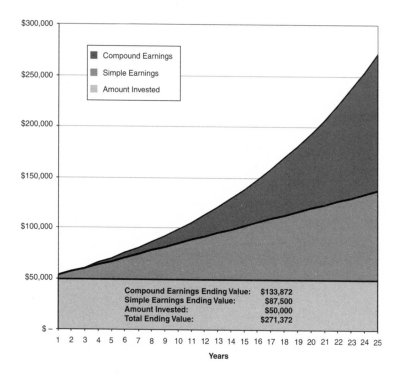

Results obtained through use of the Investment Growth Calculator on fidelity.com. ©
Copyright 1998-2000 FMR Corp. and published with the permission of Fidelity Investments.

Appendix G

Investment Growth
(Taxable, Non Inflation Adjusted)

Years of Investing:	25
Initial Balance:	$50,000
Annual Investment:	$0
Rate of Return:	7%
Inflation:	0%
Tax Rate:	28%

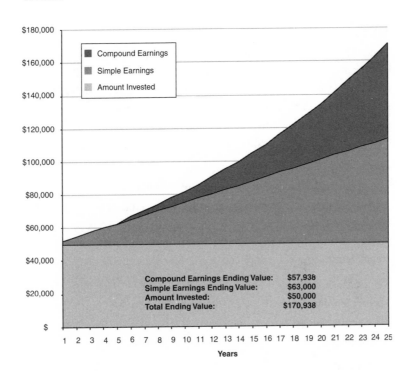

Glossary

401(a)(9)

This section of the Internal Revenue Code deals with many of the critical distribution requirements. The rules regarding Designated Beneficiaries, payments prior to or after the Required Beginning Date, and minimum distributions, among other matters, are covered in this subsection of the Code.

401(k)

This is the section of the Internal Revenue Code that describes one type of retirement plan used in the for-profit sector; like TIAA-CREF and other Section 403(b) plans, contributions from employees are derived from salary deferral or reduction agreements. Investments in Section 401(k) plans are not restricted to annuities and mutual funds, but may also include individual stocks, commonly, employer company stock.

403(b)

This is the section of the Internal Revenue Code that lays out the groundwork for retirement plans available only to tax-exempt employers, or not-for-profit institutions. Although similar in many respects to Section 401(k) plans, Section 403(b) plan investments are restricted to annuities and "regulated investment companies" or mutual fund investments.

Accumulation Phase

The accumulation phase means the period in which you are still contributing to your retirement plan. Normally this will occur while you are still employed and not yet taking any form of distribution.

Accumulation Unit

This is TIAA-CREF's term to describe the number of shares you have purchased in a variable annuity fund. The number of units that you purchase in any month is determined by the amount of your contribution and the price of the units on the day of purchase.

Annuitant

An annuitant is someone who is receiving distributions from an annuity.

Annuity

An annuity is a financial product issued by an insurance company like TIAA-CREF. An annuity provides a constant stream of payments, defined either in terms of dollars or number of annuity units. The former is a fixed annuity and the latter is a variable annuity. The length of an annuity may last a specified number of years, one or more lifetimes, or a combination of the two through a term certain or guaranteed period.

Annuity Partner

An annuity partner is the person you have chosen to share the payments from your annuity or to receive such payments after your death. This person's life expectancy is also used together with yours to calculate the size of your annuity payments if you elect an annuity based on two life-times.

Asset Allocation

Asset allocation is the term used to describe how you divide your investments among equities, fixed income securities, and cash.

Calculation Beneficiary

Your calculation beneficiary is your designated beneficiary and the person whose life expectancy is used together with yours to determine how large your annual payments must be to comply with the minimum distribution rules.

Capital Gain

A capital gain represents the appreciation of an investment from the date of purchase to a specific time in the future. An increase in value attributable to infusion of new money does not count as capital gains.

CRUT (Charitable Remainder Unitrust)

A charitable remainder unitrust is a trust in which one or more individuals have an income interest for life or for a maximum term of twenty years, and the remainder devolves to charity. The size of the annual payment is a fixed percentage, at least 5%, of the trust corpus, and the charitable remainder must equal 10% of the initial value of the trust principal.

The Code

This is the short reference for the Internal Revenue Code of 1986, as amended.

Commingled Account

A commingled account consists of many investors' assets pooled into one account. Each investor owns a pro rata share. The investor does not own specific investments in the account, only a pro rata share based on his own contribution(s).

Compounding

Compounding is the growth effect achieved by constant reinvestment of incremental growth; as a result, each successive period's growth percentage works on an increasing amount.

Contributory (or Noncontributory) Plan

A contributory plan is a retirement plan in which the employee may contribute from his or her own salary on a tax-deferred basis. A noncontributory plan is a plan in which the employee may not contribute from his or her own compensation to the plan.

Coupon

A coupon is the term used to describe the interest paid, usually semiannually, on interest-bearing bonds. The term comes from the coupons that were attached to the notes when issued and which the buyer clipped and redeemed to receive the interest payment. In today's world, most bonds are registered and issued electronically with neither physical certificates nor coupons.

Custodial Account

Section 403(b)(7) of the Code defines the term to mean an account maintained by a financial institution that is invested exclusively in mutual fund shares.

Debt Issuer

A debt issuer is a borrower.

Defined Contribution Plan

A defined contribution plan is a retirement plan in which the retirement payment is not fixed, but the plan specifies the amount or percentage of compensation that the employee and/or employer may contribute. Typically, the contributions are credited to individual accounts in the names of the participants.

DB (Designated Beneficiary)

See chapters 29 and 37.

Disclaimer

A disclaimer is a written instrument by which the beneficiary of a will, retirement plan, or trust elects not to receive the benefit specified in the applicable document.

Distribution Phase

The distribution phase is the period during which payments are made from your retirement account. This will normally occur upon retirement or at age $70^1/_2$, whichever comes later if you are a participant in a qualified plan.

Dividend

Dividends represent company earnings paid to the shareholders after management has retained what it deems necessary to keep the company healthy. Dividends are usually paid in a set amount per share on a quarterly basis.

Equity(ies)

Stock or shares in a company are also referred to as equity in the company.

ERISA

ERISA is the Employee Retirement Income Security Act, created in 1974, which deals with employee benefits, primarily retirement and pension plans.

Extended Generational IRA

This is an IRA that has been structured to allow minimum distributions from a tax-deferred account to continue into the next generation after both the participant and spouse have died.

Fixed Annuity Pool

A fixed annuity pool is the fund into which all fixed annuity premiums and the earnings thereon are paid. Annuity payments to those participants who have started the distribution phase come from this fund.

Funds

One often refers to mutual funds as "funds." They are pooled accounts under management from one source.

GRA

Group Retirement Account. See chapter 9.

GSRA

Group Supplemental Retirement Account. See Chapter 9.

Guaranteed Period

See "term certain" below.

Hedge

A hedge is an investment taken to counterbalance potential changes that may affect another investment in order to maintain a relatively balanced result in a volatile environment.

Hybrid Method

The hybrid method calculates joint life expectancy using the recalculation method for one life and the subtract one method for the other.

IRA (Individual Retirement Account)

An Individual Retirement Account is a tax-deferred custodial account whose investments are directed by the account owner. For those not participating in a retirement plan and whose income falls within certain limits, annual tax-deductible contributions of up to $2,000 may be made to IRA accounts. IRA accounts are also used to receive "rollovers" from qualified retirement plans.

IPRO (Interest Payment Retirement Option)

See chapter 21.

Life Expectancy

Life expectancy is how long you are expected to live, given your age, according to a mortality table. Such a table is compiled based on national census statistics or other large pool calculations.

Maturity

Maturity is the date on which the principal amount of a debt must be paid.

MDIB (Minimum Distribution Incidental Benefit) Rules

This is a rule created by the IRS to ensure that retirement benefits are not unduly stretched out. The rules require that in determining life expectancies, if the participant or IRA owner is living, any nonspousal DB will be treated as only ten years younger than the participant or owner. They also provide for a percentage reduction in the annuity payable to an annuity partner based upon the age difference between the annuitants.

MDO (Minimum Distribution Option)

See chapters 32 and 33.

Mortality Costs

In the case of life insurance policies or annuities, the insurance company calculates the premium based on the annual amount it thinks will be necessary to invest over a given number of years to be able to pay out the face value upon your death. In the case of annuities, the insurance company calculates how much it can afford to pay you annually based on the lump sum you pay it up front and what it thinks it can earn on that payment over a specified number of years depending on the type of annuity. Mortality costs represent the fees that the insurance company adds to the premium or deducts from the annuity payments to cover the chance that the insured dies early or the annuitant lives longer than expected.

Multigenerational IRA
The same as "extended generational IRA" (see above).

Portability
See chapter 11.

Premium
A payment made to an insurance company to pay for insurance coverage or to add to an annuity account in the accumulation phase.

Proprietary Funds
Many mutual fund companies reserve some of their accounts for customers who invest directly through the company only. They are proprietary funds. In order to move holdings in these funds to another account with another company, the shares must be sold and the investment transferred as a cash holding.

QDOT (Qualified Domestic Trust)
See chapter 44.

QPRT (Qualified Personal Residence Trust)
See chapter 40.

Qualified Plan
A retirement or pension plan that is qualified under the provisions of ERISA.

Recalculation Method
This is one of two methods of calculating individual life expectancy based on census statistics. It involves an annual recomputation, based upon the statistic that for each year that you live, your life expectancy does not decline by a year. Put colloquially, the longer you live, the longer you are likely to live.

RBD (Required Beginning Date)
See chapter 21.

Reserves
Reserves are the funds withheld by an insurance company to ensure that it will have enough cash on hand to pay its policy holders in spite of adverse investment experience or statistically unlikely mortality experience.

RA (Retirement Annuity)
See chapter 7.

RTB (Retirement Transition Benefit)
See chapter 25.

Second-to-Die Life Insurance Policy
See chapter 41.

Subtract One Method
This is the second method for calculating an individual's life expectancy. Your life expectancy is determined as of a given date or age and is not readjusted to reflect actual experience. As one ages by a year, life expectancy is reduced by one year.

SRA (Supplemental Retirement Annuity)
See chapter 8.

Surrender
In the context of annuities, surrender is the term used when an annuity owner cancels an annuity policy and receives a lump-sum payment instead.

Surrender Charges
Surrender charges are the fees charged by insurance companies to clients who surrender annuities.

Systematic Withdrawals
See chapter 21.

Term Certain
Term certain is used to describe an annuity that will pay out over a specified number of years.

Term Life Policy
A term policy, or a term life policy, is a life insurance policy the pro-

ceeds of which will be paid only if your death occurs within a specified period of time, usually one year.

Time Value of Money

The time value of money means the value that one will receive from having and using money earlier either to produce growth through investment or, to reduce the present value of a future gift because enjoyment of the money is deferred.

TPA (Transfer Payout Annuity)

See chapter 18.

Yield

Yield is another term for the effective return on an investment.

Selected Bibliography

This book is based in part on two articles that we published in 1997 and 1998 in the *Tax Management Estates, Gifts and Trusts Journal*. In addition to consulting newer versions of the library of TIAA-CREF brochures, research dialogs, *The Participant*, information on the TIAA-CREF Web site, and other TIAA-CREF literature, we found the following useful in preparing this book. Obviously, we plowed through the Internal Revenue Code of 1986, as amended, the Internal Revenue Service's regulations and proposed regulations, and private letter rulings.

For the history of TIAA-CREF, we used Greenough's *It's My Retirement Money: Take Good Care of It* (1990) and periodical literature cited in the first of the two articles.

The clearest explanation of the Byzantine rules governing retirement plans and their interrelationship with estate planning is Natalie B. Choate's *Life and Death Planning for Retirement Benefits* (3rd ed., 1999). The professional literature on TIAA-CREF and other Section 403(b) plans stands out for its sparseness. The most useful and succinct from a legal and tax point of view is Kenty and London, *Tax-Deferred Annuities—Section 403(b)* (1996), which is No. 388, 4th edition, in the Bureau of National Affairs Tax Management library of tax portfolios as updated.

As we prepared this book, we read a number of articles in the periodical literature that bore on some of the concepts that we were trying to explain. Many of them appeared in the *Wall Street Journal*, and we have listed those pieces that seemed of particular relevance to the lay reader. Those articles include the following:

Asinof, Lynn. "New IRA Policies May Mean Big Savings," *Wall Street Journal* (19 March 1999), Your Money Matters column.
———. "Oops ... How a Variety of Basic Foul-Ups Are Bedeviling the Beneficiaries of IRAs," *Wall Street Journal* (29 March 1999), Your Money Matters column.
Clements, Jonathan. "Advice Is Good; Is Ignoring It Bliss?" *Wall Street Journal* (6 July 1999), Getting Going column.

————. "Investing Ideas That Stand Test of Time," *Wall Street Journal* (4 May 1999), Getting Going column.

————. "Portfolios for the Conservative and Bold," *Wall Street Journal* (10 November 1998), Getting Going column.

————. "Riskphobes Are Taking Two Big Gambles," *Wall Street Journal* (1 December 1998), Getting Going column.

————. "Start Worrying About the Right Things," *Wall Street Journal* (27 July 1999), Getting Going column.

"Dow Jones Asset Management," Dow Jones Publishing Corp., Vol. II, No. 6 (November/December 1998).

Gopinath, Deepak. "Lost and Found," *Institutional Investor* (February 1999).

Hubler, Eric. "The New Faces of Retirement," *New York Times* (3 January 1999), Money and Business section.

Oppel, Richard A., Jr. "For Teachers, Object Lessons from the 401(k)," *New York Times* (13 June 1999), Money and Business section.

"Private Client Focus," Goldman Sachs Investment Research (29 November 1998).

Ward, Sandra. "Playing With Fire—Rivals Who Underestimate TIAA-CREF Just Might Get Burned," *Barron's Online* (11 January 1999).

Of the TIAA-CREF brochures, we found the most useful to be *"A Guide to the TIAA-CREF Accounts,"* booklet no. 3 in the Library Series, a publication of TIAA-CREF External Affairs, Corporate Publications Division (1998).

Index

DATE DUE